PLUTARCH'S THEMISTOCLES
A HISTORICAL COMMENTARY

FRANK J. FROST

PLUTARCH'S THEMISTOCLES

A HISTORICAL COMMENTARY

PRINCETON UNIVERSITY PRESS

PRINCETON, NEW JERSEY

Publication of this book has been aided by a grant from the
National Endowment for the Humanities

This book has been composed in Linotype Janson

Clothbound editions of Princeton University Press books
are printed on acid-free paper, and binding materials are
chosen for strength and durability

Printed in the United States of America by Princeton
University Press, Princeton, New Jersey

for my teacher
TRUESDELL S. BROWN

CONTENTS

LIST OF ILLUSTRATIONS

PREFACE

It was in 1963 that I first contemplated the major task of writing a historical commentary to Plutarch's *Life of Themistocles* and, with an abundance of youthful confidence and self-esteem, I announced the project in the "Arbeitsvorhaben" section of *Gnomon* 35 (1963) 432. I could not know at the time that the last page would not be written until a spring day in Athens in 1977. I can only plead that a number of circumstances interrupted the orderly progress of the work: some contributed to my understanding, others only to my age. Of the greatest utility was the time I spent editing an expanded edition of Adolf Bauer's *Plutarchs Themistokles für quellenkritische Übungen* (Leipzig, 1884; 2nd ed. Chicago, 1967). I also served for four years in elective political office, which contributed in many ways to my appreciation of practical politics (indispensable to any student of Themistocles) but severely curtailed the research I was able to accomplish. During the long interval between conception and completion, a number of fine articles and monographs have appeared dealing in various thoughtful and creative ways with early Athenian politics, the Persian Wars, and Plutarch. I may venture to hope that the contribution made to this book by classical scholarship during the last fourteen years will more than outweigh the admittedly leisurely pace I have maintained in completing it.

The career of Themistocles is contemporary with some of the most hotly discussed decades in Greek history. Let me quote the memorable phrase of Ernst Badian: "Athenian history in the fifth century B.C. has, on the whole, become a battlefield where only the trained hoplite can compete. By contrast, the period from Cleisthenes down to 480 is one where the mere peltast still has a chance" ("Archons and Strategoi," *Antichthon* 5 [1971] 1). My own role in these military affairs is somewhat ambiguous. In some disputes I will contest as vigorously as any; I will carefully skirt those skirmishes among learned scholars which remind me of Thucydides' description of the night battle around Epipolae: neither ground, nor opponents, nor objective itself can be discerned in the general darkness. In a few cases my response has simply been Archilochean.

Throughout the commentary, however, I have maintained one consistent goal: to define the various problems as carefully as possible, to show the nature of the historical tradition about problematic events, and particularly to explain how, in my opinion, Plutarch's testimony is to be interpreted. This approach has dictated two introductory chapters. In the first, I examine the various traditions—historical, political, or simply romantic—about Themistocles—from Simonides, Herodotus, and Thucydides to the pedants and rhetors of imperial Rome. The second chapter explains Plutarch's reaction to these traditions and otherwise fulfills the indispensable chore imposed on those who write about the biographer—to clarify my personal perspective in interpreting Plutarch's use of his sources. A commentary requires copious citation. To keep the notes from becoming overwhelming, I have emphasized the ancient testimonia, endeavoring to supply complete references, while limiting those from modern literature to titles I felt were illustrative or most to the point. In the case of continuing controversies, I have tried to summarize the arguments of each side with a representative sampling of modern scholarship. As a considered policy, I have rarely referred to the works of some of the most prominent scholars of the late nineteenth and early twentieth centuries to whom we all owe so much:

Karl Julius Beloch, Georg Busolt, Ulrich von Wilamowitz-Moellendorf, to name but a few. The audience for whom this book is intended will understand that continual reference to the fundamental older literature would be more distracting than useful.

I would like to thank the Academic Senate Research Committee of the University of California, Santa Barbara, for financial assistance during the writing of this book, the History Department for granting me leave in 1977 to complete the manuscript, and in particular the Director and staff of the American School of Classical Studies in Athens for kindly allowing me full use of their facilities in 1977.

FRANK J. FROST
Athens and Santa Barbara, 1977

PLUTARCH'S THEMISTOCLES
A HISTORICAL COMMENTARY

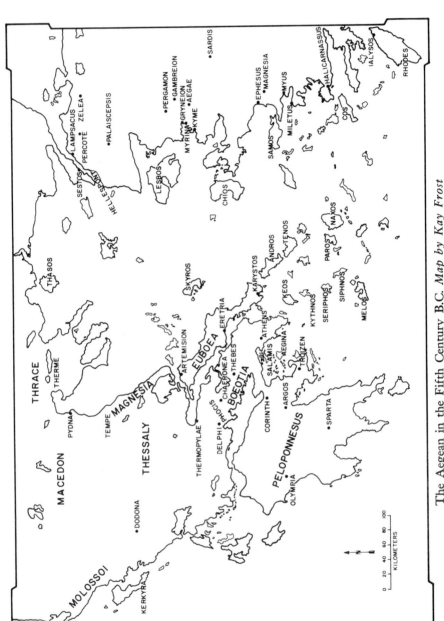

The Aegean in the Fifth Century B.C. *Map by Kay Frost*

I

THEMISTOCLES IN THE LITERARY TRADITION

A. THE FIRST GENERATION

THEMISTOCLES' deeds were first sung by two poets of his own lifetime. These first entries in the literary record indicate from the very beginning the controversy his name could provoke and would continue to provoke throughout antiquity. Simonides of Keos (c. 556-468) was a personal friend of Themistocles (Cicero, *De Fin.* 2.32, and see comment to 1.4, 5.6). He certainly mentioned the general's role in his epics, *The Seafight at Artemision* and *The Seafight at Salamis* (titles known from the *Suda* s.v. Simonides); in various unknown works, he glorified Themistocles' wise counsel (15.4) and recorded his rebuilding of the Lycomid shrine at Phlya after the war (1.4), thus indicating that Themistocles belonged to an aristocratic house.

Timocreon of Rhodes was a very different sort of writer. If Simonides was the model of a court poet, gracious and fashionable, Timocreon was in the mold of Archilochus, an athlete, brawler, and famous for his gluttony.[1] Timocreon had evidently chosen the wrong side in the Persian Wars and seems to have applied to his friend and *proxenos* Themistocles to use his influence in having him reinstated at Ialysos. But the general took a bribe not to reinstate him (the difficulties of this episode are discussed further, in the

[1] Athenaeus 415F; *Anth.Pal.* 13.30-31, 7.348. See fuller discussion in comment to 21.3.

4 PLUTARCH'S THEMISTOCLES

comment to 21.3). Note that these two poets provide valuable evidence for Themistocles' two most famous attributes:
good counsel and avarice. We know therefore that these
two traits were recognized by contemporaries.[2]

From other poets of his generation, we have next to
nothing. Although only the reference in *Persae* 353-364 is
certain, it is often supposed that Aeschylus alludes elsewhere, in this play or that, to Themistocles, or to Themistoclean policy.[3] This may be so, but the question here is the
extent to which Aeschylus established a tradition that influenced later writers on Themistocles, and for this there is
no evidence.[4]

Besides this brief and contradictory reputation in verse,
several monuments preserved the memory of Themistocles:
the shrine of the Lycomids in Phlya, one of Artemis Aristoboule in Melite,[5] the fortifications of Piraeus. Among
its documentary records Athens will have preserved the
date of his archonship (493/2) on the list inscribed sometime around 425,[6] and an unknown number of decrees he

---

[2] A. Bauer, *Themistokles* (Merseburg, 1881) 9-14; F. Schachermeyr,
"Das Bild des Themistokles in der antiken Geschichtesschreibung,"
*XXIᵉ Congrès international des sciences historiques, Vienna. Rap-
ports* IV (1965) 82. See also A. Podlecki, "Simonides: 480," *Historia*
17 (1968) 262-274; idem, *Themistocles* (Montreal and London, 1975)
49-54.

[3] E.g., A. Diamantopoulos, "The Danaid Tetralogy of Aeschylus,"
JHS 77 (1957) 227-228; W. G. Forrest, "Themistokles and Argos," *CQ*
10 n.s. (1960) 236-240; J. Carrière, "Communicazione sulla tragedia
antica greca," *Dioniso* 43 (1969) 169-174; Podlecki, *Themistocles* 47-
49.

[4] As there is evidence, for instance, that a passage in Sophocles' lost
play Ἑλένης ἀπαίτησις (fr. 178 Jebb) was widely held in antiquity to
allude to the exile's suicide by a draught of bull's blood, schol. Arist.
Knights 84, and see comment to 31.6.

[5] J. Threpsiades and E. Vanderpool, "Themistokles' Sanctuary of
Artemis Aristoboule," *Arch.Delt.* 19 (1964) 26-36, and see comment to
22.2.

[6] B. Meritt, *Hesperia* 8 (1939) 59ff.; D. Bradeen, "The Fifth Century Archon List," *Hesp.* 32 (1963) 187ff.; F. Jacoby, *Atthis* (Oxford, 1949) 171.

had moved, including perhaps a version of the famous evacuation decree. It should be remembered that Themistocles' sons returned to Athens not too long after his death and that they were well-to-do and took some care to preserve the memory of their father (Thuc. I 138.6; Paus. I 1.2, 26.4; see comment to 32.1).

B. HERODOTUS

7.143: When the assembly was pondering the meaning of the "wooden wall" in the second Delphic response, Themistocles supported those who thought this meant the fleet; his arguments persuaded the assembly to accept this interpretation. At this time he was still ἐς πρώτους νεωστὶ παριών.[7]

7.144: Themistocles proposed using the mining revenue from Laureion to build two hundred triremes for the war against Aegina. It does not seem to me that Herodotus thought Themistocles was looking ahead to a Persian War or that he ought to have thought so,[8] although this was sometimes assumed by other ancient writers (Thuc. I 14.2; Aristides II 250-251; see comment to 4.2).

7.173: Themistocles was general of the Athenians in the army sent to Tempe. He and the Spartan Evaenetus were warned of Xerxes' strength, and of a pass by which they might be outflanked, by messengers from Alexander of Macedon.

8.4: The Euboeans gave Themistocles thirty talents with

---

[7] This phrase has created difficulties for some scholars. I have argued, in "Themistocles' Place in Athenian Politics," *CSCA* 1 (1968) 114f., that Themistocles held the archonship in 493/2 as a young man of about 30-33 years, that the archonship was the first real step in a career of public service and therefore Themistocles could be accurately described, in 483, as having "recently" emerged as a leader in Athenian public affairs. Podlecki (*Them.* 68) has said that this view cannot be seriously maintained but offers no evidence to the contrary.

[8] So also E. Badian, "Archons and *Strategoi*," *Antichthon* 5 (1971) 6f.

which to persuade his fellow commanders to make a stand at Artemision. He passed on five talents to the Spartan Eurybiades, three to Adeimantus the Corinthian, and kept the rest himself. This was a famous example of the general's *pleonexia*.[9]

8.19: Here Herodotus begins to describe Themistocles' plan to detach the Ionians and Carians from the Persian fleet, but then breaks off to tell of his advice to the other generals. They should sacrifice all the Euboean flocks, light fires, and leave to him the decision when to depart. The historian's purpose in this episode is obscure—was the slaughter of the flocks necessary to fulfill the oracle of Bacis (8.20)?[10]

8.22: At sources of fresh water along the route of the Persian fleet, Themistocles placed inscriptions addressed to the Ionian contingents, asking them to change their alliance. His purpose was twofold: either the Ionians would be persuaded, or Xerxes would doubt their reliability. This was a famous stratagem (see comment to 9.2), but Herodotus, who elsewhere betrays no special regard for Ionian trustworthiness, seems to take special care in pointing out that few Ionians did in fact malinger at Salamis (8.85).

8.57-63: Here begins the controversy between Themistocles and the Peloponnesian generals that ends only with the secret message to the Persians. 8.57: Mnesiphilus advised him to persuade Eurybiades to change his mind about retreating to the Isthmus. 8.58: Themistocles so persuaded the Spartan and 8.59-60: laid the Athenian strategy and the evidence of the oracles before the other generals. This counsel—to make a stand at Salamis—was the classical example of *euboulia* in his entire career, yet Herodotus seems

---

[9] Hannelore Barth, "Das Verhalten des Themistokles gegenüber den Gelde," *Klio* 43-45 (1965) 34-36.

[10] So W. How, J. Wells, *A Commentary on Herodotus* (Oxford, 1928) ad loc.: "They were to light fires in their camp on the shore to deceive the enemy and so get away unmolested. The fires would also serve to roast the sheep which were to provide food for the fleet."

to emphasize the fact that Themistocles passed off the arguments of another man as his own.[11] 8.61: There were bitter words between Themistocles and the Corinthian Adeimantus (with whom Herodotus deals harshly throughout), but finally 8.62-63: he prevailed upon Eurybiades by threatening the desertion of the entire Athenian population.

8.75: When Themistocles saw that the actual presence of the full Persian fleet had undone the resolve of the Peloponnesians, he sent his servant Sicinnus to tell Xerxes that the Greeks were divided and planning to flee and that he should attack immediately. 8.79: Aristeides now arrived from Aegina and agreed with Themistocles to lay down their rivalry until the war was over. He brought confirmation that the western straits had been sealed off. 8.80: Themistocles admitted that the Persians had acted at his prompting and urged Aristeides to report what he had seen to the council of generals.

8.83: Themistocles addressed the troops, exhorting them to array the best in their nature against the worst. 8.92: The ship of Themistocles encountered an Aeginetan vessel commanded by Polycritus, who taunted him with the old Athenian accusations of Aeginetan medizing (6.50).

8.108-110: When the pursuing Greek fleet came to Andros, Themistocles advised sailing to the Hellespont and breaking the bridges; Eurybiades countered with the suggestion that it was better not to impede Xerxes' flight, but to get him out of Europe as quickly as possible. Themistocles then returned to the Athenian contingent and persuaded them of Eurybiades' views, once more passing off another man's arguments as his own. Consequently, he sent Sicinnus and others to tell Xerxes that he had persuaded the Greeks not to cut off his retreat. "He said this intending to lay up something to his account with the Persian, so that he would have a place to turn in case he should suffer some-

[11] C. Hignett, *Xerxes' Invasion of Greece* (Oxford, 1963) 204, calls this a "spiteful invention to deprive Themistocles of the credit for his originality and insight."

thing from the Athenians. *And this did in fact happen.*"
This is one of the rare instances where Herodotus reveals
his knowledge of later events outside the scope of his
historie.

8.111-112: These are further stories of Themistocles'
pleonexia in extorting, or attempting to extort, money from
Andros, Karystos, and Paros. Exactions from enemy cities
were of course normal, but Herodotus adds that Themistocles also took money, "unknown to the other generals."

8.123-124: When the *aristeia* were to be awarded to the
worthiest, each general voted for himself first, and the
majority for Themistocles second. But the Spartans made
up for the slight by taking him home with them and giving
him all manner of honors never before accorded a foreigner.

8.124: Timodemus of Aphidna criticized Themistocles,
saying that his honors were because of the deeds of all
Athenians. Themistocles replied that he would not have
been honored thus by the Spartans if he were a Belbinitan,
nor would Timodemus, even though he was an Athenian.
The point of this story was changed by Plato (*Rep.* 329e-
330a) and other authors.[12]

Herodotus' treatment of Themistocles has always been an
intriguing puzzle. Anyone who interprets this material does
so subjectively to a certain extent and needs to let readers
know his approach to the following questions. What was
the range of opinion about Themistocles in Athens in the
440's? To what extent was Herodotus influenced by public
opinion?

The general will have been remembered both for his accomplishments and for his traits of character. His catalogue
of deeds was ambiguous. He had contributed greatly to
victory at Salamis; he had steadfastly recommended an anti-
Spartan policy after the war; he had fled to the Great King
and (some said) promised to make all the Greeks subject to
Persia. But it was also said that he finally committed suicide

---

[12] Noted by How and Wells ad loc.; Cicero, *De Sen.* 3.8; Plut.
Apophth.Them. 185C no. 7; see comment to 18.5.

rather than carry out his promise. Athenians must have
argued the merits of this case for decades. One would think
that on balance it was favorable to Themistocles. The accusation of medism could easily be countered in the 440's
when Sparta was clearly the enemy and increasingly a
threat.[13] Themistocles, one could say, never really wanted
to go to Persia; it was the fault of malignant Spartans trying to deprive Athens of wise leadership by bringing false
accusations against him. Memories of Themistocles' deeds
were also colored by those famous aspects of his personality
about which a body of legend was already building up.
These were his *euboulia*—his uncanny cleverness at predict-
ing what would happen and devising the most appropriate
response; and his *pleonexia*—his knack for turning matters
to his own financial advantage.

I cannot agree with Podlecki that there were also memories of old *Parteikämpfe* that influenced appraisals of Themistocles in Herodotus' day. I have always maintained that
we must not inflict political parties (in German dress,
moreover) on the Marathon generation.[14] Nor do I believe
that Herodotus' critical appraisal of the general can be explained by adverse propaganda by his enemies in Athens,
be they Alcmeonids or whatever.[15] This theory attributes to
Herodotus a naïveté he nowhere else reveals. He was certainly capable of adjusting or embroidering his data for the
sake of good storytelling, but to assume that he pitched his
narrative to agree with the approved version of some faction in Athens means we must once more commence the
fruitless task of identifying Herodotus' friends at Athens.

In general, I would suspect that the great mass of Atheni-

[13] See H. Strasburger, "Herodot und das perikleische Athen,"
Historia 4 (1955) 21-22; F. Jacoby, *Atthis* 396 n. 43; idem, *RE* Supplb.
2 (1913) 239-240.

[14] Podlecki, *Themistocles* 67; see my remarks in *CSCA* 1 (1968)
105f., 123-125.

[15] How and Wells I 42-43; Hignett, *Xerxes' Invasion* 204; G. L.
Cawkwell, "The Fall of Themistocles," *Auckland Classical Essays*
(Auckland, 1970) 42f.; Schachermeyr, *Rapports* 83.

ans—who were as notoriously quick to forgive their leaders as they were to condemn them, and whose political loyalties were more determined by live personalities than by dead issues—would have remembered Themistocles with appreciation. His ambition, his quick wits, his ability to make a little money on the side—these were all qualities they admired, and if he accomplished his goals by means that were sometimes devious, it was because the world was a hard and devious place. Athenians were neither sanctimonious nor stuffy; this was the generation that watched the young Alcibiades growing up and spoiled him so with their adulation. And it may be pertinent to recall that the noble Cimon's favorite memory was not of butchering Persians but of fooling fellow Greeks.[16]

To some degree Herodotus had formed some opinions about Themistocles before he ever came to Athens. To some degree he could not help being influenced by the atmosphere of opinion he found in the city. As a growing boy he was living not far from an important city of Asia Minor ruled by the tyrant Themistocles by virtue of his submission to the Persian King. Later he came to Athens and heard the accusations of medism, the warm approval of those who saw Themistocles as an enemy of the hated Spartans, the traditions of *euboulia* and *pleonexia*. What was he to make of it all?

First of all, I think, we must agree that Herodotus does not willingly distort the truth about recent history (as opposed to popular tales about winged serpents or one-eyed Arimaspians). After hearing all sides, he put down what he believed had really happened. If we are then disappointed with what he tells us, it must be, as Fornara has nicely put it, because we wish he had told us something else.[17] If he tells us that Themistocles took bribes from the Euboeans

---

[16] Ion of Chios in Plut. *Cimon* 9; see Peter Green's instructive insight on Mediterranean attitudes to "palm-greasing" in *The Year of Salamis* (London, 1970) 131.

[17] C. Fornara, *Herodotus* (Oxford, 1971) 66-74 and especially 72f.

and extorted money from the islanders, it may actually be because it was the truth. If he seems to detract from Themistocles' *euboulia* by saying that he was merely passing on another man's advice as his own, he no doubt believed that this was so, and had witnesses to back it up.[18] If the treatment seems on balance unfavorable, it may very well be that Themistocles began to have a new vogue at Athens during the 440's and that Herodotus, who prided himself on his superiority to popular enthusiasm, was merely trying to restore perspective to what was already becoming a Themistocles romance. One might add that Herodotus, with all his complexities, was basically anti-hero. He rarely glorified Greek individuals because his theme was that the war was won by the concerted efforts of free men. When he did single out individuals for praise, they tended to be hoplites from the ranks rather than generals and politicians.[19] But Herodotus' treatment of Themistocles will probably never be satisfactorily explained. Later writers, both modern and ancient, have felt they could do a better job. The first, and most influential, was Thucydides.

C. THUCYDIDES

I 14.3: Themistocles persuaded the Athenians to build the fleet. Herodotus' implication that only the Aeginetan war was considered at the time (7.144) was tacitly corrected by Thucydides: τοῦ βαρβάρου προσδοκίμου ὄντος.

I 74: Thucydides' belief in the general's foresight is further revealed in the speech of the Athenian answering the Corinthian accusations at Sparta: the battle of Salamis was the deciding contest of the Persian War. To this the Athenians brought the most ships and the general Themistocles, without whose counsel the battle would not have been

---

[18] On the Mnesiphilus episode, see my remarks in "Themistocles and Mnesiphilus," *Historia* 20 (1971) 20.

[19] E.g., Dieneces (7.226); Polycritus, Eumenes, and Ameinias (8.93); Sophanes (9.74).

fought in the favorable waters of the straits. The Spartans were pointedly reminded that they had honored Themistocles beyond precedent at that time.

I 90.3-91: When Spartan ambassadors tried to dissuade the Athenians from rebuilding their walls, Themistocles went in turn to Sparta and put them off until the walls were as high as necessary, meanwhile persuading the Spartans to send ambassadors to Athens where they could be held as unwitting hostages to ensure his own safety once the truth was known.

I 93.3: Themistocles persuaded the Athenians to fortify Piraeus. He had already started this project during his archonship (this is a most difficult and controversial passage).[20]

I 135: The Spartans had found evidence during their investigation of Pausanias that implicated Themistocles as well. The Athenians agreed to try him, and both states cooperated in hunting him down (he had been ostracized and was living in Argos). I 136: But Themistocles fled to Kerkyra, thence to Epirus, where Admetus sheltered the suppliant and sent him on to Pydna. I 137: Here he took ship for Ephesos, but was delayed by a storm at Naxos, where he was in danger of being caught by the Athenian fleet. By a combination of threats and promises he extricated himself from this difficulty, landed in Asia, and wrote to Artaxerxes, "newly come to the throne."[21] He reminded the king of his two messages, "the report from Salamis about the withdrawal and that about the bridges."[22] I 138: After learning Persian, Themistocles went up to court and was honored by him, both because of the Persian's hope that

[20] See special note, "The Archon Year 493/2," in chapter III of the commentary.

[21] The date 465/4 seems fairly well established by the regnal intervals in Manetho, *FGrH* IIIC pp. 50-51; Diod. XI 69.6: Artaxerxes reigned forty years; Thuc. IV 50.3: he died in 425/4.

[22] I.e., the messages described by Herodotus 8.75, 8.110. So A. W. Gomme, *A Historical Commentary to Thucydides* I (Oxford, 1945) 440-441 and see comment to 28.2.

Themistocles would lead a new expedition against Greece and even more because of his obvious brilliance.

Thucydides now concluded his digression with an unusual detour into character analysis. Themistocles, he said, was unequaled at arriving at an immediate appreciation of any situation, deciding instantly what ought to be done about it, and explaining his plan to others. His gifts of statesmanship were natural, not acquired—a view to which later writers would take exception. Thucydides had made three important contributions to the Themistocles tradition. First, he had put in the mouth of an Athenian diplomat the statement that Themistocles had made the most decisive contributions to the victory of the Greeks, thus substantially improving on the general picture drawn by Herodotus. Second, he had drawn a narrative framework of the general's postwar career, flight, and exile. Third, he had, in his concise way, described what he felt constituted the man's great intellectual gifts. We are certain that all later writers of any stature were aware of Thucydides' treatment of Themistocles. Furthermore, because of the historian's style, it was almost impossible to misunderstand him. Therefore when Diodorus, or Nepos, or Plutarch (who are most obviously following the Thucydidean outline) differ with Thucydides, we must assume that there were available alternate stories about the great man's career. The fact that Diodorus, Nepos, and Plutarch, while differing with Thucydides, also disagree among themselves makes it clear that there was more than one account. Unfortunately, none of these writers explains why he preferred such an account to the authority of Thucydides.

D. MINOR FIFTH-CENTURY WRITERS

For fourth-century writers, as for modern scholarship, the accounts of Herodotus and Thucydides represented the major part of the written record. The few fragments of the fifth-century writers whose works are no longer extant

contribute almost nothing to our understanding; we must
assume however that these works were available to authors
in succeeding generations who wished to dig for information not found in Herodotus or Thucydides. The sources
discussed below may have added a detail or two that supplemented the narrative of the two major historians, or
even a variant tale from another branch of the oral tradition. But the thesis that there was a single major non-
Herodotean tradition about the Persian Wars that was
drawn on heavily by Ephorus and others and which can be
reconstructed from the accounts of Diodorus, Plutarch, the
Suda, and a variety of other writers has so little in the way
of real evidence to support it that it cannot be seriously considered.[23] On the other hand, we do know of an alternative to Thucydides' sketch of the Pentecontaetia: the work
of Hellanicus of Lesbos. Hellanicus lived till the end of
the fifth century[24] and wrote three works that may have
supplemented or differed in matters of detail with the works
of the two major historians. A *Persica* in two or more books
was consulted by Plutarch for the events of 480/79.[25] The
Priestesses of Hera at Argos undertook the task of arrang-
ing, in the form of a chronicle, Greek history from the
Flood down to historical times.[26] The famous *Atthis* treated
local Athenian history in the same fashion, tying events in
this case to Archon years.[27] One is put in the uncomfortable
position of having to assume that all of these works dealt

[23] The thesis of E. Obst, "Der Feldzug des Xerxes," *Klio* Beiheft
12 (1914); see F. Jacoby, "Herodotus," *RE* Supplb. ii (1913) 392ff.;
G. Gottlieb, *Das Verhältnis der ausserherodoteischen Überlieferung
zu Herodot* (Frankfurt, 1963) 48, 135; Hignett, *Xerxes' Invasion*
12-15.

[24] *FGrH* 323a FF 25 and 26 deal with the events of the year 407/6;
see Jacoby *FGrH* IIIb suppl. 2-4.

[25] *De Hdt.mal.* 869A, *FGrH* 323a F 28, and Jacoby ad loc.

[26] This work was perhaps the first attempt to create a method for
dating Greek antiquity. The method seems to be tacitly recognized
by Thucydides II 2 and IV 133 but otherwise rejected by him as a
method of dating (cf. V 20).

[27] Full discussion in *FGrH* IIIb suppl. 1-57.

with Themistocles, without being able to say how, as no fragment that mentions Themistocles has survived. One scholar has suggested Hellanicus' *Atthis* as a major source for the author(s) of the fictional Themistocles letters,[28] but such exercises in scholarly guesswork are barely capable of supporting their own weight and should not be used as bases for further conjecture—as the author himself was the first to admit. It should be noted if Hellanicus did in fact date Themistocles' movements during the two decades after the Persian Wars, in either the *Priestesses* or the *Atthis*, no subsequent author found his dates particularly compelling.[29]

The *Persica* (or perhaps the *Hellenica*) of Charon of Lampsacus, a contemporary of Herodotus,[30] recorded the meeting of Themistocles with Artaxerxes, but we have only this bare statement (in 27.1) and no idea how Charon treated the subject. The existence of such a historian, nearly contemporary with events and a native of one of Themistocles' later tributary cities, has however proven too much of a temptation for modern scholars to resist and there have been attempts to show that this or that piece of information derives from Charon.[31] These will be discussed further in the commentary.

[28] Norman A. Doenges, *The Letters of Themistocles* (Diss. Princeton, 1953) 184-185.

[29] Thuc. I 97.2; implied by Plut. *Them.* 27.2. A. Mosshammer believes Eusebius was misled by Hellanicus on the date of the fortification of Piraeus, "Themistocles' Archonship in the Chronographic Tradition," *Hermes* 103 (1975) 222-234.

[30] *De Hdt.mal.* 859AB; Dion.Hal. *De Thuc.* 5, *Ad Pomp.* 3.7 (*FGrH* 262 T 3).

[31] R. Lenardon, "Charon, Thucydides and Themistokles," *Phoenix* 15 (1961) 28-40; Carl Nylander, "Assyria Grammata: Remarks on the 21st Letter of Themistokles," *Opuscula Athen.* 8 (1968) 119-136, shows that the change in official Persian usage from Aramaic to Achaemenid cuneiform (c. 520) is accurately described by the author of this Letter and must be derived from a nearly contemporary source; R. Schmitt, "Die achaemenidische Satrapie TAYAIY DRA-YAHYA," *Historia* 21 (1972), shows that the title of the satrapy

A useful comment is preserved from the *Epidemiae* of Ion of Chios, a dramatist and philosopher who knew many of the great at Athens and seems to have left this memoir of his meetings with them.[32] At a dinner given sometime in the 450's, Ion heard the guests describe Themistocles as unable to sing or perform on the kithara but skilled in making a city great and wealthy.[33] This is our only evidence that the statesman was regarded as *amousos* by his own generation and that this aspect of his character was not simply invented by later writers for the sake of contrast. Other than this we know only that Ion referred to the daughter of Themistocles as an Ἀθηναία ξένη.[34]

Of all the minor writers of the fifth century, the one contributing the most supplementary information (or misinformation) was that curious figure Stesimbrotus of Thasos. According to his work *On Themistocles, Thucydides and Pericles* (the title is from Athenaeus 589E; all other fragments are in Plutarch), Themistocles studied with Anaxagoras and Melissus (2.3, *FGrH* 107 F 1). He passed the shipbuilding bill against the opposition of Miltiades (4.3, F 2); while at the court of Admetus, his family was sent to him by Epicrates, who was later indicated for this by Cimon (24.5, F 3). Comment on these passages is reserved for later. It suffices to say that Plutarch trusted Stesimbrotus neither in these passages nor very much elsewhere (*Cimon* 4.4, 16.1; *Pericles* 13.16, 26.1). Modern scholarship has been

given to Artabazos in Letter 16 (p. 755 Hercher) is a direct translation of one of the previously uncertain satrapies in the Behistun inscription. He suggests Charon as a source. See also a recent survey of Charon by Mauro Moggi, "Autori greci di *Persika*: Carone di Lampsaco," *ASNP* Serie III 7 (1977) 1-26.

[32] *FGrH* IIIb pp. 192-194; Jacoby, "Some Remarks on Ion of Chios," *CQ* 41 (1947) 1-17.

[33] *Cimon* 9.1, *FGrH* 392 F 13. For the implied date see Jacoby, *CQ* 41 (1947) 2 n. 7.

[34] Photius, *Lex.* s.v., 392 F 11. The interest of the lexicographer was in the use of the ethnic only and little is to be gained from speculation about the exact context of the citation. See comment to 32.2.

much concerned over Stesimbrotus' "tendenz," over which there is no agreement.[35] His work may have been a tract attacking the Athenian empire in general, or it may have been designed to support one or another of the factions within Athens in the later fifth century. A third possibility is that the work had less to do with politics than with the training and moral character of great men. Stesimbrotus was a professional rhapsode, or Homeric expounder,[36] was probably therefore hostile to sophism and wished to show in his work the bad effects of sophistic influence on men like Themistocles and Pericles. The main problem in analyzing Stesimbrotus' work is that there are virtually no prose works of any genre whatsoever from this period of Greek history with which we might compare it. The few remaining fragments are simply not enough to reconstruct the nature or tendency of the tract. Nor can one say with any confidence what influence it had on the developing Themistocles tradition, because Stesimbrotus is not cited by any authority known to us until Plutarch and Athenaeus.

The Athenian aristocrat and political adventurer Critias, whose ruthless character is chillingly depicted in the speeches attributed to him by Xenophon,[37] wrote a number of political works from which a handful of fragments have survived. Timocreon and Herodotus had mentioned the *pleonexia* of Themistocles; Critias developed this theme and supplied some details. Before entering public life, Themistocles' οὐσία πατρῷα had amounted to three talents, but when he was exiled and his goods confiscated, he was found to be worth more than a hundred.[38] This is oral tradition, of course, but it is a tradition that came to be standardized, as the Socratic school took delight in reciting the catalogue

---

[35] Older literature cited by Jacoby, *FGrH* IID 343f.; cf. R. Laqueur, *RE* II 3 (1929) 2464-2467; M. A. Levi, *Plutarco e il V secolo* (Milan, 1955) 12-13; Podlecki, *Themistocles* 56-58.

[36] Plato, *Ion* 530cd, *FGrH* 107 T 3; Xen. *Symp.* 3.6 T 4; see FF 21-25 from the scholia to Homer.

[37] *Hellenica* II 3.24 50sq.   [38] Quoted by Aelian *VH* 10.17.

of Athenian statesmen who had been punished by the Demos.[39]

Surprisingly enough, Old Comedy, from which we should expect much, seems to have contributed little to the Themistocles tradition. In two passages of the *Knights* (813, 833), Aristophanes characterized Themistocles as a great benefactor of the Demos; to see implied criticism in this, however, is to take a narrow view of the poet's goals. As with so much of comedy, the point here must remain obscure. The reference to the exile's suicide by bull's blood in *Knights* 84 is informative, on the other hand, for it is solid evidence that the story was already current in 425/4. There is also a fragment from a lost play by the comic poet Platon, referring to the building of the general's tomb by the entrance to Piraeus, which may mean that Themistocles had been officially rehabilitated by the beginning of the fourth century (see comment to 32.4). Other than this, we have only the statement of Sophocles' biographer about those "comic poets who did not even keep their hands off Themistocles"—οὐδ'ἂν ὑπὸ τῶν κωμικῶν ἄδηκτος ἀφείθη τῶν οὐδὲ Θεμιστοκλέους ἀπεσχημένων.[40] This evidently means that there was some hostile comment which the biographer, unaccustomed to the style of Old Comedy so many centuries before his own day, found offensive.

In the fifth century, two great historians had told parts of Themistocles' story with a minimum of interpretive zeal. In general, both writers were more interested in events than in ideas. But the explosive broadening of intellectual horizons that began during the Peloponnesian War brought with it a host of new literary genres for which history was a means rather than an end in itself. During the fourth century, two new groups of scholars—the moral philosophers

---

[39] E.g., Plato *Gorgias* 515e-516d. That records were kept of such confiscations seems indicated by the citation of Theophrastus in *Them.* 25.3.

[40] *Vita Sophoclis* 1. I interpret this in the same way as Podlecki, *Themistocles* 58.

and the political scientists—sought to explain the phenomenon of Themistocles, to fit him into the tidy patterns of
their disciplines, and thus wrought major changes in the
tradition.

E. The Philosophers

When Thucydides offered his opinion that Themistocles
was naturally gifted, συνετὸς φύσει, he was adding his voice
to a discussion that had begun in his day and continued for
half a century, involving not only Themistocles but all
statesmen. The question was whether one could become
σπουδαῖος and acquire ἐπιστήμη by trusting to natural gifts
alone, or whether it was necessary to have some sort of
guidance or instruction. The argument seems quaint today
and more sterile than most raised by the schools. Yet it cannot be dismissed on this account, as discussion of this sort
had a profound influence on the creation of a tradition
about Themistocles, especially about his youth.[41]

The first generation of sophists introduced the idea that
statesmanship was a *techne* and could be taught, an idea
that was persuasively expounded by men like Protagoras
and Gorgias. The famous friendship between Anaxagoras
and Pericles promoted this concept; regardless of the real
nature of their relationship, the sophists and teachers of
rhetoric saw what they wanted to see and did their best to
advertise the teaching of the philosopher and the success
of his pupil as cause and effect, pure and simple. In succeeding generations it became necessary for a writer who
had any respect for philosophy to link up every successful
statesman with his own personal mentor.[42] When the author
of the pseudo-Platonic *De virtute* claimed that the teachers

[41] Much of the following discussion was first presented in my
article "Themistocles and Mnesiphilus," *Historia* 20 (1971) 20-23.

[42] Cicero, *De Orat.* 3.34-35; that this type of discussion about
Themistocles went on among the Socratics was first suggested by
Adolf Bauer, *Themistokles* 71f.

of Themistocles, Thucydides, Aristeides, and Pericles were unknown (376C), it was merely for the sake of his argument; Stesimbrotus confidently (if mistakenly) named the teachers of Themistocles, and all Athens know that Pericles studied with Anaxagoras and Damon.[43]

Plato, of course, took no part in the debate. To him, Themistocles was a false statesman, a classic example of the leader who advises only what is useful, with no consideration of what is just; he and Pericles had filled the city with foolishness—walls and dockyards and so forth (*Gorgias* 455E, 519A)—he had created the navy and the navy had promoted the unfettered license of the democracy (*Laws* 706C). But the other Socratics showed no such idealistic standards. To them, Themistocles was a model of successful statesmanship—one of the great national heroes, to be held up as an example to the young. Their goal was to demonstrate, by this example, the statesman's dependence on the philosopher.

In Xenophon's *Memorabilia* (IV 2.2) we see the young Euthydemus perplexed by the question whether it was by association with wise men or by natural gifts that Themistocles so distinguished himself that the citizens turned to him when an experienced man was needed. Socrates then answered that it was foolish to suppose one needed instruction in minor skills if it were possible to learn statesmanship —the most difficult of all arts—by oneself.

This thesis was supported by the argument of the Socratic Aeschines of Sphettos in his dialogue *Alcibiades*, part of which can be reasonably reconstructed.[44] Socrates reported a conversation he had with Alcibiades. The young man

[43] Contemporary comment about Damon is quoted by Plut. *Per.* 4.4; the influence of Anaxagoras on Pericles is mentioned by Plato, *Phaedr.* 270a, also quoted by Plut. *Per.* 8.2.

[44] H. Dittmar, *Aischines von Sphettos* (Berlin, 1912) 155-158; Grenfell and Hunt, *The Oxyrhynchus Papyrus* xiii (1913) pp. 88-94 (commentary to no. 1608, Aeschines Socraticus, *Alcibiades*); G. C. Field, *Plato and His Contemporaries* (London, 1930) 147-148; E. G. Berry, "The Oxyrhynchus Fragments of Aeschines," *TAPA* 81 (1950) 1-8.

seems to have claimed that he need only rely on his natural gifts to become great—as he said Themistocles had done. But Socrates showed that Themistocles was φαῦλος as a youth, and had even been disinherited by his father. He then demonstrated that just as one must be *amousos* before becoming *mousikos* and *aphippos* before becoming *hippikos*,[45] so was Themistocles *phaulos* before he became a great statesman. His greatness was adequately proven by his deeds and leadership in the Persian Wars.[46] Themistocles' change of character was accomplished through a course of self-improvement, and although Socrates neglected to specify what this consisted of in the case of Themistocles, we know that for Alcibiades he was suggesting closer association with someone who could teach him virtue—Socrates himself.

It seems abundantly clear that both Xenophon and Aeschines started with the premise that natural gifts were not enough, that it took instruction and guidance to make a gifted man great. They then forced the story of Themistocles to fit this theory, selecting, rejecting, or improving upon whatever data they felt necessary to make his case a good example. But for the philosophers, as for us, several things were not particularly clear: the identity of the wise man whose existence was implied by Xenophon and appropriate details about Themistocles' riotous youth—way back in the sixth century. I suspect that the schools had very little real information about either matter. But when colorful details are needed for convincing illustration they have a way of coming into existence by themselves, as it is not only nature that abhors a vacuum.

Herodotus had mentioned Mnesiphilus only as an acquaintance of Themistocles; by Plutarch's day, this person has become a full-fledged pre-Socratic philosopher, neatly fitted into a διαδοχή,[47] this being a necessary credential for

---

[45] *POxy* xiii 1608 fr. 1.

[46] Aristides, *For the Four* II 292ff. (fr. 8 Dittmar).

[47] *Them.* 2.6; *Sept.sap.conv.* 154C, 156B: *An seni* 795C; Clement

all philosophers. I suggest that the primary reason for this interest in Mnesiphilus was the connection the fourth century philosophers saw between him and Themistocles; one assumes in the absence of any evidence that his doctrine (or what passed for a doctrine) reached Plutarch through the agency of one of the Alexandrian scholars who compiled φιλοσόφων διαδοχαί according to their doctrines.[48] In the same fashion, stories about Themistocles' dissolute youth became more and more spectacular, I suggest again, for no other purpose than to contrast with his later sagacity and eminence, until we find him dashing through the streets of Athens in a quadriga drawn by four prostitutes, whose very names are known.[49] There is no way to prove all these stories. But even the least skeptical must ask how all these sensational details were preserved for the edification of philosophers a century later. All the grand young men entertained the greater public with their youthful exuberance—it was almost expected of them. Why then should the young Themistocles' misdeeds in particular be remembered?

There is one good reason for the development of these tales. The juvenile delinquent par excellence was Alcibiades, and during his later career and after his death, I believe it was inevitable that he came to be compared with Themistocles. They were the two greatest combat generals in Athenian history; they both became renegades because of the jealousy of the Demos (as the anti-democratic Socratics would have been likely to claim); no doubt, men would conjecture, Themistocles too had lived life to the fullest during his youth. Who then played the role of Socrates and persuaded Themistocles to give up frivolous things and make use of his true gifts? It must have been that obscure

---

Alex. *Stromateis* I 14, 65.3 (which derives from an epitome of the *diadochai*).

[48] Plut. *Them.* 2.6: ἐπιτήδευμα πεποιημένου καὶ διασῴζοντος ὥσπερ αἵρεσιν ἐκ διαδοχῆς ἀπὸ Σόλωνος. See comment to this passage.

[49] Idomeneus in Athen. 576C, 533D, *FGrH* 338 F 4.

figure Mnesiphilus, the philosophers would say, and thus the legend developed.

F. THE POLITICAL THEORISTS

While the moral philosophers were developing the general's character to suit their arguments, political theorists were debating his place in Athenian partisan politics with no less attention to the demands of pure reason. Neither Herodotus nor Thucydides had anything to say about Themistocles' political tendency. The former describes domestic politics at Athens as a series of clashes between individual personalities,[50] with no question of differing political philosophies. Thucydides was contemptuous of political labels, seeing them only as false beacons in man's eternal quest for power (III 82.8). To Thucydides, there were only two political parties anywhere—those in power and those out of power. Nevertheless, less than a century later, when Aristotle had finished reducing the entire human political experience to symmetry and order, Themistocles was firmly entrenched in the Athenian political spectrum as a radical democrat, προστάτης τοῦ δήμου, creator of the ναυτικὸς ὄχλος and deadly opponent of the Areopagus. Obviously certain forces had been at work upon the Themistocles legend between the era of the historians and Aristotle's day. These forces must be analyzed for two reasons. First, it was the Aristotelian picture of Themistocles that was accepted by Plutarch (and, it must be admitted, by many modern scholars as well). Second, one hopes to answer the question for its own sake: did Themistocles consciously promote the growing power of a party of the Demos or oppose an older, aristocratic polity, during the period between Cleisthenes and Pericles?[51]

[50] See V. Ehrenberg, "Origins of Democracy," *Historia* 1 (1950) 527f.

[51] Much of this argument was first published in "Themistocles' Place in Athenian Politics," *CSCA* 1 (1968) 105-124.

During the fourth century, the orators of the Athenian democracy made a secure place for the general in the pantheon of national heroes. At the very beginning of the century, Lysias listed the names of Solon, Themistocles, and Pericles as the model *nomothetae* to whom Athenians should look.[52] He also reminded the Athenians, humiliated by the destruction of their walls, of Themistocles' accomplishment in building them.[53] The later orators invariably presented Themistocles as the modest hero of an older, better Athens,[54] whose wise counsel led to the victory at Salamis,[55] and to the building of the walls.[56] The only implied criticism of the general was found in passages like Demosthenes 23.205: an older and more virtuous Athens never hesitated to punish its greatest heroes (Themistocles, for example) for thinking themselves better than others, and 20.73-74: the building of the walls by Conon was a greater deed than their original construction by Themistocles because the latter worked by stealth. As can be seen, the memory of Themistocles was such that all factions within the democracy used him as a convenient symbol of the city's glorious past.

Even to the conservative Xenophon[57] and to Isocrates, the champion of the Areopagus constitution, Themistocles was just as much the hero-stereotype of the Persian Wars.[58] Isocrates' pupil Theopompus, in his digression on the Athenian demagogues in the tenth book of his *Philippica*,[59] took a morbid delight in describing the bribery of and by Athe-

[52] *In Nicomachum* 27-28.

[53] *In Eratosthenem* 63; the *Epitaphios* attributed to Lysias echoes Thucydides I 74: at Salamis, Athens supplied the best general and the most ships (42).

[54] Demosthenes 23.196-198; [Demosth.] 13.21-22, 29; Aeschines, *Tim.* 25.

[55] Demosth. 18.204; 19.303.

[56] Demosth. 20.73-74; Dinarchus, *In Demosth.* 37; other praise in Aesch. *Falsa legat.* 9; *Ctes.* 181; Hypereides, *Epitaph.* 37.

[57] *Mem.* II 6.13; IV 2.2; *Sympos.* 8.39.

[58] *Panegyr.* 4.154; *Pax* 1.75-76; *Antidosis* 233; *Panath.* 51-52.

[59] Athenaeus 166DE, *FGrH* 115 F 100; cf. W. R. Connor, *Theopompus and Fifth-Century Athens* (Washington, 1968) 6.

nian leaders. He reported that Themistocles had bribed the Spartans not to oppose the building of the walls[60] and that his fortune, at the time of his exile, had risen to the sum of one hundred talents.[61] But there would seem to be no ideological content here; from what is known about the sardonic historian one may be sure that he combed the tradition for outrageous stories. There is no reason to suppose he made any distinction between Athenian leaders of differing political persuasions.[62]

The earliest ideological opponents of the sovereign Demos, by the decade preceding the Peloponnesian War, had already made the equation: large navies lead to democratic polities. This is a recurring theme in the work we know as the pseudo-xenophontic *Athenaion Politeia*.[63] The development of this thesis is not attested in what remains of literature between the Old Oligarch and Aristotle, but it is interesting to note that when Plato (*Laws* 706) describes the awful consequences of allowing hoplites to become accustomed to the rowers' bench, Plutarch automatically assumed that the philosopher had in mind Themistocles' creation of the Athenian navy.[64] It is possible to assume the existence of a theory prevalent among anti-democratic political thinkers of the fourth century. Themistocles created the navy, thus creating a politically potent commons with neither the education nor the emotional stability to resist demagogues; therefore, this was what he had intended. Reasoning of this sort could have converted Themistocles into an ideologue in the minds of oligarchic theoreticians. Unfortunately, it is impossible to attribute this theory to any writers we know

[60] Plut. *Them.* 19.1, F 85; cf. Andocides, *Pax* 38.

[61] *Them.* 25.3, F 86.

[62] See the comment on F 90 by Connor, "Theopompus' Treatment of Cimon," *GRBS* 4 (1963) 107-114.

[63] Cf. E. Schuetrumpf, "Die Folgen der Atimie für die athenische Demokratie," *Philologus* 117 (1973) 152-168; R. Sealey, "The Origins of *Demokratia*," *CSCA* 6 (1973) 253-263, favoring a date for the Old Oligarch c. 443-431.

[64] See comment to 4.4, 19.4-6.

by name. It is often suggested that the Atthidographer Androtion was a conservative of this stamp and that his work was a primary source for Aristotle,[65] but there is no evidence that Androtion ever mentioned Themistocles either favorably or unfavorably. It would be risky, not to say unmethodical, to see Androtion adding anything to the Themistocles tradition.

Another Atthidographer, Cleidemus, by contrast, is often thought to be the voice of the democrats, replying to the hostile interpretations of Athenian history that were later accepted by Aristotle.[66] But his story that Themistocles ransacked the luggage of those embarking for Salamis and provided pay for the sailors, in the form Plutarch told it, proves nothing about Cleidemus' purpose, political or not (see comment to 10.6-7).

The *Athenaion Politeia* of Aristotle, which made use of all the political literature and traditions of the preceding century, became for succeeding generations the standard work on Athenian political history; for modern historians it remains an enigma. In chapters 22-25 it is often very difficult to discover just what Aristotle is trying to say, or to decide whether some of the confusion is due to his sources or to a lack of clarity in his own thinking. Generations ago it was heresy to suggest that Aristotle could be anything less than clear, and some of these passages, when the treatise was first published were used as arguments to show that the great philosopher could not possibly have written such a web of errors. Criticism since that time has shown that previous generations underestimated the extent to which Aristotle was dominated by his theories of political behavior and the extent to which he forced an interpretation of the facts to fit his theories.[67]

[65] J. Day and M. Chambers, *Aristotle's History of Athenian Democracy* (Berkeley and Los Angeles, 1962) 7ff.

[66] F. Jacoby, *Atthis* 75-76, followed with some doubts by Day and Chambers 10.

[67] K. Beloch, *Griechische Geschichte* (Strassburg, 1893-1904) II.2, 134-135; Day and Chambers, 17-24; K. von Fritz and E. Kapp, *Aris-*

It is now clear that he believed the whole human political experience could be reduced to an orderly structure, like any other field of human knowledge; that polities could be ranged in some sort of spectrum; and that certain opposing forces were at work within every polity, causing it to incline now toward rule by the few and now toward rule by the many. In Athens specifically, he saw two parties emerging after the Cleisthenic reform, one of the *gnorimoi* and one of the Demos, and he seems to have assigned every famous Athenian leader to one or the other party. Modern scholarship has done valuable work in showing where he found his historical data,[68] but it is not so clear that his political interpretations were anything but his own, except for the canon of political forms derived from the constitutional theory of the Academy.[69]

His concept of the years between the Cleisthenic constitution and the restriction of the Areopagus (c. 508-462) seems to be as follows. The constitution of Cleisthenes introduced radical democracy. Ostracism—a democratic institution—was established at the start and was followed by election to the archonship by lot (487/6) and Themistocles' creation of naval power, both of which Aristotle considered harmful to a sound polity.[70] During much of this period, Miltiades was the leader of the *gnorimoi* and Xanthippus was leader of the Demos; later in the period Aristeides and Themistocles also became leaders of the Demos (*AP* 28.2).[71] After Sal-

totle's *Constitution of Athens* (New York, 1950) 32ff.; M. Pavan, *La grecità politica* (Rome, 1958) 161-168; R. Weil, "Philosophie et histoire," *La Politique d'Aristote* Entretiens Hardt 11 (1964) 161-189.

[68] Surveyed by Day and Chambers, 5-11; cf. Jacoby, *Atthis* 234-235, long n. 36.

[69] Plato, *Politicus* 291d sq.; Diog.Laert. 3.82.

[70] Ostracism: *AP* 22.1, *Pol.* 3.1284^{a}17-18; sortition: *AP* 22.5, *Pol.* 4.1294^{b}8, 6.1317^{b}20; naval democracy: *Pol.* 5.1304^{a}22, 7.1327^{b}7.

[71] Προστάτης τοῦ δήμου, which Aristotle took to mean party leader, meant at this time only patron of the whole people against the tyrants: H. Schaefer, "Prostates," *RE* Supplb. 9 (1962) 1293-1296; cf. Ehrenberg, *Historia* 1 (1950) 529 and note.

amis, there was a *metabole*, a change of constitution, because of the prestige which the Areopagus had won through their provisioning of the fleet, and this body was prominent for seventeen years. While the Areopagus now presided over the *gnorimoi*, Aristeides and Themistocles continued to be leaders of the Demos. Aristeides proposed that the revenue of the empire be used to support a movement of people into the city where they would be put on the public payroll in one capacity or another (*AP* 24); Themistocles finally aided Ephialtes in the attack on the Areopagus (*AP* 25). This brought an end to the Areopagus constitution and left the way open for a radical democracy again, in which the assembly and courts became sovereign.

Themistocles thus emerges in the *Athenaion Politeia* as a democrat by definition. First, althouth Aristotle admits he was ἐπιεικής—that is, a member of the aristocracy[72]—some tradition of his hostility to Miltiades made it necessary that he be assigned to the opposite side of the political aisle. Second, he was one of the leaders of the Demos at a time when the Demos was adopting institutions typical of radical democracy—sortition, ostracism, and a large navy—and he was specifically responsible for introducing the naval bill. Third, after the Persian Wars, he continued as a democratic leader and with Aristeides opposed the party of the Areopagus.[73] Finally, he cooperated with Ephialtes in putting an end to the Areopagus constitution.

It is easy to reject this interpretation on the basis of method alone; the idea that human behavior—especially political behavior—can be explained by some sort of logic is now rejected by even the most casual observer of the human

---

[72] *AP* 28.1: the Demos first chose leaders from those who were not ἐπιεικής after the death of Pericles. For the meaning of this term and the natural opposition between ἐπιεικής and πλῆθος, see *Pol.* 5.1308b27.

[73] In Aristotle's system of opposites, this is what seems to be meant: Aristeides and Themistocles are both democratic leaders opposing the Areopagus (*AP* 23.3, 28.2).

condition in the twentieth century. And yet there is no question that the polity of the Athenians came into the fifth century with an aristocratic orientation but on the eve of the Peloponnesian War had become dominated by a Demos jealous of its authority and prerogatives. Aristotle saw Themistocles as a force tending toward this change in polity. Can we in fact argue that he was not?

It suffices here to summarize an argument I have presented in some detail elsewhere.[74] A close survey of every known event with any political significance in Themistocles' life reported by writers prior to Aristotle produces no evidence whatever of political tendency, if in fact we can even speak of such a thing in the early fifth century. So far as we can interpret Themistocles' actions, he never once promoted any policy that would have given the Demos greater power. In fact, in one of his three attested appearances before the assembly,[75] he recommended that the mining revenue *not* be distributed among the citizen body—scarcely the line we should expect to see taken by a stock demagogue. He appears to have enjoyed popular support during the 480's and needed it to survive a series of clashes with other public figures—some of them Alcmeonids or Alcmeonid connections, who are in turn said to be famous for soliciting popular support. But there is not one scrap of evidence that can show him responsible for the change in the method of selecting archons in 487, for instance, if indeed sortition was a "liberal" reform. Nor does the mass of ostraca recently excavated from Kerameikos make the issues of the ostracophoriae any clearer, as was once hoped. If anything, they seem to show that much of the voting depended upon personal animosities rather than upon political issues.[76]

If there is one thing obvious in the 470's it is that Themistocles was losing popular support and that Cimon, who serves as Aristotle's symbol for aristocratic leadership (*AP*

[74] *CSCA* 1 (1968) 120-124.   [75] Ibid. 117f.; Hdt. 7.144.
[76] E. Vanderpool, "Ostracism at Athens," *Louise Taft Semple Lectures* second series (Cincinnati, 1970), gives numerous examples.

28.2) had seized it by his stylish series of victories in command of the *nautikos ochlos* that manned the fleet. On the other hand, Themistocles seems to have been much more comfortable dealing with powerful persons on an individual basis, which is the way things got done most of the time in the Athenian democracy (and in most other democracies I know of, as well). Even on his hazardous flight, Themistocles was at his best using exactly the right approach to King Admetus and to the Great King himself; it was the democracy of the Kerkyreans with which he had trouble.[77]

The political struggles of the Marathon generation are far from clear; they will be examined in more detail in the commentary in an attempt to come to more precise conclusions about Themistocles' political activity.[78] It suffices here to make the negative point that Aristotle's picture of left-wing and right-wing politics in fifth-century Athens is based on false premises and that his portrayal of Themistocles as a leader of the left is merely this general fallacy carried out to

[77] See comment to 24.1-2.

[78] In a forthcoming contribution to a collection of studies honoring Professor Malcolm F. McGregor, I have tried to answer the question: what were the actual goals of political activity in early fifth-century Athens? I believe this can only be answered if we first define the nature of government by identifiable function. Governmental functions scarcely existed at Athens right down to the Persian Wars and can be practically limited to religious supervision, military and diplomatic leadership, and administration of justice. Therefore, I doubt there were either any ideological motives or any great advantages to being "in power." Why then would anyone wish to be a "politician," a word which is practically an anachronistic term at this stage of Athenian governmental development? I have tried to show that the real goals of all young Athenian aristocrats were to compete successfully for honor and esteem and that political activity was just one of many ways of earning this sort of respect from one's fellows. In other words, the average Athenian aristocrat wished to be admired as a community leader without necessarily having to do any leading. Themistocles was an exception to this general rule because every time we see him he is actually trying to get something accomplished, some program put across.

a particular fallacious conclusion. In any event, the meta-
morphosis of Themistocles from statesman of the Persian
Wars to radical democratic party leader was completed in
the *Athenaion Politeia* of Aristotle. Partly because of the
stature of the great polymath, and partly because the Athenian Demos itself did not survive him, subsequent inquiry
into the Athenian polities was forced to accept his view, not
as one generation's contribution to a continuing organic
debate, but as a final summation, a sort of fossilized logos
frozen into permanence and no longer subject to revision.
Future thinkers might question Aristotle's judgment—
whether sovereign democracy was all that bad—but never
the rigid symmetry of the structure he gave to politics,
never the roles he assigned to the various players that had
to be located in the political spectrum, never the political
logic that made Themistocles a democrat.

G. EPHORUS

To complete the history of the development of the Themistocles tradition during the fourth century, something
needs to be said about Ephorus of Kyme. This historian, a
student of Isocrates, wrote a universal Greek history in
twenty-nine books, from the return of the Heraclidae to
the siege of Perinthus.[79] The work has not survived, but
enough fragments are found in later writers to give a fairly
consistent picture of its worth. Everyone seems to have
read the work, but its status as a classic depended mainly
on the fact that Ephorus was the first, and for a long time
the only, writer to attempt such a history,[80] for otherwise
he was dull, long-winded, and uncritical.

There can be no doubt that Ephorus had access to, and
reported information that supplements or differs from, both
Herodotus' account of the Persian Wars and Thucydides'

[79] Diod. XVI 76.5, *FGrH* 70 T 10.
[80] Polybius V 33.2, T 7.

sketch of the Pentecontaetia.[81] But it must be considered a mistake of method to go on and assume, as some scholars do, that every novelty found in later writers—Phanias, Nepos, or Polyaenus, for instance—must be part of the Ephoran tradition. This is the first undoubted convenience a methodical historian must attempt to deny himself. The second is the common assumption that the greater part of Diodorus Siculus, books 11-15, is an epitome of Ephorus, for this widely practiced shortcut of historiography is not a "fundamentalsatz der quellenkritik" but only a highly convenient hypothesis that is justified in only a fraction of the cases where it is applied.[82]

One can, however, assume something about the nature of the information Ephorus assimilated and reported in his history. Herodotus and Thucydides he knew of course; he often followed the former with little change,[83] whether consciously or because the information was *communis opinio*. He had to supplement Thucydides' spare sketch of the Pentecontaetia but otherwise often excerpted him sensibly for the years of the Peloponnesian War.[84] Beyond these historians he seems to have read and used almost everything, giving all equal weight as reliable authorities. The best demonstration is *FGrH* F 196, an account that shows, despite shortening and juggling by Diodorus (XII 38-41), that Ephorus had blended Thucydides, Aristophanes, Eupolis, and common anecdotes into a survey of the causes of the Peloponnesian War that has bothered both ancient and modern investigators.[85]

Extant fragments of Ephorus show that he treated Themistocles several times between c. 485-465. I list the frag-

[81] Steph.Byz. s.v. Paros, F 63; Plut. *De Hdt.mal.* 869A, F 187; see the fragments discussed below.

[82] See M. Casevitz, *Diodore de Sicile: Bibliothèque historique* Book XII (Budé, 1972) xiii-xv.

[83] Schol. Pindar, *Pyth.* 1.146, F. 186.

[84] E.g., Steph.Byz. s.v. Boudoron, F. 198.

[85] Schol. Arist. *Peace* 605; Aristodemus 16-19; Jacoby, *FGrH* IIIb Supple. 484-496; see my remarks in *Historia* 13 (1964) 392-399.

ments chronologically only for convenience; we know that Ephorus himself wrote his history *kata genos*—by subjects (Diod. V 1.4).

F 64, schol. Aristides 515.22: "Ephorus in Book One [corrected to Eleven, probably rightly, by Mueller, *FHG* IV 642] says that he [Cimon] acquired the fifty talents by marrying a wealthy woman." This may well be the story that Diodorus has in fuller form (X 32): a rich man (cf. Plut. *Cimon* 4.10) approached Themistocles looking for a rich marriage connection for his daughter, Isodice. Themistocles, in turn, advised him to seek not unmanly money but a moneyless man. The aphorism is timeless and no doubt originally anonymous, but it may well have been Ephorus who first put it in Themistocles' mouth.

F 189, Plut. *De Hdt.mal.* 855F: "Concerning Themistocles, Ephorus said that he knew of Pausanias' treason and what he was doing with the generals of the King. 'But,' he says, 'he was not persuaded to accept a role in the affair or to share the rewards.'" This story is elaborated in the Life (23) without attribution; it is probably the source of Diodorus XI 54.3-4 and the inspiration for Letter 14 (Hercher p. 754).

F 190, Plut.*Them.* 27.1: "But Ephorus . . . and most other writers say that he [Themistocles] came to Xerxes himself." See comment ad loc.

F 191: *POxy* XIII 1610 cannot be convincingly shown to be a fragment of Ephorus.[86] Of fragments 1-3, which deal with Themistocles, fr. 1 actually seems to quote Thucydides on the exile's plea to Artaxerxes: λέ]γουσι δ' οἱ μὲν ὅ[τι ὑπέ]μνησεν αὐτ[ὸν ὢν] περί τε τῆς ν[αυμα]χίας καὶ τῆς γ[εφύρας προ]ήγγειλε very closely echoes Thuc. I 137.4: γράψας τήν τε ἐκ Σαλαμῖνος προάγγελσιν τῆς ἀναχωρήσεως καὶ τὴν τῶν γεφυρῶν κτλ.

Fragment 3: ἐκ[εῖνον] μὲν ὑπὸ τῆς πόλε[ως] ἠτιμασμένον, τ[ὴν] δὲ πόλιν διὰ τ[ὰ]ς ἐκείνου πράξε[ι]ς τῆς μεγίστης τιμῆς ὑπὸ τῶν Ἑλλήνων ἀξιωθεῖσαν is in turn very similar to the stock

---

[86] See especially T. W. Africa, "Ephorus and Oxyrhynchus Papyrus 1610," *AJP* 83 (1962) 86-89.

tribute in Diodorus XI 59.3: εὕρωμεν ἐκεῖνον μὲν ὑπὸ τῆς πόλεως ἠτιμασμένον, τὴν δὲ πόλιν διὰ τὰς ἐκείνου πράξεις ἐπαιρομένην κτλ.; but clichés like this, of all the passages in the *Bibliotheca*, are most likely to be Diodorus himself speaking.[87] The eclectic author of *POxy* 1610 is therefore better left anonymous.

It is aggravating to have only these bits from Ephorus, for the historian undoubtedly gave full attention to the man whose character and achievements colored his whole age. One is therefore once more put in the position (as with Hellanicus) of having to claim that Ephorus discussed Themistocles, collected all the traditional tales about him, and created a picture of the man and his age that influenced writers of the succeeding centuries—one must claim this, and then admit inability to identify with any confidence just what anecdotes from later writers are based on Ephorus.[88]

H. HELLENISTIC LITERATURE

In the centuries between Aristotle and Plutarch, the Themistocles traditions were received and passed on by two different sets of literati. Some were scholars, with an interest in serious *historie*, who had therefore only a limited audience. Others were raconteurs, doing their best to fill the insistent demand of the Hellenistic and Graeco-Roman age for popular literature. There were, of necessity, men who did both, who composed commentaries of impeccable scholarship on one hand, and light reading for the masses on the other—men like Demetrius of Phalerum, Theophrastus, and Phanias.[89]

[87] R. Drews, "Diodorus and his Sources," *AJP* 83 (1962) 383-392, gives several examples.

[88] See also Podlecki, *Themistocles* 92-99.

[89] Demetrius' Socrates was evidently intended for the larger reading public; the author seems to have written it without having consulted his own *Archonton Anagraphe*, FGrH 228 F 44 (Plut. *Arist.*

The serious scholars were indebted to Aristotle and the successors of his school for the techniques involved in the systematic collection and investigation of documents. Before Aristotle, research into annalistic history and constitutional law, and the combination of the two into a dull but reliable and well-documented chronological record was carried on only by the Atthidographers at Athens and their counterparts in other poleis. Aristotle and his students—Theophrastus, Demetrius, Craterus, for instance—succeeded in making this sort of research a prerequisite for anyone who intended to acquire a reputation as a scholar and a position at one of the Hellenistic libraries. Such research flourished until the dark days of the Second Sophistic, when *historie* became the handmaiden of rhetoric.

One of the most difficult tasks for the scholars was to fit the life and deeds of a historical personality into some chronological canon. As an artificial convenience, they adopted the *akme*. When a man's birth date was unknown, the chronographers selected the most important event in his career and arbitrarily assumed him to have been forty years old at the time.[90] But for Themistocles, two traditions seem to have developed ten years apart, depending on whether he had reached his *akme* during his archonship (493) or when he passed the navy bill (483).[91] It can similarly be shown that there was a ten-year difference of opinion about the year of his death and about other dates as well. It is unfortunate that two such canons developed, for the eclectic Plutarch only contributes to the chronological confusion by assuming the early canon in one place (e.g. Themistocles

---

5.9). Philoponus, *Comm. in Arist.Graeca* XIII.1 p. 7.16, gives some of Phanias' scholarly titles; the character of his other work can be seen in *Them.* 7.5 sq. 13.5, 26-29 (see comment ad loc.).

[90] Jacoby, *Apollodors Chronik, Philol.Untersuchungen* 16 (1902) 41-51; see the analysis by M. Miller, *JHS* 75 (1955) 54ff.

[91] R. J. Lenardon, "The Archonship of Themistokles," *Historia* 5 (1956) 401-419; J.A.R. Munro, "The Chronology of Themistocles' Career," *CR* 6 (1892) 333-334.

at Marathon, *Arist.* 5.4) and the late one elsewhere (his death in c. 450, *Them.* 31.4).[92]

But later scholarship could be useful as well. The most typical scholarly endeavor of the Hellenistic age was the learned commentary. The extant Byzantine scholia, based on the earlier commentaries, are often condensed and confused, but the Didymus scholia to Demosthenes, discovered on papyrus at the turn of the century, show how thorough and well-documented the originals could be. For instance, Demosthenes (19.303) said that Aeschines, in the course of a speech, had the clerk read (among other documents) the decree of Themistocles calling for the evacuation of Athens and the embarkation upon the triremes. Although extant scholia to this speech preserve only an echo, learned editions from the age of Didymus would perhaps have contained more of the text; the Didymus papyrus contains much of an Amphictyonic decree as a note to what is probably Demosthenes' second Philippic.[93]

Again, we see Symmachus, one of the later editors and annotators of Aristophanes (c. A.D. 100), rejecting an anecdote about the burial of Themistocles on the grounds that Herodotus and Thucydides had said nothing about it, and denying that a verse from Sophocles alluded to the exile's suicide (schol. Arist. *Knights* 84).

The reconteurs, whether learned or not, had a far different aim from the scholars—to sell books to the general public. Therefore they wrote whatever was provocative, edifying, or scandalous. For the life of Themistocles they had several themes to enlarge upon: *pleonexia* (from Herodotus and Timocreon), youthful *phaulotes* (from the Socratics), *euboulia* and *synesis* (from Thucydides). The school of Aristotle, with its interest in human character, is

[92] Lenardon, "The Chronology of Themistokles' Ostracism and Exile," *Historia* 8 (1959) 23-48, gives all the evidence for the two canons.

[93] Diels and Schubart, *Didymos Kommentar zu Demosthenes* (Berlin, 1904) 14-15, comment to col. 4.1 sq.

best represented by the anecdotes of Phanias, preserved for us by Plutarch. The tales of other Hellenistic writers who are little more than names to us have survived because of the special interests of Athenaeus: men like Idomeneus, Amphicrates, and Clearchus of Soli.

There is no need here to carry further the accumulation of anecdotal material or, rather, as it often seems, the custom of taking anecdotes about greed or political cleverness or depraved youth and inserting the name of Themistocles —this will be treated more fully in the commentary where it seems useful. It suffices to say here that during the flowering of theatrical rhetoric during the Second Sophistic, everything that had ever been written about Themistocles and the other famous personages of what was by then ancient history was assiduously collected and catalogued in the form of ethical or historical exempla for the convenience of students of rhetoric. A good example of a rhetorician's handbook is the *Varia Historia* of Aelian. Any anecdote will do here, with no attempt at consistency. In 2.12, for instance, Themistocles is *asotos*, and disinherited; but in 3.21, he is *eugenes* and *megalophron* even as a boy, refusing to give way to Peisistratus (!) on the street. Perhaps most absurd (2.28), Themistocles noticed the courage of fighting cocks and used this example successfully to exhort the Athenians before Salamis.

Of the same order of reliability was the tradition of the periegetae. ἐντὸς δὲ τῆς πόλεως ἔστι τὸ διδασκαλεῖον τοῦ Σωκράτους . . . κατὰ δύσιν δὲ τούτου ἵστανται τὰ παλάτια τοῦ Θεμιστοκλέους, wrote an anonymous guide of the fifteenth century.[94] His descendants are still at work today; and one supposes his ancestors, escorting Roman tourists through Athens, were no different.

Pausanias was shown Themistocles' grave and his portrait in the Parthenon (I 1.2); statues of Miltiades and Themis-

[94] Le Cte. de Laborde, ed., *Documents sur l'histoire et les antiquités d'Athènes* (Paris, 1854) 3.

tocles were displayed in the Prytaneion (I 18.3-4). The information that their names had been changed to those of a Roman and a Thracian respectively most probably came from an enthusiastic guide.[95] Plutarch also was shown a statue of Themistocles. It was in the temple of Artemis Aristoboule, which the general was said to have erected after the Persian Wars, and stood near his house in Melite.[96] Plutarch, and Pausanias to a lesser extent, were not to be taken in by the more obvious fictions, but we should assume that even the most outrageous inventions of the periegetae found currency somewhere and thus added to the tradition.[97]

This brief survey would not be complete without mentioning the role of the Hellenistic schoolroom in preserving and enriching the Themistocles tradition. As one might expect, the stories that were passed on from master to student tended to be epideictic moral parables rather than the results of scholarly inquiry. As an educated youth of the Hellenistic or later Graeco-Roman world matured and attended symposia or wrote thoughtful essays for the edification of his circle, his learning would be displayed by his ability to illustrate the right point with a suitable anecdote; he would concern himself with the historical accuracy of a story about Themistocles no more than he would with one about Achilles.

By all these diverse paths of communication a corpus of Themistocles stories developed and was passed on during the centuries between the Pentecontaetia and the Pax Romana—a corpus with no rigid limits, compounded of various parts of romance, moralizing, political theory, and scholar-

[95] The evidence for this sort of re-inscription with different names was collected by J. G. Frazer, *Pausanias's Description of Greece* II 174.

[96] For the authenticity of temple, statue, and house, see comment to 22.2-3.

[97] I have tried to show that Plutarch's account of the Covenant of Plataea, for example, was largely drawn from the tradition of the official guides: *Class. et. Med.* 22 (1961) 185-189.

ship around the original core of *historie* provided by Herodotus and Thucydides. At any time, the corpus could be
added to by a casual remark in a barber shop. At any time,
part of the tradition could be effectively lost by the burying
of a dull and tedious *Atthis* in the darkest corner of some
archive, where a scholiast might or might not find it. This
is the tradition that reached a man like Nepos, whose confusion at the profuse and contradictory elements is evident
and whose relief at being able to quote Thucydides is
equally apparent.[98] And this is the same tradition, a generation or so later, that reached the young Plutarch, attending
the school of Ammonius in Athens.

[98] Nepos, *Them.* 9.1, 10.4; *Paus.* 2.2-4; and notice in *Cimon* 2 what
happens when he doesn't bother to look up the passage in Thucydides.

II

PLUTARCH, BIOGRAPHY, AND HISTORY

THE *Lives* of Plutarch of Chaeronea have had a varied career. From the time of their rediscovery during the age of the Renaissance until the nineteenth century they enjoyed a universal popularity rarely accorded any work. During the seventeenth and eighteenth centuries especially, in England and on the Continent, the *Lives* became the plaything of an intellectual *haut monde* that shared Plutarch's preoc-

A version of this chapter under the title, "Plutarch and Clio," has been published in *Panhellenica: Essays in Greek History and Historiography in Honor of T. S. Brown*, ed. by Stanley M. Burstein and Louis A. Okin (Lawrence, Kansas: Coronado Press, 1979). I thank the Coronado Press for permission to publish in this form.

I did much of the research for this chapter and reached many of the conclusions many years ago while working on my doctoral dissertation, *The Scholarship of Plutarch* (University of California, Los Angeles, 1961). Since that time, the tide of Plutarchean criticism has swung back from *Hochkritik* to common sense. Several important books have been written about Plutarch in the last decade and I have been pleased to see that their authors have independently arrived at a judgment of the biographer very close to my own. These works (cited hereafter by author's name alone) are: P. A. Stadter, *Plutarch's Historical Methods* (Cambridge, Mass., 1965); R. H. Barrow, *Plutarch and His Times* (London, 1967); C. P. Jones, *Plutarch and Rome* (Oxford, 1971); and D. A. Russell, *Plutarch* (London, 1975). That there was anything left to say after these fine scholars were through is a tribute to Plutarch's complex nature as human being and writer. There will always be something new to say about Plutarch.

cupation with virtue and his interest in man as a moral
animal. It is not difficult to see why. Plutarch is unique in
his ability to be inoffensive without being dull. His stric-
tures against inhumanity and abuse of privilege have
warmed liberal spirits to a degree comfortably below the
point of combustion while his obvious preference for en-
lightened autocracy has found him a favored position in
the libraries of the most unenlightened despots.

For centuries, Plutarch was the most popular single source
for classical antiquity. An eighteenth-century reader who
wished to turn to the ancient world for information or inspiration needed to look no further than one of the fifty
assorted biographies, covering a period from the mists of
prehistory to the Year of the Four Emperors. The same
audience that saw him as a teacher of virtue also accepted
him with very little question as a historian of critical ability
and independent value. It was in his secondary role as historian that Plutarch came to grief.

In the midst of the great scientific inventions and dis-
coveries of the nineteenth century, history followed the
fashionable trend and became a "scientific" discipline while
historians cloaked their intuition, sound or otherwise, under
the name of "scientific method." Some of the worst ex-
cesses in the name of "method" took place in the study of
classical antiquity, certainly not because the field attracted
inferior talent, but because most of the data necessary for
the reconstruction of the era had disappeared. In a physical
science, data may be inferred once the natural law has been
established; the extension of this process into Greek historiography often led to a cruel betrayal of common sense.

Many names are involved in the application of higher
criticism to Plutarch, but the imprimatur of genius and the
final seal of approval of the process was added by the
grandest name of all: Eduard Meyer. In a close analysis of
Plutarch's *Cimon*,[1] Meyer concluded that the biographer

[1] "Die Biographie Kimons," *Forschungen zur alten Geschichte* II
(Halle, 1899) 1-87.

had used an intermediary source. To support this contention he compared Plutarch with one of his own contemporaries who might be composing a biography of Charles V or Frederick the Great for a popular audience. Like these authors, Plutarch would not have consulted original sources; he would have turned to convenient secondary material, in general, ". . . the deposit of the learned work of generations, from the golden age of scholarly investigation in the third and second centuries B.C. . . ."[2] and specifically, that giant of learning and industry, Didymus Chalcenterus of Alexandria. Meyer's general argument was as follows: Plutarch gives the same information as A. A cites Didymus. Therefore Plutarch must also be using Didymus, including his citations of earlier authors.[3] Meyer's reputation was so impressive and his arguments so reasonable that no one raised some obvious objections, for instance, that almost nothing was known about Didymus,[4] that Plutarch cited other authors thousands of times, but Didymus only once.[5]

But these little flaws are minor details. The original mistake was one of perspective when Meyer elected to compare Plutarch to popular writers of his own day and neglected to recognize the biographer as a unique figure even in antiquity. The failure of communication between Plutarch and Eduard Meyer was the eternal one between the classical humanist and the historian who convinces himself of his scientific method—or, as Meyer might have put it,

---

[2] Ibid. 69.   [3] Ibid. 36-50.

[4] The fragments were collected by M. Schmidt (Leipzig, 1854). A papyrus fragment of a lexicon to Demosthenes' *In Aristocratem* had been published by F. Blass, *Hermes* 17 (1882) 150ff. The large fragment of Didymus' commentary to Demosthenes, purchased in Cairo in 1901 and published by H. Diels and W. Schubart in 1904, was unknown when Meyer wrote his study.

[5] *Solon* 1.1, only to refute him. Plutarch's information is in fact at variance with Didymus several times in the *Cimon*. 4.4 contradicts Didymus in schol. Pindar, *N.* 2.19 on the relationship of Miltiades and Thucydides; 4.3 contradicts Didymus in Marcellinus, *Vita Thuc.* 32, on the death of Thucydides.

between *Classicismus* and *Historismus*. The great man was always intolerant of the former.[6] Most people recognize, for instance, that Plutarch and Nepos[7] had nothing in common in education, method or perception, yet from Meyer's perspective all writers of less than genius seemed to have the same stature: they were all classical aesthetes or literary dilettantes.

Another aspect of Meyer's reasoning comes from a chance statement: "Plutarch knew the great classical authors Herodotus and Thucydides well, of course, and his knowledge shines through again and again; but he did not use them. . . ."[8] By his distinction between the terms "know" and "use," Meyer assumed the method of a modern research historian, who is always "using" sources, i.e., consulting material or notes as he writes. But to find Plutarch's counterpart among modern writers, we should look last in the ranks of the research historians. Consider, on the other hand, Gilbert Murray, most representative of the classical humanist, as opposed to the scientific historical tradition. In the beginning of the second chapter of his *Five Stages of Greek Religion*, he gives us Xenophon's famous description of the agonized Athenian reaction upon hearing the news of the naval catastrophe—so Murray says—at Cynoscephalae(!). Using Meyer's reasoning, we would have to say that Gilbert Murray "knew" Xenophon but was using a secondary source that misquoted Xenophon. In all probability, however, Murray wasn't using anything at all except his own thorough knowledge of classical antiquity, and that a trifle casually.[9]

6 V. Ehrenberg, "Eduard Meyer" in *Aspects of the Ancient World* (New York, 1946) 224 and passim.

7 Meyer did not distinguish between Plutarch and Nepos: *Forschungen* II 67; *Geschichte des Altertums* III 153.

8 *Forschungen* II 68.

9 "He deeply admired German scholarship, and confessed the difference: he was an amateur and an *animateur*." M. Henderson, "Gilbert Murray," *JHS* 77 (1957) xvi.

Meyer's analysis of Plutarch's sources was typical of his generation's attempt to introduce some sort of artificial order into classical historiography. Each ancient author—and especially those existing only in fragments—had to be tied into a line of communication either as a source or receiver of any given bit of information.[10] These lines of communication gradually became so canonized that one could dispense with proof of their existence merely by citing the eminence by whose august lucubrations they were first evolved.[11] Once this system was adopted it was no longer necessary to treat later, extant authors such as Plutarch (and Diodorus and Athenaeus) as if they were real persons, but only to chat learnedly about their sources in a manner that became increasingly confident in inverse proportion to the amount of indisputable information available about such a source.

It is sufficient here, without going further into the bibliographical details of Plutarchean *Quellenkunde*, to state the consensus of the first part of this century: it was agreed that the biographer made consistent use of historical and biographical handbooks. It was from this type of reference work, and from commentaries on a few famous works that he drew his narrative, including his citations and variant accounts. His own contribution consisted of no more than a literary style and a frequent insertion of moral judgments.[12] But since the second World War, there has been a vigorous reaction to higher criticism. In the introduction

[10] E.g., Callisthenes-Hermippus-Didymus; Critias-Androtion-Aristotle; Herodotus-Ephorus-Diodorus.

[11] E.g., Busolt's theory of Plutarch's reliance on Idomeneus for the life of Aristeides, *Griechische Geschichte*[2] II 628ff., widely followed by Jacoby, *FGrH* IIIb 88; C. Hignett, *Xerxes' Invasion of Greece* 20; I. Calabi Limentani, *Plutarchi vita Aristidis* (Florence, 1964), xv; et al.

[12] In addition to Meyer, see K. Beloch, *Griechische Geschichte*[2] I.1, 34; F. Leo, *Die griechische-römische Biographie* (Leipzig, 1901) 174-177; W. Uxkull-Gyllenband, *Plutarch und die griechische Biographie* (Stuttgart, 1927) 114f.

to his commentary on Thucydides, the late Arnold Gomme devoted thirty pages to an analysis of Plutarch, and concluded with one of the sharpest statements on record against the old view: "I do not in fact believe that a man, universally declared to be widely read and universally admitted to be honest, used only one or two books for an essay or a *Life*, keeping closely to their form and content, using all their learning . . . , pretending to quote from so many authors, criticizing some of them and suppressing the name of one author in particular—the one from whom he took nearly everything he knew."[13]

Konrat Ziegler, who had devoted more than half a century to the study of Plutarch when he wrote his article for Pauly-Wissowa, also attributed far more original research to Plutarch.[14] The Swedish scholar Carl Theander mounted a full-scale attack upon hypercriticism in his *Plutarch und die Geschichte*. He insisted on the importance of autopsy and oral tradition for the study of the biographer's sources[15] and reevaluated Plutarch's relationship to the various historians of previous centuries. He concluded that the biographer had indeed read not only the major historians, but also the countless minor writers cited throughout his works.[16] Since that time, the stature of Plutarch as scholar and historian has undergone continuing reevaluation; one can say that at the present time his talents (uneven as they are), his industry and his profound knowledge of ancient literature are esteemed as at no time since the age of Voltaire.[17]

[13] A. W. Gomme, *HCT* I 82.

[14] *Plutarchos von Chaironeia* (Stuttgart, 1949) 273-291 (a separately published edition of Ziegler's *RE* article).

[15] *Bulletin de la Société Royale des lettres de Lund* (1950-1951) I 2-32.

[16] Ibid. 37-66.

[17] See, for instance, K. Herbert, *Ephorus in Plutarch's Lives: A Source Problem* (Diss. Harvard 1954); E. Meinhardt, *Perikles bei Plutarch* (Frankfurt, 1957) 9-22; Helmbold and O'Neil, *Plutarch's*

Most discussions of the biographies turn to the sources first and to their author second, if at all. My tendency has been to reverse this process, not without a certain feeling of vulnerability. For the scholar who deals in *Quellenforschung*, who counts citations, compiles lists of authors, and traces stories from source to source like an exercise in electrical circuitry can easily convince himself and others of the scientism of his method and the statistical nature of his results. An attempt, on the other hand, to recreate Plutarch's method by analyzing him as a human being, and a product of his age, must remain in the realm of speculation. But I believe this sort of speculation is necessary: to reconstruct Plutarch's approach, not to his sources, but to his subjects, from his first acquaintance with their names and deeds to the easy familiarity with which he treats them in his later years.

Plutarch's family had lived in Chaeronea for generations; his great-grandfather Nicarchus recalled the entire citizenry pressed into service to carry supplies down to the gulf of Corinth for Antony's fleet in 31 B.C.[18] Both his grandfather, Lamprias, and father, Autobulus, were educated men of means, position, and experience. Lamprias was a wit and bon vivant, Autobulus more reserved,[19] but both men were fond of wine, company, and conversation. Whether or not the *Quaestiones conviviales* and other dialogues were verbatim reports, Plutarch felt it in character to show his grandfather quoting Homer, Hesiod, Theophrastus, and others,[20] and his father appealing to Homer, Aristotle, and a wide range of other poets, playwrights, and philosophers.[21]

The values of the family were those of a large, friendly

Quotations (American Philological Association Monographs XIX, 1959) vii-ix.

[18] *Antony* 68.

[19] *Quaestiones conviviales* [henceforth *Qc*] II 8, 641F.

[20] *Qc* I 5, V 5, V 8.

[21] Homer: *Qc* I 2, 615F; Aristotle: III 8, 656C; others: *De soll.animal.* 959C, E; 961A, C; 964CD; 956 A, C.

country household: there is easy banter; good advice is not only given but taken;[22] and the warmth, generosity, and understanding of the relationship of son, father, and grand-father seem as remarkably unfashionable to our age of gen-eration "gaps" as they would have been to Aristophanes' incessantly warring fathers and sons.[23]

Family tradition guaranteed that Plutarch and his broth-ers would become educated men according to the standard of the day, which was high. Family means made it possible, and after such early schooling as was available in Chae-ronea, the young Plutarch left to attend the school of Am-monius in Athens.[24] Here, over the course of years, Plu-tarch became intimately acquainted with the entire rich literary heritage of Greece. No one will doubt that his early education was the finest possible, and his juvenilia, bristling with citations, betray his satisfaction with his mastery of ancient literature.[25]

But no boy encounters history first in a book. I suggest that Plutarch had acquired the usual intelligent boy's knowl-edge of the history of his country long before he looked into his first roll of papyrus. First, there is his knowledge of the terrain. In the *Life* of Sulla, the biographer's detailed and loving description of the ground traversed before and after the second battle of Chaeronea is obviously drawn from first-hand experience:[26] this is the country in which he grew up, explored, chased rabbits, and played with friends. And who can doubt that on an early trip to Athens, on the road up Kithairon, it was pointed out to the boy: here stood Pausanias and the Spartans; yonder, Aristeides

[22] *Praec.ger.reip.* 816D.

[23] Cf. R. Flacelière, *Plutarque Vies* I (Paris, 1957) x-xi; Russell, 3-5.

[24] Ziegler, *Plutarchos* 15-17; Jones, "The Teacher of Plutarch," *HSCP* 71 (1966) 205-213.

[25] See, for instance, *De glor.Ath.* and Ziegler's judicious comments, *Plutarchos* 90.

[26] *Sulla* 15-19; see N.G.L. Hammond, "The Two Battles of Chae-ronea," *Klio* 31 (1938) 186ff.

and the Athenians; while across the Asopus, the Persians covered the plain; and so forth. The point is this: that Plutarch had undoubtedly become familiar with Plataea, with Salamis, and with dozens of other sites long before he first looked into Herodotus. First impressions are usually the strongest, and one must always be aware that the biographer writes many battle pieces, not from books or maps, but with a clear picture of the action and the ground in his head.

Plutarch probably also formed his impressions of the great men of Greek history as a youth, and before he had begun any serious study. Anecdotes about these men were common fare in the lower schools of his day, where they were produced on cue by schoolmasters to illustrate traits of character tending toward, or away from, virtue.[27] When the young Plutarch first read Herodotus, Thucydides, and Xenophon, one should assume that he knew the subject matter already, and that the only novelty he faced was the impress of a famous author's personality upon his materials. In exactly the same way, intelligent students in the lower schools today form their first impressions about the great egalitarian Andrew Jackson or the great reactionary William McKinley. But higher learning today is happily in an atmosphere of continual revisionism, with any number of Jacksons or McKinleys available to jar the preconceptions of the beginning graduate student; the most depressing aspect of Greek education is its stultifying orthodoxy. And even if revisionism had been acceptable in Plutarch's day, there is no such tendency evident in the man who wrote the *Lives*. His scholarship is obvious in his works on science, on philosophy, and in his literary commentaries; the corpus of his surviving work reveals an almost encyclopedic knowledge of Greek literature from Homer to his younger contemporary Favorinus; but in him there is not the mischief of a Beloch, nor the passion for setting people straight of an Arnold Gomme.

[27] Russell, 46.

To a store of information thus acquired through hearsay, observation, and the vagaries of lower schooling, the academy of Ammonius will have added the tools of scholarship. We should assume that Plutarch had already committed Homer and much of the canon of tragedy to memory; higher education of his day added analysis and exegesis to basic texts already encountered, and required extensive additional reading in all branches of literature.[28] Although many of the works dated to Plutarch's youth have a rhetorical-epideictic quality, we should not conclude that Ammonius' school put literature to the service of rhetoric, as did so many institutions of learning during the later age of the Second Sophistic; the picture Plutarch gives us of Ammonius is that of a philosopher, not a trainer of rhetoricians.[29] Plutarch himself admits that the young are tempted to concentrate on those areas of learning that are most glamorous;[30] but the corpus of his work demonstrates that his enduring love was for philosophy in its literal sense, wisdom for its own sake, as opposed to rhetoric.[31]

Many young men of his caste would have been driven to their schooling and promptly forgot the major part of what they had learned. It is clear from any given page of Plutarch that education was for him a lifelong process and did not end with his schooling under Ammonius. His 221 references to Homer, 41 citations from Aeschylus, 34 from Sophocles, 137 from Euripides, betray by their very inexactness a superbly educated man quoting casually from an enormous store of learning.[32] His 600-plus appeals to Plato

[28] The best description of early training in literature is by H. I. Marrou, *History of Education in Antiquity* (English trans. New York, 1956) part II, chap. 7. Evidence for the most popular required and recommended authors during the Pax Romana is collected by Tom Jones, *The Silver Plated Age* (Sandoval, 1962) 46-58.

[29] E.g., *Them.* 32.6, where he is "Ammonius the philosopher," and again in *De def.orac.* 410F. Cf. *De E Delph.* 385B sq., 391E.

[30] *De prof.in virt.* 78EF.

[31] Ziegler, *Plutarchos* 291ff.; Jones, 14ff.

[32] Ziegler, *Plutarchos* 277ff.; Barrow, 156ff.; Russell, 42ff.

make it unnecessary to demonstrate further his command of the philosopher's thought.[33] But this is only one aspect of his knowledge. It is instructive to turn from books to the contribution environment made to Plutarch's education.

Athens, during the lifetime of Plutarch, was a living museum. For a visitor with an inquiring mind, it offered not only the libraries and intellectual circles of a great university city, but also an unending panorama of antiquities, explained for the tourist by professional guides, and for more scholarly visitors by written guidebooks.[34] As a student in Athens and a frequent resident thereafter, Plutarch had the opportunity to augment his knowledge of Athenian history by inspecting the monuments himself, by discussing points of interest with learned companions and teachers and by unconsciously absorbing the popular tales of guides and rhetors.

There is abundant evidence to show that Plutarch recognized the value of autopsy and took a keen interest in places and objects of historical interest.[35] For example, in *Nicias* 13.3 and *Alcibiades* 18.6, 21.3, the biographer describes the mutilation of the herms—except for the one belonging to the tribe Aigeis, near the house of Andocides. Is there any reason to suggest Ephorus,[36] or indeed any "source," for this piece of information? "The herm," says Plutarch, "is even now called that of Andocides, and all so name it, although the inscription on it proves otherwise." Nothing could be clearer. Here is a spot in Athens, obviously so well known that people no doubt arranged to meet by it. It is exactly in such passages of Plutarch that source-hunting is least needed.

Among the other antiquities of Athens from various ages, the biographer noted the wooden tablets, or *axones*, upon

[33] R. M. Jones, *The Platonism of Plutarch* (New York, 1916); Ziegler, *Plutarchos* 113f.

[34] E.g., P. *Hawara* 80/1, *FGrH* 369; the works of Diodorus the periegete and Heliodorus, *FGrH* 372-373; Polemon's work on the monuments, *FHG* III, p. 116ff.

[35] Theander, loc.cit. [n. 15] 2-32.

[36] As does Jacoby, *FGrH* IIIb Suppl. i 506.

which were written the laws of Solon,[37] the bronze lion dedicated to the memory of Leaena, a companion of Harmodius and Aristogeiton,[38] the palladium and tripods dedicated by Nicias,[39] the tomb built by Harpalus for his mistress,[40] and many many more items of antiquarian interest.[41]

Besides the environment of antiquities, there was the environment of learned men. All the companions with whom we find him in the dialogues were informed, well educated, and fond of displaying their knowledge.[42] Sometimes they gave the source of their information, and even when they did not, we should assume that if pressed they would have been able to recall—somewhere in Thucydides, or Aristotle, or Polybius.[43] It is quite understandable that a story should have occurred to Plutarch and his friends first, before the name of its author, or authors. They feel no compulsion to annotate with the overwhelming and heavy-handed bibliomania of an Athenaeus. But there were also times when the name of an author would be totally irrelevant, as the anecdote was so much a part of the tradition. The following examples show how the informal chatter of the dialogues can turn up in the *Lives*.

Qc I.2, 651F: Plutarch's father mentioned that Aemilius

[37] *Solon* 25.1; cf. Pausanias I 18.3.

[38] *De garrul.* 505EF; cf. Paus. I 23.2; Pliny, *NH* 34, 72; Polyaenus 8.45.

[39] *Nicias* 3.3; cf. Plato, *Gorgias* 472A. Dinsmoor, *AJA* 14 (1910) 478f., thought Plutarch had seen the *neos* set up by the younger Nicias, with the dedication preserved in *IG* ii² 3055, and assumed it to belong to the older Nicias.

[40] *Phocion* 22.1; cf. Paus. I 37.5; Theopompus and Dicaearchus in Athenaeus 594E sq.

[41] Phocion's house, *Phocion* 18.8; the shrine of Artemis Aristoboule, *Them.* 22.2-3, published by Threpsiades and Vanderpool, *Deltion* 9 (1965) 26ff.; the Cimoneian monuments, *Cimon* 4.3, 19.5; and many others.

[42] Barrow, 26f.; Russell, 44-46.

[43] E.g., *De def.orac.* 422D; *Qc* V 3, 677AB; and especially *Qc* V 2, 675B: "when many were surprised and demanded proof because the story seemed incredible, I remembered by chance that Acesander reported it in his work *On Libya*."

Paulus, after the defeat of Perseus at Pydna, took a great deal of care over the proper seating at a banquet, saying that the same skill is required both for organizing a battle and an entertainment. The biographer preserved the story both in the *Apophthegmata* 198B and in the *Aemilius* 28.7-9. When his father introduced the story with "they say," he could have meant Polybius 30.14, or Livy 45.32, or just what everyone knew.

Qc I.6, 623E: In a discussion of Alexander's drinking habits, Philinus—a frequent member of these symposia—quoted from the *Ephemerides* to show that Alexander was a heavy drinker. Theophrastus was then cited for the king's "hot" constitution and its causes. Much of this conversation is repeated in the *Alexander* 4.2.

Qc I.10, 628F: In a discussion of the Aeantis tribe and its history, Plutarch noted the oracle which required the tribe to perform special sacrifices after the battle of Plataea; the story is repeated in *Aristeides* 19.6.

Qc VIII.4,723F-724A: Protogenes remembered just having read in *ta Attika* that Theseus made the palm the prize, when he first held games at Delos. As one can see, when Plutarch repeated this information in *Theseus* 21.3, with the phrase, "they say," he could be referring to the Atthidographers or to Protogenes; or he could even mean that everyone knew this about Theseus, and that it is the authoritative tradition.

These examples suffice to show the importance of oral transmission and learned discussion in Plutarch's life. It may be thought strange that one should even need to prove that such discussion went on; the necessity arises because of the impression left by Meyer and his school that Plutarch began writing his *Lives* in a vacuum, with his mind wiped clean like a slate, and that every word, every event described, every quotation, is the result of research accomplished only moments before—like a modern graduate student writing a seminar paper in an utterly unfamiliar field.

It would seem probable that the *Lives* were written in

Plutarch's maturity, and that they were written as one unified project.[44] But I would qualify this statement by suggesting that the composition of the *Lives* was by no means a new undertaking for Plutarch, but only the putting into order for publication of subjects that had occupied him throughout his life. Certainly the goal of pointing out the way to virtue by biographical anecdotes, as is his fashion, drawn from both Greek and Roman history, had occurred to him as early as his first visits to Rome, where he was in demand as a lecturer and teacher.[45] Later on in life, it may have seemed to the biographer, as it did to Tacitus, that an age of toleration and freedom of expression had begun under Trajan and that the time was ripe for bringing his life's work to fruition, for collecting these anecdotes and examples from both notebooks[46] and memory and putting them into final form as biographies.

Plutarch's whole life as a teacher was dedicated to the promotion of virtue. Although he liked to show off his erudition, his works were not (with a few exceptions) intended for the edification of fellow scholars, but for the guidance of the young. We would suppose that a group of male college undergraduates would be exactly the sort of audience he was trying to reach when he said that he began his writing of *Lives* to benefit others.[47] This should never be forgotten as one reads the *Lives*. Their primary purpose of instructing the young was not to be obscured by too much learned argument,[48] or by slipping into a historical narrative.[49]

In an age that tends toward cynicism it is sometimes

[44] Ziegler, *Plutarchos* 77, 257f.; cf. C. P. Jones, "Toward a Chronology of Plutarch's Works," *JRS* 56 (1966) 72.

[45] *Demosth.* 2.2; *De curios.* 522D; Jones, 21, 103ff.

[46] The custom of collecting notes is mentioned in *De cohib.ira* 457D; *De tranq.anim.* 464F. See titles of non-extant works in the Lamprias catalogue: no. 62, *Stromateis historikoi*; no. 125, *Apomnemoneumata*; Barrow, 153ff.

[47] *Aemilius* 1.1.   [48] *Solon* 27.1.

[49] *Alexander* 1.1

difficult to judge a moralist, particularly one who is virtually unknown to us except through his own writings. At the Fourth International Congress of Classical Studies, held at the University of Pennsylvania in 1964, that learned and respected scholar B. A. van Groningen launched an attack on the intellectual world of the Pax Romana. Plutarch was a typical representative of this age, he said. His philosophy was shallow and unoriginal, his moralizing tiresome and, from a literary standpoint, third-rate. As I listened to this talk, I could not help agreeing with many of his points. But neither could I help thinking of the founder of the great University whose guests we were. Was Benjamin Franklin's philosophy profound and original? Did his moral precepts sparkle? Was he a literary immortal? In fact, what impression might we have of Franklin if we had only his written works by which to judge him?[50] Both men were genial, wise, and didactic by nature. Above all, both men were empirical, preferring to instruct, advise, and offer solutions on the basis of past experience rather than on the promise of some ideal doctrine. I may be forgiven for not wishing to press this parallel too far. For the times into which Franklin was born required the most of him while the Pax Romana required of Plutarch only that he occupy several magistracies in an age of profound order and continuity. And we must sympathize with him when we realize that the *Praecepta gerendae reipublicae*, freighted though it is with tales of Phocion and Cato and Pericles and Scipio, was written specifically to instruct a man who wished to adorn a provincial bureaucrat's desk in Sardis.

If moral guidance was the most important consideration for Plutarch, literary art and dramatic unity would have come second, and *Quellenforschung*—the darling of the moderns—a poor third and subordinated wherever need be to art. But because of accidents of survival, it is often Plu-

[50] A task surprisingly attempted by D. H. Lawrence, "Benjamin Franklin," *Studies in Classical American Literature*, a petulant and unworthy diatribe.

tarch, and Plutarch alone, to whom one must turn for solutions to historical problems. These encounters are often
exasperating and are no doubt responsible for the harsh
treatment the biographer has received at the hands of highly
respected modern scholars who are impatient with moral
guidance and rhetoric and dramatic balance when they
would really like each *Life* to be a stack of fragments from
well-regarded, lost authors: "Hellanicus says . . . , Callis-
thenes says . . . , Philochorus says . . . ," and so forth. But
if one expects to use Plutarch as a historian, one must accept
him on his own terms. I set forth a few selective rules—
probably a minimal list—the historian should use in understanding and interpreting Plutarch.

Herodotus 1.61: ". . . not wishing to have children by
his newly wed wife, Peisistratus had sex with her in an
unnatural manner."

Plutarch, *De Herodoti malignitate* 16, 858C (citing Herodotus): ". . . the girl said to her mother, 'Look, mama,
Peisistratus is having sex with me in an unnatural manner.'"
This perhaps unintentionally hilarious example suffices to
show that Plutarch, when claiming to cite directly from the
works of another, does not always quote with the exact-
ness that would be required of a modern scholar. And
sometimes he simply cites erroneously.[51] On the other hand,
where his Latin sources can be checked he is quite accurate.[52] This would seem to suggest a general rule: that the
more familiar Plutarch was with his source, or story, the
more likely he was to be a bit casual with his data; when
on unfamiliar ground, he is more careful and has perhaps
made more precise notes. This is by no means an unknown
tendency in scholarship. In the present age we can count on
editors to catch our most embarrassing blunders (although

---

[51] E.g., *Them.* 21.1, where he cites Herodotus 8.111 out of context,
thus distorting the historical facts.

[52] See Jones, 83.

through three editions and many printings no one caught
Gilbert Murray's mutilation of Xenophon, noted above);
Plutarch had no editor, of course, and therefore the modern reader must be aware that the biographer is capable
of distorting his source.

I believe, however, that it is the biographer's own mistake, and not that of some intermediary source. The safest
assumption is that Plutarch had at one time or another read
every author he cited, except when he specifically admitted
to be citing at second hand[53] or third hand.[54] Even when
he displayed a cluster of citations almost identical to a group
found in some other author,[55] one should not assume that
both men were using the same bibliographical handbook,
but only that the nature of the subject or the argument had
by Plutarch's day called forth a standard list of authorities
and a more or less standard order in which to cite them.[56]

One should be aware of Plutarch's opinion of his source.
When he names his authority, one should know whether he
approved of the man's work, and bear in mind that his approval was not always based on qualifications a modern
historian would insist upon. In *Pericles* 29-32, for instance,
he evidently gave equal weight to Thucydides, Ephorus,
and Aristophanes—and then said, as if truly bewildered,
"the truth is not clear."[57] Nor was he always consistent in
his attitude to any given author. He at times used the information of writers he otherwise held in profound distrust
because they offered something he found congenial to his
immediate purpose. For instance, Duris of Samos had described Pericles' barbaric cruelty in putting down the
Samian revolt. But Duris, said Plutarch, tends to exaggerate
even where his personal feelings are not involved; in a case
concerning his own country he is even more likely to

---

[53] *Solon* 1.1; *Alex.* 53.2; *Demosth.* 30.1.
[54] *De def.orac.* 422D.
[55] For example, *Pericles* 24 and schol.Plato *Menex.* 235E.
[56] Noted by Gomme, *HCT* I 82 n. 3.
[57] I have treated this passage at length in "Pericles and Dracontides,"
JHS 84 (1964) 69ff.

magnify calamity.[58] Two chapters previously, however, the biographer had retained an account of the branding of prisoners by both sides, which was also from Duris—a fact which he neglected to mention.[59] Plutarch could also turn unexpectedly from a show of scholarship to repeat traditional tales that were inconsistent with what he had just been saying.[60]

Because of the variable nature of Plutarch's attitude to his sources, when he does not name his authority one must resist the constant temptation to supply a name. To suggest, without convincing evidence, that Plutarch was repeating something he found in this or that author is to make a meaningless statement—even if it is true—unless one can also show both his attitude to that author and his reasons for following that author's version.

The composition of every *Life* was dictated not by canons of biographical art established by previous generations (for which there has never been any real evidence) but by the subject of the biography himself: his career, his "image" after history, political theory, and rhetoric had had their way with it, and the sources available. If anecdote provided the bulk of a life, the *Cimon*, for instance, it was because his career fell into a period that had been ignored by the historians. The treatment of some figures had to take into account the storm of philosophic and rhetorical argument that raged about their memory. The biographer could hardly ignore Plato's criticism of Pericles, for example, in the *Gorgias*.[61] Here the issue was exactly philos-

[58] *FGrH* 76 F 67, in *Per.* 28.3.

[59] *Per.* 26.4. The story was perhaps in the ancient scholia to the *Babylonians* of Aristophanes, where it was found by Photius s.v. Σαμίων ὁ δῆμος and attributed to Duris, *FGrH* 76 F 66.

[60] In *Them.* 27.1, he cites all the sources that said Themistocles came to Artaxerxes, rather than Xerxes and says that their chronology is preferable. But in the ensuing narrative it becomes clear that he is following a source who believed Xerxes and his eventual assassin Artabanus were still alive.

[61] In *Per.* 9, Plutarch got around the conflicting judgments of Plato

ophy versus rhetoric and was hardly a dead one in his day, as witness the *Pro quattuorviris* of his near contemporary, Aelius Aristides.

Every *Life* is different. The *Theseus* seems to have required special research into the *Atthis*; it smells of the lamp in places, unusually so for Plutarch. The *Artoxerxes* is a careful blend of Xenophon and Ctesias and displays the biographer's usual disregard of source analysis. Stories are chosen which fit the drama, and historical veracity is not an issue.[62] No passage in Plutarch should be read out of context—a context that is often wider than at first suspected. This warning applies particularly to the fragments of writers who have not otherwise been preserved. The *Lives* are not a collection of fragments; every item has its place and is part of a dramatic logic, although the logic can sometimes be a mystery Plutarch did not feel obligated to share. It is precisely because of this logic that one must always beware of Plutarch's attempts to synthesize, to combine various elements of his source material that may have had nothing to do with each other. In *Cimon* 13.4-5, for example, he would have us believe that the Peace of Callias was the direct result of the battle of the Eurymedon, about twenty years earlier, and was itself commemorated by the erection of an Altar of Peace—a monument that Philochorus, for one, dated seventy-five years later.[63]

---

and Thucydides by deciding that Pericles was a demagogue first and a statesman later.

[62] He disapproved of Ctesias' long rambling account of Cyrus' death in *Artox.* 11, which he said killed off Cyrus as if with a blunt knife; but in *Alex.* 75 he ridiculed the accounts of those writers who felt it necessary to bring the man off with a sudden stroke, ". . . as if devising a moving and tragic ending for a great drama." In the latter instance Plutarch preferred to follow the version of the *Ephemerides* (*FGrH* 117 F 3b) which dragged out Alexander's death interminably. In one case he has selected his source on the basis of "fitness"; in the other, on the basis of reliability. This example was pointed out to me long ago by Truesdell Brown.

[63] *FGrH* 328 F 151 (Didymus, *In Demosth.* 7.62 sq.); see Jacoby

If there is an exception to this rule of dramatic logic, it is Plutarch's habit of slipping into free association—of writing "as each matter came to mind," as he said he wrote his *Quaestiones conviviales*.[64] It is clearly the habit of a man who knew almost too much and had a tendency to ramble, which in our day and age would be severely curbed by a stern editor. In that case, of course, we would be without the anecdotes about Aspasia and her later namesake in *Pericles* 24: "Since these matters occurred to me while I was writing it would be contrary to human nature to pass over them." And quite contrary to Plutarch's nature, we might add. On the other hand, after describing the uproar at the Isthmian games when Flamininus announced the liberation of Greece, the biographer added that the noise knocked birds dead out of the sky—which is perhaps appropriate to mention—but one scarcely needs the meteorological speculation which follows and interrupts the entire narrative.[65] No *Life* is entirely free of such loosely woven bits that occur whenever Plutarch's memory is jogged.

It is far easier for the modern historian to analyze the work of an epitomizer like Diodorus, or a drudge like Diogenes Laertius, or Harpocration, and others of his genre, who looked things up and put down exactly what they found in response to a specific question. And it is annoying to have to subject every passage of Plutarch used as historical evidence to the most searching analysis—and still not be sure one is right. But it is to Plutarch the historian we turn—not to the biographer, the teacher, the moralist—and if one is to use Plutarch as a historian, one is committed to just such analysis. History herself has left us no alternative.

---

ad loc. *FGrH* IIIb Suppl. 523f. I have discussed the passage in "Some Documents in Plutarch's Lives," *Classica et Mediaevalia* 22 (1961) 192-194.

[64] *Qc* II proem. 629D.   [65] *Flam.* 10.

III

THEMISTOCLES' PRE-WAR CAREER: COMMENTARY TO CHAPTERS 1-5

1.1 Θεμιστοκλεῖ δὲ

Some scholars have suggested that the beginning of this Life is missing.[1] There may have been a paragraph explaining Plutarch's reasons for comparing Themistocles and Camillus—reasons we would be delighted to know, as the parallel is hardly a striking one—and ending with the observation that both were *novi homines*.

Nothing is known of his father, Neocles. Anecdotes and later fictions, such as the pair of orations composed by Libanius (*Declam.* 9, 10 Foerster) seem to be mere amplification of the story of his father disowning him (see comment to 2.8).

Φρεαρρίου τῶν δήμων ἐκ τῆς Λεοντίδος φυλῆς

E. Kirsten once located Phrearrhioi in the heart of the Laureion mining district; we know there was a mine in the vicinity.[2] But in 1970, E. Vanderpool published an inscription of the deme Phrearrhioi that had been found near a wooded hill just south of the small village of Olympos, in

---

[1] E.g., C. Sintenis in his 1851 Leipzig edition; B. Perrin, Plutarch's *Themistocles and Aristides* (New York, 1901) 173. Doubted by Flacelière, *Vie de Thém.* ad loc.

[2] "Der gegenwärtige Stand der attischen Demenforschung," *Atti del terzo congresso internazionale di epigrafia greca e latina* (Rome, 1957) 162, 168; see his map in *Westermanns Atlas zur Weltgeschichte* (Braunschweig, 1956) 13. Evidence of a mining lease in M. Crosby, *Hesp.* 26 (1957) 4.35-36: τὸ Φρ]εαρροῖ μέταλλον.

the area of the 48th-kilometer post on the inland road to
Athens from Anavyssos.[3] Vanderpool believes the deme
center to have been between Olympos and the hill. I surveyed the area in the spring of 1977 and found substantial
remains of walls and a spring on the southwestern slope of
the hill as well. There is no reason to doubt the location of
Phrearrhioi in this general vicinity.

Plutarch spelled Leontis with *omicron*, not *omega* (Frost,
CP 61 [1966] 216f.); editors since Blass have often emended
to *omega*, but this is a correction of Plutarch's spelling, not
manuscript error, and should be rejected.

1.1-2 . . . νόθος δὲ πρὸς μητρός, ὡς λέγουσιν·
᾿Αβρότονον Θρήισσα γυνὴ γένος· ἀλλὰ τεκέσθαι
τὸν μέγαν ῞Ελλησίν φημι Θεμιστοκλέα.

The same couplet is quoted from Amphicrates' *On Famous
Men* by Athenaeus (576D); it is also found in the *Anthology*
under the heading, "for Abrotonon the mother of Themistocles" (*Anth.Pal.* 7.306). Plutarch knew a variant account:
Phanias said Themistocles' mother was Carian and her name
was Euterpe. Neanthes of Cyzicus confirmed this name and
added that she was from Halicarnassus (*FGrH* 84 F 2ab;
Athenaeus 576D said this information came from the third
and fourth books of Neanthes' *Hellenica*).

Compare Nepos, *Them.* 1.2: *Pater eius Neocles generosus
fuit. Is uxorem Acarnanam civem duxit, ex qua natus est
Themistocles.*[4] There is not only the problem of determin-
ing which version is correct, but the usual doubts about the
reliability of either account. It should come as no surprise
that the mother of Themistocles was not well known; Plutarch admits elsewhere (*Alcib.* 1.3) that the mothers of
Nicias and Demosthenes were unknown too, and they lived
in an era about which far more was known.

[3] "A *Lex sacra* of the Attic deme Phrearrhioi," *Hesp.* 39 (1970)
47-53.
[4] Acarnanam *Gif PA B M*: acornanam *F*: arcananam *R*: halicarnas-
siam *Aldus*; karinam *Richter* (*ZGym* 11, 336).

The earliest writer represented here is Phanias of Eresos (Amphicrates is probably the orator of the first century B.C. mentioned by Plut. *Lucul.* 22.6; so Mueller, *FHG* IV 300). Phanias was a contemporary and countryman of Theophrastus (Plut. *Non posse* 1097B, fr. 7 Wehrli) and was born between 376-373 (*Suda* s.v. Phanias). It is possible that both he and Neanthes followed the same source, Phanias saying only that Themistocles' mother was a Carian named Euterpe and Neanthes adding the information that she was from Halicarnassus, but it is impossible to speculate about such a source. It is safe to say only that in the mid-fourth century, in one or more works, this information was available, that Phanias repeated it, and that in the late third century, while writing his *Hellenica*, Neanthes found the same report (for Neanthes' dates, Jacoby, *FGrH* IIC, 144f.).

I would guess that Nepos came across the same version and that either he or his sources before him distorted Καρίνη into *Acarnana*. He also said specifically that the bride of Neocles was a *cives*. Habrotonon, on the other hand, was a common slave name and became almost a synonym for an easily available serving girl and concubine, perhaps because of the character of the same name in Menander's *Epitrepontes*.[5]

The various meanings of *notheia* at this period of history (the last quarter of the sixth century) are complex. The first implication of *notheia* is that Themistocles was born to Neocles by a concubine. This does not seem probable. The first and only hint of illegitimacy comes from the couplet quoted here, four centuries or so after the event. But both Lysias and Aristotle imply that Themistocles, like other statesmen of his day, was from an aristocratic house.[6] The second implication of *notheia* is that Neocles had married

---

[5] Plut. *Amat.* 753D.

[6] Lysias 30.27-28 contrasts Nicomachus' servile origins with the families of Solon and Themistocles. *AP* 28.1 says the Demos first chose leaders who were not of noble birth after the death of Pericles.

the daughter of a prominent Halicarnassian. At the time of
Themistocles' birth, it was quite common for grander
Athenians to consider themselves part of an international
aristocracy and to seek rewarding marriage connections
abroad.[7] But by the citizenship law of c. 451,[8] offspring of
such marriages, μητρόξενοι, would be considered *nothoi*. At
the time of passage of this law, the most prominent *me-
troxenos* at Athens was Cimon, whose mother Hegesipyle
was a Thracian (Hdt. 6.39; Plut. *Cimon* 4.1). It is possible
that at the time people speculated about great Athenians of
the past who would have been *nothoi* under the new law,
including Themistocles and even Cleisthenes (Hdt. 6.130f).
This is a logical explanation (but not the only one, of
course) for the tradition of Themistocles' *notheia*.[9]

1.3 διότι καὶ τῶν νόθων εἰς Κυνόσαργες συντελούντων
Athenians of mixed descent were enrolled at this gymnasium
sacred to Heracles. They were subject to the duties of
parasitoi during certain sacrifices (Polemon, in Athen. 234E;
cf. *IG* i[2] 129) and no stigma attached to their status.[10] The
anecdote about Themistocles cleverly obliterating the distinction between νόθοι and γνήσιοι is no doubt a late invention; as shown above, there was no such distinction. Testimonia to Kynosarges were collected in Frazer's *Pausanias*
(II 193f.) where, however, it was mistakenly located northeast of the city. It is to the southeast, in fact, outside and
near the Itonian gate and the Ilissus.[11]

[7] See the survey by J.-M. Hannick, "Droit de cité et mariages
mixtes dans la Grèce classique," *L'Antiquité Classique* 45 (1976)
133-148.

[8] *AP* 26.4; Plut. *Per.*; Jacoby, *FGrH* IIIb Suppl. 471ff.; Hignett,
History of the Athenian Constitution 343ff.

[9] See S. C. Humphreys, "The Nothoi of Kynosarges," *JHS* 94
(1974) 94.

[10] Demosth. 23.213; Plut. *Amat.* 750F; see K. Latte, "Nothoi," *RE*
17 (1936) 1069ff.; preceding note.

[11] [Plato] *Axiochus* 364a,b,d; Judeich, *Topographie von Athen*[2]
422; see now complete bibliography in J. Travlos, *Pictorial Dictionary of Athens* (London, 1971) 340.

1.4 ὅτι μέντοι τοῦ Λυκομιδῶν γένους μετεῖχε, δῆλόν ἐστι

Simonides reported that Themistocles had restored and adorned the shrine of the Lycomids at Phlya after the Persians had burned it. This final story concludes Plutarch's device of offering varying accounts in increasing order of probability. First is the popular tradition of his day as quoted in the couplet; then comes a more authoritative account for which Phanias and Neanthes are cited; finally, as the language makes clear, we have what Plutarch considered the real facts. Neocles may have been a member of a cadet branch of the Lycomids that had moved to Phrearrhioi. The main branch of the clan remained at Phlya (*IG* i² 302.29, 31, ii² 2670). He may have married into a prominent family of Halicarnassus in order to enhance his status. These are all possibilities. But Thracian Habrotonon seems to have stuck in the minds of prominent scholars right down to the present and we continue to hear statements like: "Das Bildnis des Themistokles [the Ostia herm] zeigt den Sohn einer thrakischen Mutter."[12]

Phlya is located in the modern suburb of Chalandri about nine kilometers north of the Athenian agora.[13] The Lycomids were an ancient priestly clan of Attica with possibly a feud of long standing with the Alcmeonids.[14] They celebrated mysteries at their shrine in Phlya at which were sung hymns to Demeter by Musaeus (Paus. I 22.8, IV 7.5, 7) and hymns by Orpheus and Pamphus (Paus. IX 27.2, 30.12). According to Hippolytus (*Ref.omn.haeres.* V 20.4-6 Wendland), Bacchic mysteries and mysteries of the Great Goddess were celebrated there. Hippolytus says there was a *pastas* (an enclosure of some sort) in which there were descriptions of the rites: περὶ ὧν καὶ Πλούταρχος ποιεῖται λόγους ἐν

[12] G. Hafner, *Geschichte der griechischen Kunst* (Zurich, 1961) 174f.

[13] E. Meyer, *RE Supplb.* 10 (1965) 535-538.

[14] Suggested by G. Ferrara, "Temistocle e Solone," *Maia* 16 (1964) 61ff., on the basis of *AP* 1.1; Plut. *Solon* 12.4

ταῖς πρὸς Ἐμπεδοκλέα δέκα βίβλοις (Lamprias cat. no. 43: εἰς Ἐμπεδοκλέα βιβλία ί). An honorary decree by the Eumolpids and Lycomids was dated ἐπὶ ἱερείας Φλαουίας Λαοδαμείας τῆς Κλείτου Φλυέως θ[υγατ]ρός (IG ii² 3559). The lady is well attested (IG ii² 3546, 3557-60, 4753-54) and was, coincidentally, the daughter-in-law of Plutarch's schoolmate Thrasyllus, the son of his teacher Ammonius.[15] I draw attention to Plutarch's lost work and to his possible acquaintance in later life with a priestess from Phlya to support my continuing conviction that he generally knows a lot more about most subjects than he chooses to tell and that his mistakes are more likely to derive from an unmanageable information surplus than from a dearth.[16]

Themistocles seems to have felt a special relationship with the Mother Goddess; see comment to 30, 31.1.

2.1-3. Ἔτι δὲ παῖς ὢν ὁμολογεῖται φορᾶς μεστὸς εἶναι καὶ τῇ μὲν φύσει συνετός, τῇ δὲ προαιρέσει μεγαλοπράγμων καὶ πολιτικός

Almost nothing in the first three paragraphs of this chapter requires much attention. What we find here are Themistocles' lifelong qualities of σύνεσις and φιλοτιμία projected backward into the period of his youth, about which nothing was known.[17] The λόγοι κατηγορικοί and συνηγορικοί that Themistocles was supposed to have spent his time practicing are obvious anachronisms. According to a lost work of Aristotle quoted by Cicero (Brutus 12.46), the science of rhetoric was first put into organized form after the end of the

---

[15] Stemma in C. Jones, "The Teacher of Plutarch," HSCP 71 (1966) 210.

[16] On the telesterion at Phlya, see also Harriet B. Hawes, "A Gift of Themistocles: the Ludovisi Throne and the Boston Relief," AJA 26 (1922) 293ff., an ingenious attempt to prove that Themistocles commissioned these monuments for the Lycomid precinct—generally met with disbelief.

[17] On these qualities, see, H. Martin, "The character of Plutarch's Themistocles," TAPA 92 (1961) 326ff.

Syracusan monarchy (c. 465); in general one would not go far wrong in attributing all these stories to the Hellenistic schoolroom.

Themistocles was supposed to have scorned subjects tending toward a life of cultured enjoyment, but τῶν δ'εἰς σύνεσιν ἢ πρᾶξιν λεγομένων δῆλος ἦν ὑπερορῶν παρ' ἡλικίαν, ὡς τῇ φύσει πιστεύων. Because the language seems to call for contrasting attitudes to these various subjects, Madvig suggested ὑπερερῶν for ὑπερορῶν despite the unanimity of the best manuscripts, and this emendation has been accepted by Ziegler and Flacelière (e.g., ". . . il montrait une passion extrême et au-dessus de son âge pour celles qui se rapportent, comme on dit, à l'intelligence et à l'action, parce qu'il avait confiance dans ses dons naturels). But ὑπερορῶν can make sense as well: ". . . he clearly showed an indifference far beyond his years, as though he put his confidence in his natural gifts alone" (Perrin's Loeb translation). I believe this is what Plutarch meant to say. For one thing, ὑπερεράω is not attested in Greek literature, and to make such a word the basis of a conjecture is a chancy business. Second, the character of Themistocles as seen here—scorning study and relying on natural gifts—is exactly his character as seen by the Socratics, of whose influence on Plutarch there can be no doubt. And the example of Themistocles was used by the philosophers of the fourth century more than once to convince other young men that natural gifts must be supplemented by the guidance of older and wiser men.[18]

2.4 ὅθεν ὕστερον

He used to say at convivial gatherings that he didn't know how to play the lyre or kithara, but how to make a small and obscure city great and illustrious. By contrast with the foregoing anecdotes, the statement comes from the contemporary account of Ion of Chios, who had heard Athenians quote Themistocles to this effect.[19] Without the

[18] Xen. *Mem.* IV 2.2; Aesch.Socr. in *POxy* xiii 1608; cf. H. Martin, "Plutarch's Themistocles 2," *AJP* 85 (1964) 192-195.

[19] *FGrH* 392 F 13, Plut. *Cimon* 9.1; on the circumstances, see

chance attribution to Ion in the *Cimon* we would no doubt assign this anecdote as well to the Hellenistic raconteurs.

2.5 καίτοι Στησίμβροτος (*FGrH* 107 F 1) Ἀναξαγόρου τε διακοῦσαι τὸν Θεμιστοκλέα φησὶ καὶ περὶ Μέλισσον σπουδάσαι τὸν φυσικόν, οὐκ εὖ τῶν χρόνων ἁπτόμενος.

The nature of Stesimbrotus' work *On Themistocles, Thucydides and Pericles* (title from Athenaeus 589DE) remains a mystery. We know only that the author was from Thasos and perhaps lived at Athens in the later fifth century and that he was a Homeric rhapsode—a professional teacher of the wisdom of Homer (see 107 FF 21-25) like Socrates' contemporary, Ion of Ephesus (Plato, *Ion* 530CD; Xen. *Symp.* 3.6). Plutarch thought him malicious, especially toward Pericles, and inaccurate as well. The Homeric expounders were not fond of the new education and perhaps Stesimbrotus claimed Themistocles was uncultured because he consorted with physicists like Anaxagoras and Melissus.[20] At any rate it is interesting to note that Plutarch can be aware of really gross chronological errors, pointing out that Anaxagoras and Melissus were contemporaries of Pericles, "who was much younger than Themistocles."[21]

2.6 Μᾶλλον οὖν ἄν τις προσέχοι τοῖς Μνησιφίλου τὸν Θεμιστοκλέα τοῦ Φρεαρρίου ζηλωτὴν γενέσθαι λέγουσιν

Some scholars in the past have suspected that all references

Jacoby, *CQ* 41 (1947) 2, and note 7. The tale is repeated by Augustine, *Ep.* 118.13 ad Diosc.; Procopius I 1.7 Haury (both authors probably saw it in Plutarch); cf. Cicero, *Tusc.* I 2, 4.

[20] B. Perrin, *Plutarch's Themistocles* 177; Jacoby, *FGrH* IID 345; M. A. Levi, *Plutarco e il 5 secolo* 12.

[21] An understandable method of comparative dating: there was confusion about both Anaxagoras' and Melissus' *akmai*. Apollodorus, in Diog.Laert. 9.24 (*FGrH* 244 F 72) put Melissus' *akme* at the 84th Olympiad (444-441). But another tradition cited by Diogenes held that he was a pupil of Parmenides and had met Heraclitus, both of whom had flourished at the 69th Olympiad (504-501), Diog. 9.1, 9.23. Apollodorus dated the *akme* of Anaxagoras at 460 (Diog. 2.7, 244 F 31), but Demetrius' *Archon List* (*FGrH* 228 F 2, in Diog. 2.7) put him in Athens at the age of twenty during the archonship of Callias (456/5).

to Mnesiphilus are inferences or pure fictions based on his
brief appearance in Herodotus (8.57f.). Plutarch goes on
in this paragraph to say that Mnesiphilus was a "successor"
of Solon, preserving a scheme of practical political wisdom,
an example of which is given in the *Septem sapientum
convivium*. Mnesiphilus is introduced as a guest (154CD)
and later on (156BC) quotes the doctrine that the ἔργον of
every human or divine activity is the product (τό γιγνόμενον)
rather than the medium of production (δι' οὗ γίγνεται), that
is to say, a builder's *ergon* is a temple, not carpentry or
the mixing of mortar.

Evidently the earliest writers to concern themselves with
the succession of the various philosophical doctrines had
constructed the succession Solon-Mnesiphilus-Themistocles,
although such a succession required an enormously long
life for the middle man. The tradition was preserved by
Clement of Alexandria (*Stromateis* I, 14, 65.3) who seems
to have been consulting an epitome of *Successions*. As suggested above, Mnesiphilus probably found his way into the
literature about philosophic successions because by fourth-
century school standards every statesman was required to
have a mentor.[22]

We now know that Mnesiphilus not only existed, he was
well enough known to appear on hostile ostraca, probably
during the ostracophoria of 487/6. One of the new Kerameikos ostraca bears Mnesiphilus' name and joins with another piece bearing the name of Megacles (at this date still
unpublished). I have suggested elsewhere (*Historia* 20
[1971] 23-25) that either Mnesiphilus was blamed for the
conduct of his student (as Socrates was for Critias) or
(more likely) that he was in some way responsible for the
rise of his protégé to political significance. This can only
be speculative, however, as the existence of political spon-
sorship and clientship at Athens is more implied than attested by the limited evidence.

[22] Long ago noted by Bauer, *Themistokles* 72f.; Munro, *CAH* IV
303 note.

2.7 ἐν δὲ ταῖς πρώταις τῆς νεότητος ὁρμαῖς

Stories of Themistocles' dissolute youth may just possibly date all the way back to the sixth century, but I believe it more likely that they are based on a tendency to compare Themistocles with Alcibiades (see above, pp. 22-23). What is obvious is that the schools could not have done without Themistocles as an *exemplum*. The earliest rumor of his depraved behavior in surviving literature is no earlier than Aeschines Socraticus' *Alcibiades*, written in the first third of the fourth century. Here he is compared to the good horseman or the cultured man; both have to be unskilled at their art before they can become *hippikos* or *mousikos*. In the same way, Themistocles, by an absurd syllogism, had to be *phaulos* before he could be statesmanlike, a claim specifically denied by Thucydides (I 138.3). By the end of the century, the Epicurean Idomeneus had contributed details (*FGrH* 338 F 4ab) and by the Second Sophistic, Themistocles' juvenile delinquency and subsequent conversion to decency had become a staple of the *exempla* (Aelian, *VH* 2.12; *Rhetores Graeci* IV 690, VII.1 585 Walz). Plutarch here puts the moral into Themistocles' own mouth: "the wildest colts make the best horses." This is not true, incidentally.

2.8 ἃ δὲ τούτων ἐξαρτῶσιν ἔνιοι διηγήματα πλάττοντες, ἀποκήρυξιν μὲν ὑπὸ τοῦ πατρὸς

"Some writers," e.g. Aeschines Socraticus (the earliest), and the sources consulted by Nepos (*Them.* 1.2) and Valerius Maximus (VI 9, ext. 2). The inclusion of the topic in the *Controversiae* of Seneca the Elder (I 8.6) shows that the disinheritance had become a rhetorical commonplace by the first century B.C. Although Plutarch denied the story as fiction, it lost no currency in later centuries.[23] To refute the tradition of estrangement of father and son, Plutarch supplies an anecdote even less worthy of belief. Neocles showing the young Themistocles the old and neglected

[23] Aelian, *VH* 2.12; Alex.Aphr. *Comm.in Arist. Graec.* II.2 p. 179.26; Stobaeus IV 117.9; Libanius, *Declam.* IX and X.

triremes is to us an obvious anachronism, as the first triremes owned by Athens were those built by Themistocles' Navy Bill.[24]

There is very little one can add to Plutarch's impressionistic treatment of Themistocles' youth, except perhaps his approximate year of birth. The data are these: Themistocles lived sixty-five years (*Them.* 31.6). He died when Egypt revolted, and Greek triremes sailed as far as Cyprus and Cilicia, and Cimon was master of the seas (*Them.* 31.4; *Cimon* 18.6-7). Whether Plutarch realized it, he was saying two different things. Themistocles died *either* when Egypt revolted (c. 459) *or* when Cimon sailed as far as Cyprus and was master of the seas (c. 450, Thuc. I 112.3). According to the biographer's arithmetic, therefore, he was born in either 525 or 516.

This brings us to the third, and independent, datum. Dionysius of Halicarnassus informs us (*AR* VI 34.1): "After this, Aulus Verginius Caelimontanus and Titus Veturius Geminus took over the consular offices, when Themistocles was archon at Athens, AUC 260, being the year before the seventy-second Olympiad (492), in which Tisicrates of Croton won for the second time." Obviously, if Themistocles were archon in 493/2, he cannot have been born in 515. One is forced therefore to reject either Dionysius' date or the later chronology implied by Plutarch. Both writers had their weaknesses, but in this case the question is, specifically, whose chronology is to be considered more reliable. Fortunately, it is an easy question to answer. Dionysius' accuracy in dating has been noted frequently[25] and if one cares to substantiate the impression of accuracy it

---

[24] Thuc. I 14.3; noted by Perrin, *Plutarch's Themistocles* 181, and many others, pace J. Labarbe, *La loi navale de Thémistocle* (Paris, 1957) 127; cf. Frost, *CP* 66 (1971) 264.

[25] E.g., Munro, *CR* 6 (1892) 333; Cadoux, *JHS* 58 (1948) 87.

will be found that Dionysius gives thirty-three archon dates, twenty-two of which are attested independently.[26] His date for Themistocles is particularly firm, being reinforced by the synchronisms AUC 260 and the name of the victor in the stadion the following year. Plutarch's chronology, on the other hand, is notoriously unreliable because it was not normally a concern to him. Here, specifically, the inexactness of his statement: "When Egypt revolted . . . and Cimon was master of the seas" betrays the fact that he is thinking in terms of eras and not of precise years. Compare his claim in *Cimon* 13.4 that the general's victory at the Eurymedon caused the King to make the Peace of Callias. My inclination is to suspect the data provided by Plutarch for dating purposes, including his statement that Themistocles lived sixty-five years, for this figure, after all, may derive from Plutarch's own arithmetic.

Left only with Dionysius' date, and the assumption that Themistocles was young when elected—thirty or so[27]— one can still say fairly confidently that Themistocles was born about 525. The chronology of Themistocles' later career is discussed further on. Of modern comment on his dates, one should note J.A.R. Munro, "The Chronology of Themistocles' Career," *CR* 6 (1892) 333f., who demonstrated in masterfully concise fashion that there were two chronologies of the general in antiquity with a ten-year discrepancy. The later chronology has been recently argued by R. Flacelière, "Sur quelques points obscurs de la vie de Thémistocle," *REA* 55 (1953) 15-19, and mentioned as a possibility by Gomme, *HCT* I 261f. Their objections to the early chronology are well met by R. Lenardon, "The Archonship of Themistokles," *Historia* 5 (1956) 401-419.

[26] The list may be scanned most conveniently in Hiller's *Fasti, IG* i² pp. 268-301, to which add *SEG* X 352; Hill, *Sources for Greek History*² (Oxford, 1951) 397-401.

[27] H. T. Wade-Gery, "Themistokles' Archonship," *Essays* 171 n. 1, who compares Aristeides in 490/89 and Miltiades in 524/3.

3.1-3 ταχὺ μέντοι καὶ νεανικῶς ἔοικεν ἅψασθαι τοῦ Θεμιστοκλέους τὰ πολιτικὰ πράγματα

At this point in the *Life* the theme of the rivalry between Themistocles and Aristeides suits Plutarch's biographical purpose admirably. It is developed at greater length at about the same place in the *Life* of Aristeides (2-4). The *fact* of the rivalry need not be doubted (Hdt. 8.79; Timocreon seemed to take note of the contrast between the two men in *Them.* 21.4), but the details given by Plutarch are surely embroidery from Hellenistic writers neither more nor less reliable than Ariston, quoted here and in the *Aristeides* (2.3) and Idomeneus, quoted in *Arist.* 4.4 (*FGrH* 338 F 7). The very mention of the office of τῶν δημοσίων προσόδων ἐπιμελητής in the latter story is enough to condemn it; in the early fifth century one would be thinking of the *kolakretai*.[28]

There are other anachronisms. *Them.* 3.3: Aristeides resisted Themistocles, "who urged the Demos on to great innovations"—a projection backward from the post-Periclean age of demagogues and the Demos of Aristophanes' *Knights*. *Arist.* 2.5: Themistocles joined a *hetaireia*; in the early fifth century this was certainly not the sort of political association described by Thucydides (e.g., *synomosiai* in 8.54).[29]

3.4 νέος ὢν ἔτι, τῆς ἐν Μαραθῶνι μάχης πρὸς τοὺς βαρβάρους γενομένης

Nothing could more clearly illustrate Plutarch's freedom from the sort of tiresome consistency that tyrannizes modern historians. In the *Aristeides* (5.4), Themistocles and Aristeides are ranged side by side in their respective regiments at Marathon, and compete with each other in valor.

[28] *IG* i² 19.13, 338.10, etc.; see Calabi Limentani, *Vita Aristidis*, comment to 4.3; Jacoby, *FGrH* IIIb 88 and IIIb Suppl. 117ff. ad Androtion 324 F 5; R. Thomsen, *Eisphora* (Copenhagen, 1964) 136-138.

[29] Cf. F. Sartori, *Le eterie nella vita politica ateniese del vi e v secolo A.C.* (Roma, 1957) 43, 61; Perrin, *Plutarch's Themistocles* 270.

But here, and elsewhere in Plutarch, Themistocles is still a youth, sleepless over Miltiades' fame (*Thes.* 6.9; *Prof.in virt.* 84C; *Praec.reip.ger.* 800B, etc.). Although this latter story was frequently recalled in antiquity (Cicero, *Tusc.* IV 19, 44; Val.Max. VIII 14 ext. 1; Libanius, *Declam.* IX 12), it is more probable that Themistocles was in fact present at Marathon, although no early evidence puts him there. The argument is circumstantial: as he was about thirty-five years of age and had served as archon a few years previously, he would have been, if not *strategos*, at least an officer of some distinction in the regiment of the Leontis tribe.[30]

Plutarch ignores the rest of Themistocles' early career until the year of the Maroneia strike and the Navy Bill (c. 484/3). Some information may be inferred: he was probably at some time a *bouleutes* from the tribe Leontis. Leontid colleagues more or less contemporary will have included the grandfather of the historian Thucydides of Halimous and Cleinias of Skambonidai, the father of Alcibiades, who performed so notably at Artemision (Hdt. 8.17). Inferences aside, there are several crucial and well-attested events from Themistocles' early career not mentioned by Plutarch, and these need brief treatment before continuing.

THE ARCHON YEAR 493/2

1. The Archonship

Some have wondered how Themistocles could have attained "the highest office in the state" in 493/2 only to

---

[30] Lenardon, *Historia* 5 (1956) 409-411, is inclined to see Themistocles at Marathon, although I cannot agree that it is "inherent in the narrative that Themistokles was one of the *strategoi*." Flacelière, believing that Themistocles was born in 515, naturally denied the tale, *REA* 55 (1953) 17; other references in Calabi Limentani, *Vita Aristidis* 22f., where Lenardon, however, is misquoted. C. Fornara, *The Athenian Board of Generals*, Historia Einzelschriften 16 (1971) 41-42, rejects the strategia of both Aristeides and Themistocles.

drop out of sight for a decade.[31] But was the archonship the highest office in the state? Is it to be seen as equivalent to the office of Roman consul or First Minister of some modern parliamentary state? The answer must be a qualified no. First, our only knowledge of the duties of the eponymous archon comes from the brief survey in chapter 56 of the *Athenaion Politeia*, which makes it clear that the archonship was an administrative office rather than an executive one. The Athenians did not in fact delegate executive power to any officials, except generals in the field. Second, the archonship may have been the highest administrative office in the state but was in any case of minor importance because the Athenians did not much care for people in offices. I have dealt with this question at some length elsewhere;[32] the argument is as follows.

The evidence seems to show that young men of thirty or so became archons approximately *ad annum* under the Peisistratids and that the custom continued under the Cleisthenic constitution.[33] But the Athenians are known other-wise to have put a premium on age and experience. "Who of those over fifty years of age wishes to speak, and then other Athenians in turn?" was the herald's question, opening discussion in the assembly,[34] and there is evidence for an age qualification in other posts from time to time (e.g. *IG* i² 57.17). Moreover, the most influential and powerful individuals in the Athenian state were not office holders, but private citizens, whose power was based on reputation, achievement and probably wealth as well. The archonship may once have been worth fighting over (*AP* 13.2) but we

---

[31] Gomme, *HCT* I 261; Flacelière, *REA* 55 (1953) 18.

[32] *CSCA* I (1968) 114-115.

[33] Miltiades, Peisistratus the younger, Themistocles, Aristeides, and Hipparchus are all noted by H. T. Wade-Gery, "The Laws of Kleisthenes," *Essays* 146 n. 1, 171 n. 1; see also H. Schaefer, "Besonderheit und Begriff der attische Demokratie im V Jahrhundert," *Probleme der alten Geschichte* (Göttingen, 1963) 142.

[34] Aeschines 3.4, and see G. T. Griffith, "Isegoria in the Athenian Assembly," in *Ehrenberg Studies* (Oxford, 1966) 119f.

shall never know why; when in 487/6 the Athenians began to select archons by lot (if this is in fact what they did, see following note) this was only a natural consequence of the disesteem into which the office had fallen. A recent survey by Badian has convincingly demonstrated the obscurity of almost every person who held the archonship both before and after the reform during the year of Telesinus.[35]

The archonship in the late sixth and early fifth centuries, therefore, is to be seen as a proving ground for young men of promise, and Themistocles in this office might be compared to a Roman quaestor, but not to a consul. If this interpretation is accepted, then Herodotus' description of Themistocles' status in 483 as ἐς πρώτους νεωστὶ παριών (7.143) makes more sense because archons and junior Areopagites were not considered to be among the *protoi*.[36]

2. The Fortification of Piraeus

Thuc. I 93.3: ἔπεισε δὲ καὶ τοῦ Πειραιῶς τὰ λοιπὰ ὁ Θεμιστοκλῆς οἰκοδομεῖν (ὑπῆρκτο δ' αὐτοῦ πρότερον ἐπὶ τῆς ἐκείνου ἀρχῆς ἧς κατ' ἐνιαυτὸν ᾿Αθηναίοις ἦρξε). Cf. Eusebius, *Chron.* vers. Arm. Ol. 71.1; Pausanias I 1.2; schol. Thucydides ad loc.

If we are to take the most obvious interpretation of this difficult passage and assume that the historian is referring to the eponymous archonship,[37] then the beginning of fortification at this time is quite understandable, considering both the continuing hostilities with Aegina (on which see below) and the apprehension of informed Athenians following the disastrous failure of the Ionian revolt in the previous year. The project may have been a policy moved by Themistocles; it is just as likely that as archon he was instructed by the assembly to administer the project; given

---

[35] "Archons and *Strategoi*," *Antichthon* 5 (1971) 9-17.

[36] Podlecki, *Themistocles* 68, says that this "cannot seriously be maintained," but adduces no evidence to the contrary, nor does R. W. Wallace, "Ephialtes and the Areopagus," *GRBS* 15 (1974) 259-269—an unreconstructed, Aristotelian picture of the era.

[37] See below, comment to 19.3.

the nature of the man, he would have taken credit for the initial construction when work resumed in 478.[38]

The fortification in 493/2 should not be seen as the far-sighted commencement of the larger system of walls which it was to become but as (1) a long overdue protection for Attica's second largest population center, and (2) a replacement as naval station for Phaleron, whose vulnerability had been revealed twice in the past twenty years (Hdt. 5. 63, 5.81).

3. Phrynichus

It may have been during this year that the tragedian Phrynichus presented the play ἡ Μιλήτου ἅλωσις (or ἡ Μιλήτου ἅλωσις ὑπὸ Δαρείου, according to Callisthenes in Strabo XIV 1.7, FGrH 124 F 30). Herodotus said (6.21) that the poet was fined 1,000 drachmae because in his vivid portrayal of the sack of Miletus by the Persians he had reminded them of οἰκήια κακά—"family" tragedies, which probably refers to the legend that Miletus was a colony of the Athenians.

Ancient authors disagreed over the reasons for the wrath of the Athenians. The scholiast to Aristophanes' *Wasps* 1490 and Aelian (*VH* 13.17), both explaining a reference to Phrynichus in collections of proverbs, claimed that the playwright's work was cowardly and defeatist, perhaps implying that the poet was suggesting peace at any price with Persia. But Ammianus Marcellinus (XXVIII 1.3-4) said Phrynichus was reproaching the Athenians by showing them the suffering of a city they themselves had founded and which they allowed to be destroyed without sending aid. Ammianus added that the Milesians burned themselves and their goods along with their city. This is obviously the opposite interpretation from that of the scholiast, and there

---

[38] On the passage of Thucydides, see Lenardon, *Historia* 5 (1956) 406-411; Wade-Gery, *Essays* 171f. A. Mosshammer, "Themistocles' Archonship in the Chronographic Tradition," *Hermes* 103 (1975) 222-234, sees the apparent confirmation of Thucydides by Eusebius as a mistake attributable to Hellanicus.

is no help from the other testimony to the incident (Callis-thenes, cited above; Plut. *Praec.ger.reip.* 814B; *Suda* s.v. Phrynichus). It is therefore impossible to say what political propaganda, if any, was involved in the play. Nevertheless, several modern scholars have seen Themistocles involved in the production of this play.[39] But the only connection is the fact that Themistocles sponsored Phrynichus' play, *The Phoenician Women*, in 477/6, seventeen years later (Plut. *Them.* 5.4, probably quoting from the *didaskalia*). Political interpretation of surviving tragedies is unreward-ing enough without going on to base theories on works of which not one word has survived; with no more evidence than this one must deny any connection between this play and a Themistoclean policy of vigilance against Persia.

4. Miltiades' Return

During the same archon year Miltiades arrived in Athens, having seen correctly that he could not hold the Chersonese against the systematic advance of the Phoenician fleet (Hdt. 6.40-41, 104). One can only assume that the un-expected arrival of an imposing ruler, with great wealth, military skill, and wide experience in dealing with Persians, portended an eclipse for all ambitious men in Athens. Some were not willing to see their primacy challenged, and they brought Miltiades into court on a charge of "tyranny in the Chersonese" (Hdt. 6.104). Although persuasive arguments have been advanced to make Themistocles an ally of Milti-ades in this trial,[40] there is no evidence for Themistocles'

[39] E. Walker, *CAH* IV 171f.; Wade-Gery, *Essays* 177f.; V. Ehren-berg, "Die Generation von Marathon," *Ost und West* (Prague, 1935) 117; W. G. Forrest, "Themistokles and Argos," *CQ* 10 n.s. (1960) 235f. Podlecki, *Themistocles* 6f., is more cautious, saying only that Themistocles must have been sympathetic with the theme.

[40] Wade-Gery, *Essays* 165: "I believe that Themistokles was his judge, resolved . . . to override the evidence." Cf. Walker, *CAH* IV 171f.; C. A. Robinson, "The Struggle for Power at Athens," *AJP* 60 (1939) 232ff.; M. McGregor, "The Pro-Persian Party at Athens," *HSCP* Suppl. I (1940) 94; Burn, *Persia and the Greeks* 226.

relationship with the great man. I reiterate my interpretation of the archonship: that Themistocles was still a young man, perhaps owing his position to older and more powerful sponsors from the great houses. I believe it unlikely that he would have taken a strong position on either side in this dangerous political feud.[41] His first strenuous political challenge, so far as we know, was still seven years off.

THE OSTRACOPHORIAE

The most fascinating—and tantalizing—aspect of domestic politics at Athens in the 480's is the series of ostracism contests. The evidence is twofold. According to the *Athenaion Politeia*, Hipparchus, son of Charmus, was ostracised in 488/7 (*AP* 22.3-4), Megacles in 487/6 (*AP* 22.5), and "friends of the tyrants" for the next two years (*AP* 22.6). But in 484/3 they ostracized Xanthippus, the first exile who "had nothing to do with the tyranny." Finally, in 483/2, Aristeides was banished (*AP* 22.7).

All these names, plus many others, have been found on ostraca. The most recent finds, from the Kerameikos since 1966, have added greatly to our evidence, if not to our understanding. The huge numbers of ostraca naming Megacles and Themistocles seem to show that the find spot in Kerameikos was a dump for the ostracophoria of 487/6. This is confirmed by a pair of ostraca broken from the same pot, one bearing the name of Themistocles, one with that of Megacles.

It is certainly tempting to see Themistocles involved in all these contests, but despite the new finds our ignorance of the personalities, factions, and issues remains as great as ever. Any strong opinions about the ostracophoriae should be tempered by the following considerations.

[41] E. Gruen, "Stesimbrotus on Miltiades and Themistocles," *CSCA* 3 (1970) 91-98, suggests that the debate between Miltiades and Themistocles (4.4, below) should be dated to 493; I believe this goes beyond what can safely be deduced from the evidence.

The fact that one politician could not really ostracize another is often neglected, as we are reminded by A. R. Hands.[12] To do so, he would first have to persuade the assembly to hold an ostracophoria during the sixth prytany (*AP* 43.5). He would have to be convinced of his ability to collect enough personal supporters to vote against his enemy in the eighth prytany (Philochorus, *FGrH* 328 F 30). But even in this case, a valid contest required a total of 6,000 votes.[43] A politician hoping to exile another would therefore have to collect as close to 6,000 votes as possible, hoping that his opponent's counter-campaign and the inevitable scatter vote would bring the total to over 6,000. One cannot deny categorically that such a campaign ever took place; the mechanics make it unlikely that a contest of this sort could be successful.

The obscurity of some of the names found in contexts datable to the 480's demonstrates just how uninformed we are about the politics of the period.[44] What our evidence shows is limited to the following: (1) Themistocles had, by 487, become sufficiently powerful to arouse the fears and jealousy of a significant number of other Athenians in public life. (2) His enemies were well organized, as demonstrated by a cache of 190 ostraca, prepared in advance with his name on them, but seemingly never used.[45] We know a little more about the campaign against Megacles. Some of the new ostraca are talkative: one calls him an adulterer,

[42] "Ostraka and the Law of Ostracism," *JHS* 79 (1959) 69-79; good summary by Podlecki, *Themistocles* 185-194.

[43] So Plut. *Arist.* 7.6, to be accepted over the excerpt from Philochorus in a rhetorical lexicon (328 F 30), which seems to say that over 6,000 votes had to be cast against *one* person. I follow the arguments of Jacoby, *FGrH* IIIb Suppl. 316-317; other references in Calabi Limentani, *Vita Aristidis* xlviii-xlvix; E. Vanderpool, "Ostracism at Athens," *Semple Lectures* 218.

[44] E.g., Callixenus, Cydrocles, Habronichus, all found in conjunction with Themistocles and Aristeides ostraca, Vanderpool, *Hesperia* Suppl. 8 (1949) 395.

[45] O. Broneer, *Hesp.* 7 (1938) 228-243.

another blames him for loss of a piece of land, another perhaps because of an affair with a boy. But so far no one is able to say with certainty what issues or traits of character led to the involvement of Themistocles in the ostracophoriae, until 483/2, when the issues become a little clearer.

4.1 Καὶ πρῶτον μὲν τὴν Λαυρεωτικὴν πρόσοδον ἀπὸ τῶν ἀργυρείων μετάλλων ἔθος ἐχόντων 'Αθηναίων διανέμεσθαι

The debate over the use of the Laureion-Maroneia silver strike must be treated first as a historiographical problem. The first extant narrative is that of Herodotus, who says there was a great deal of money in the treasury from the Laureion mines; that the Athenians were about to allot the money ὀρχηδόν (or ὀρχιδόν) to the amount of ten drachmas;[46] that Themistocles persuaded the Athenians to stop the distribution and build two hundred ships instead (7.144).

The next account is *AP* 22.7, which differs in these particulars: the surplus (of 100T) came from a specific strike in the region of Maroneia;[47] a proposal was before the assembly to distribute the money when Themistocles proposed instead to lend one talent to the one hundred richest men in Athens, not saying what they were to do with it,

[46] Whatever the MS reading, the word occurs only here in extant literature, and in the lexicographers' explanation of this passage: ὀρχηδὸν ὡς ἠβηδόν, Ἡρόδοτος (Hesych., *Suda*, s.v.), that is, "youths and older." Despite the minute analysis of J. Labarbe, *La loi navale de Thémistocle* 61-73, it is difficult to propose a more exact meaning than this. *LSJ*⁹ derives ὀρχηδόν from ὄρχος = row of trees or vines, i.e., "one after another; man by man."

[47] Maroneia is a district or village, not a deme, of the Laureion mining district (Demosth. 37.4), named frequently in mining leases: e.g., *Hesp.* 10 (1941) 17 no. 1.59; *Hesp.* 19 (1950) 261 no. 19.18. It is conjecturally located near the modern Kamareza, Ardaillon, *Les mines du Laurion* (Paris, 1897) 138-140. The district was probably named after the rich mining district in Thrace; there was also an area named Pangaion in the deme of Besa which may have been near Maroneia. See M. Crosby, *Hesp.* 19 (1950) 207 no. 2.17-18, 255 no. 18.6, comment on p. 258; cf. Labarbe *Loi navale* 32-36.

but suggesting that if their use of it was approved, the city would assume the expense; in this way one hundred triremes were built.

Since all subsequent reports of the episode are based on Herodotus, Aristotle, or various traditions available to Aristotle, it is necessary to analyse the differences between the two accounts.

1. The variants Laureion-Maroneia do not necessarily conflict. Aristotle is simply specifying the area of the major strike.

2. There is no reason to reject out of hand the story that the construction was turned over to wealthy men operating more or less like private contractors. Public works were in their infancy at Athens and state-run shipyards no doubt nonexistent. That this method of construction was kept secret from the assembly, however, is difficult to believe. First, Herodotus specifically stated that Themistocles proposed to use the ships in the Aeginetan war. Second, can we picture the assembly approving an undisclosed expenditure as an alternative to a public distribution? Podlecki points out that Miltiades persuaded the assembly to approve an expeditionary force with an undisclosed destination in 489 (Hdt. 6.132), but the circumstances are quite different. Keeping a military venture secret makes sense; concealing the nature of a major domestic disbursement of funds simply does not seem possible, particularly when we remember what happened to Miltiades and his catastrophic expedition.

3. As to the discrepant numbers of ships, it is generally assumed that Herodotus is in error and has taken the number two hundred from the approximate number of ships owned by Athens three years later on the eve of Salamis.[48] This

---

[48] He seems to have forgotten that Athens already had fifty ships (6.89). On the eve of battle, Athens owned two hundred ships, of which they had the use of one hundred and eighty (8.44), having loaned twenty to Chalcis (8.1, 8.46). But the round number two hundred is otherwise given (8.61) and was accepted by tradition: Diod. 15.78; Nepos, *Them.* 2.2; Plut. *Them.* 11.5; cf. *Hesp.* 31 (1962)

is not at all improbable. The most frustrating problem for modern scholars remains the knowledge that Aristotle had one or more sources that specified the archon year of the debate over the Naval Bill and gave details like the secret award of contracts and the number of ships—and yet no one can say with any certainty who those sources were and where they got their information.

We learn little more from later writers. It seems obvious that all our other ancient sources (with the exception of Justin II 12.12, probably copied uncritically out of Herodotus) decided to ignore the number given by Herodotus and to accept the number one hundred, whether because of the authority of Aristotle or because this number was given by writers like Ephorus whose works are lost.[49] Polyaenus has also preserved the story of the one hundred richest men; he may have seen this in the *Athenaion Politeia*. There was also a tradition that the Athenians had made regular distributions of the mining revenue. This was repeated by both Nepos[50] and Plutarch. It is not certain, however, that the biographer had seen this in a specific source; he may simply have inferred it from Herodotus, whom he seems to be following fairly closely (although not on the number of triremes).

τὸν πρὸς Αἰγινήτας πόλεμον

For this "undeclared war," we are almost entirely dependent upon the vague and disjointed narrative of Herodotus. The Aeginetans attacked Attica in c. 505 at the urging of the Thebans (5.80-81). The Athenians were prevented from

---

311 line 14 (the Themistocles Decree); How and Wells ad 7.144. Labarbe, *Loi navale* 37-42, pressing his sources too hard, as usual, proposed to resolve the difference by claiming a revenue of 100T from Maroneia and a revenue of 100T from the rest of Laureion in 483/2. He claimed that Herodotus combined the two items to get enough money for two hundred ships. Regular use of Occam's razor is needed to deal with this sort of reasoning.

[49] See Nepos, *Them.* 2.2; Plut. *Them.* 4.3; Polyaenus I 30.6; Libanius, *Declam.* 10.27.

[50] On which, see Podlecki, *Themistocles* 202f.

retaliating by the threat of a Spartan invasion (5.90). In
about 491, Aegina gave earth and water to the Great King,
on which pretext the Athenians encouraged Cleomenes of
Sparta to attack the island (6.49-50). The Aeginetans surrendered to Cleomenes and gave hostages, who were then
handed over to the Athenians (6.73; that Themistocles was
involved may be implied by the later rage of Polycritus,
son of one of the hostages, who taunted Themistocles during the battle of Salamis for having accused Aegina of
medism, 8.92). But after the death of Cleomenes, c. 489/8,
Athens refused to return the hostages; this led to renewed
hostilities during which the Athenians were forced to bor-
row twenty ships from Corinth (6.85-94; cf. Thuc. I 41.2).
For the purposes of this inquiry it suffices to say that the
war continued right down to the eve of the Persian invasion, at which time it was ended, together with lesser
Greek quarrels, by the common threat (7.145). Most of the
other dates during the course of the war are disputed.[51]

The later tradition typically made Themistocles' pleading
of the Aeginetan war a stratagem: in reality he knew all the
time that the real threat was Persia (e.g., Aristides II 250f.).
But Herodotus never implied this (7.144), and Thucydides
sums up the situation (I 14.3): "Themistocles persuaded the
Athenians to build the ships while they were fighting the
Aeginetans and at the same time awaiting the barbarian. . . ."
That is to say, the most pressing business at hand was the
war with Aegina, but the Persian threat was not entirely
ignored. This must be the true picture. The Athenians were
never unaware of the Persian threat, nor did they care to
sweep matters under the rug. It is certain that in this crucial
assembly session every single ramification of Themistocles'
proposal was discussed.

The political theorists of the fourth century, of whom
Plato is most important (see below, comment to 4.4), saw

[51] Walker, *CAH* IV 254ff.; Andrewes, *BSA* 37 (1936/1937) 1-7;
N.G.L. Hammond, *Historia* 4 (1955) 407; Podlecki, "Athens and
Aegina," *Historia* 25 (1976) 396-403.

in this episode the foundation of Athenian naval democracy
with all its supposed attendant ills, and consequently they
interpreted the debate that took place in the assembly as
being on the question whether to have a navy. But this
obscures what must have always been the real issue: whether
the Athenians should enlarge the war with Aegina *to the
extent* of building a large modern navy.[52] Themistocles'
opponents will not have been oligarchs who foresaw the
awful effects of naval democracy, but a combination of
forces—the ignorant and indigent who wished a cash distribution; those conservatives present in any society who
resist innovation and novelty; most important, those who
favored better relations with Aegina—men with close
bonds of friendship with prominent Aeginetans, probably
including Melesias, the father of the politician Thucydides.[53]
If [Demosthenes] 26 ii 6 is correct in claiming that Aristeides spent his exile on Aegina, we may assume him to be
one of this group as well, if not in fact its leader.

4.2 ᾗ καὶ ῥᾷον ὁ Θεμιστοκλῆς συνέπεισεν, οὐ Δαρεῖον οὐδὲ
Πέρσας . . . ἐπισείων
Darius died sometime between 487 and 485. Scholars apply-
ing various sorts of addition and subtraction to the Pharonic
canon of Manetho (*FGrH* 609 F 2-3c, p. 5of.) have arrived at any number of dates, from Boeckh's 23 December
488 (Mueller, *FHG* II 605) to Eduard Meyer's "Herbst,
485."[54] The only relatively firm date to calculate back
from is the year 425/4 for the death of Artaxerxes (Thuc.
IV 50). Artaxerxes ruled forty or forty-one years according
to the variants in Eusebius' chronology, derived originally
from Manetho; Artabanus usurped the throne for seven
months; Xerxes ruled for 21 years: 40 (41) plus 7 months

[52] So also Calabi Limentani, *Vita Aristidis* lxiv.
[53] Pindar, *Ol.* 8; *Nem.* 4, 6; cf. *Nem.* 5.49: χρὴ δ' ἀπ' 'Αθανᾶν' τέκτον'
ἀθληταῖσιν ἔμμεν; noted by Wade-Gery, *Essays* 243-246; Davies, *APF*
7268 I.
[54] *Geschichte des Altertums* IV.1 317.

plus 21 plus 425/4 adds up to approximately the year 487—
or a little later.

Plutarch, however, thought Darius was alive when the
debate took place. An error of three to five years is not excessive for the biographer. It is difficult enough for us to
correlate Greek and oriental systems of chronology; for
the biographer it would have been, if not impossible, totally
uncharacteristic. As noted above, in spite of Plutarch's glib
assertion that the Persian threat was far away and uncertain,
it is difficult to believe that it was not discussed during this
debate.

4.3 Ἑκατόν

Plutarch follows here the almost unanimous verdict of ancient writers in rejecting the 200 triremes of Herodotus.
See comment to 4.1, above.

4.4 Ἐκ δὲ τούτου κατὰ μικρὸν ὑπάγων καὶ καταβιβάζων τὴν πόλιν
πρὸς τὴν θάλατταν

Themistocles urged this strategy supposedly because the
Athenians were not equal to their neighbors in infantry, but
in naval strength were able to ward off the barbarian and
to rule Greece. This notion of Plutarch's is obviously *post
eventum* and looking forward to chapter 19.3. That Themistocles ever told the Athenians that they were τὰ πεζὰ . . .
οὐδὲ τοῖς ὁμόροις ἀξιόμαχοι is most doubtful. In 483/2, he was
addressing the recent victors of Marathon, hoplites who had
soundly thrashed both Boeotians and Chalcidians on the
same day (Hdt. 5.77; cf. Meiggs and Lewis, *GHI* no. 15).
The thinking here, wherever Plutarch encountered it, is
closer to the strategy of the Peloponnesian War.[55]

ὥς φησιν ὁ Πλάτων

Normally an admirer of the philosopher, Plutarch differs
with him throughout the rest of this chapter on two counts:
the argument of *Laws* 706cd, which claims that "stalwart
hoplites" are made cowardly by close naval support because

[55] As in [Xenophon] *AP* 2.1: τὸ δὲ ὁπλιτικὸν αὐτοῖς ὃ ἥκιστα δοκεῖ εὖ
ἔχειν Ἀθήνησιν, κτλ.

they can always flee back to their ships (the passage is familiar to Plutarch; it is quoted again in *Philop.* 14.3); and *Laws* 707bc, where the philosopher's spokesman argues that the infantry battles of Marathon and Plataea were responsible for the salvation of the Greeks, not the naval battle of Salamis.

Plutarch chooses first to answer the broader implication of the whole passage of the *Laws*: that maritime power corrupts the purity of the state. Here he differs not only with Plato but also a host of other writers known to him but only dimly perceived by us, including the author who said that Themistocles τὸ δόρυ καὶ τὴν ἀσπίδα τῶν πολιτῶν παρελόμενος εἰς ὑπηρέσιον καὶ κώπην συνέστειλε τὸν ᾿Αθηναίων δῆμον (perhaps a comic poet).[56] The biographer evidently felt he should inject a note of practical common sense: whether the purity of the state was harmed by the possession of a navy was an academic concern. The fact is that the salvation of the Greeks did come from the sea.[57] This brought him to the second point—the most decisive battle of the Persian War. As Plato exaggerated the significance of the infantry conflicts, so did Plutarch magnify the victory at Salamis. "For Xerxes fled after the defeat of his ships as if he were no longer *axiomachos* and he left Mardonius behind, as it seems to me, more to hinder the pursuit of the Greeks than for the purpose of enslaving them." Plutarch's argument is for the most part a paraphrase of Thucydides I 73.5-74.1 (cf. Hdt. 8.103). The interpretation of Mardonius' force as a mere rearguard is Plutarch's own contribution. Hignett has a good discussion of the military situation after Salamis (*Xerxes' Invasion* 264ff.).

4.5 ὡς ἱστορεῖ Στησίμβροτος (*FGrH* 107 F 2)

According to Stesimbrotus, Themistocles ἔπραξε δὲ ταῦτα Μιλτιάδου κρατήσας ἀντιλέγοντος. What does ταῦτα refer to? Is it the specific passage of the naval bill, or does it mean

[56] Suggested by Perrin, *Plutarch's Themistocles* 186.

[57] Aristides, II 274, while specifically criticizing the *Gorgias*, is also aware of *Laws* 706cd and includes it in his polemic.

that Themistocles made mariners of the Athenians against the *continual* opposition of Miltiades? In the context, it could mean either. Plutarch also uses the verb ἀντιλέγω elsewhere in both senses.[58] In any case it is difficult to resist the idea that Stesimbrotus made Miltiades a spokesman for hoplite primacy and against naval power. The fact that Miltiades died five years before the naval bill would not have occurred to Plutarch any more than the anachronism involving Darius, noted above. Jacoby is probably correct in claiming that Plutarch didn't know when Miltiades died, and Stesimbrotus didn't care (*FGrH* IID 345f.). But his assertion that 4.4sq. is mostly from Stesimbrotus, with the citation from Plato added by Plutarch, is surely wrong. The biographer was concerned first and foremost with the philosophical question raised by Plato; it was the Stesimbrotus citation that was parenthetically added to the discussion because it just happened to occur to Plutarch at that moment.[59]

The fifth chapter of the *Themistocles* is almost entirely ancedotal. The stories are grouped under three topics: 5.1-2, Themistocles' hunger for money; 5.3-5, his *philotimia*; 5.6-7, methods by which he sought popularity.

5.1-2 Σύντονον δ' αὐτὸν γεγονέναι χρηματιστὴν οἱ μέν τινές φασι δι' ἐλευθεριότητα

Some say he wanted money only to be able to spend it in a grand manner. Others claimed he was simply miserly. We are told that Themistocles' estate as a young man was "only"

---

[58] In *Adv.Colotem* 1115B the verb means to differ in a general sense; in *Per.* 8.5 it means specific opposition during an assembly debate.

[59] On this episode, see also Wilamowitz, *Aristoteles und Athen* (Berlin 1893) II 84 n. 20; Perrin, *Plutarch's Themistocles* 186f.; Gottlieb, *Ausserherodoteischen Überlieferung* 99f.; on the question of sea power, see G. Morrow, *Plato's Cretan City* (Princeton, 1960) 97-100; A. Momigliano, "Sea Power in Greek Thought," *CR* 58 (1944) 1-7; A. Raubitschek, "Meeresnähe und Volksherrschaft," *WS* 71 (1958) 112ff.

three talents (25.3; "three to five talents" in *Arist.Cat. comp.* 1.4, both passages probably resting on the authority of Critias, in Aelian, *VH* 10.17). Themistocles was not truly wealthy, like Callias, but an estate of three talents was considered substantial by Isaeus (3.18, 25) more than a century later.

Selling the food sent as a gift is a story also told of Themistocles' friend Simonides (Chamaeleon in Athenaeus 656C, fr. 33 Wehrli).

Diphilides the horse breeder, whom Themistocles threatened with domestic discord, is unidentifiable. A Diphilides ἐκ κεραμέων of early fifth-century date is known from a dedication[60] but it is doubtful whether this, or indeed any anecdote from this chapter, merits much belief.

5.3-5 τῇ δὲ φιλοτιμίᾳ πάντας ὑπερέβαλεν
Three stories illustrating his pursuit of fame and honor. (1) He invited the musician Epicles of Hermione to practice at his house; (2) he tried to outdo Cimon in luxury and pomp at Olympia; and (3) as winning choregus he erected a memorial of his victory.

These illustrations were chosen carelessly and uncritically. The first is pointless to us at least, although Plutarch's audience may have known more of the background of the story. Recent social history shows that the alliance of politicians and entertainers is a natural one. Epicles is unrecorded elsewhere in surviving literature.

It is difficult to think of a time when a young Themistocles could have appeared at Olympia with Cimon and offended the Greeks with a parvenu display of wealth. In 496, for instance, he would have been about thirty, Cimon still an adolescent. In 492, such a display would not have been inappropriate for a young man who had just laid down the archonship. That he was "in no way *gnorimos*" is simply

[60] Even the date is suspect; *IG* i² 575 is usually identified as a deliberately archaizing production of imperial times, A. Raubitschek, *Dedications from the Athenian Akropolis* (Cambridge, 1949) 149.

not true. If there is something significant in this ancedote, it is lost on us.

Plutarch's report of Themistocles' choregic victory, on the other hand, has every appearance of authenticity; he may have seen the tablet himself (cf. *Arist.* 13.; *Nic.* 3.3) or found a report in the Didaskalia. But the datum hardly demonstrates Plutarch's point: in 476, when the drama was performed, Themistocles was one of the most famous individuals in Greece, and a choregic victory would have been only a minor triumph. Scholars since Nauck have assumed the play to be the *Phoenissae.* Adeimantus' archon year is also reported by the Marmor Parium, A 54.

5.6-7 οὐ μὴν ἀλλὰ τοῖς πολλοῖς ἐνήρμοττε
The common people liked him, first, because he knew every citizen's name by heart, and second, because he always volunteered his services as a dependable judge in business disputes (κριτὴς ἀσφαλής περὶ τὰ συμβόλαια).

Simonides was famed as the originator of a mnemonic system which he offered to teach to Themistocles.[61] He in turn replied that he would rather learn how to forget (Cicero, *De fin.* II 32, 104). Traditionally, Themistocles had what we would call a photographic memory and this was especially noted by Latin writers.[62]

Nepos also testifies to Themistocles' frequent involvement *in judiciis privatis* (*Them.* 1.3). The word κριτής used by Plutarch does not here refer to a specific position defined by the constitution (except the judges of dramatic contests, e.g. Andoc. 4.21, which is obviously not the case here), and the biographer is evidently being no more precise than his anecdotal sources required him to be.[63] The ancient

---

[61] Marmor Parium A 54; Cicero, *De orat.* II 86, 351; Pliny, *NH* 7.24; Longinus, *Rhet.* 1.2 p. 201 Hammer; et al.

[62] Cicero, *De senect.* 21; *Acad.prior* II 1, 2; Val. Max. VIII 7, ext. 15.

[63] It might be thought that he is thinking of the well-known position of *diaitetes* (*AP* 53; cf. 16.5, 26.3), but in *Qc* 617A, Plutarch

tradition was of two minds as to whether Themistocles was an honest judge. The story about Simonides not receiving the favor due a friend is often cited elsewhere by Plutarch.[64] In the *Praecepta*, however, Plutarch contrasted this story with another: Themistocles said, "Never let me sit on such a throne where my friends will receive no more than those who are not friends" (807 AB); this is an ancient testimonial to the *rousfeti* system with which modern Greeks are so familiar.[65]

The next anecdote is an afterthought, perhaps thrown in while the biographer was on the subject of Simonides. The poet did not actually "abuse" Corinth; the Corinthians felt themselves insulted by his line: Κορινθίοισι οὐ μανίει [sc. τὸ Ἴλιον] οὐδὲ Δαναοί.[66] Simonides is otherwise known to have written much on behalf of the Corinthians. See the Simonidean verses cited by Plutarch in *De Hdt.mal.* 870E[67] and especially 872DE.

τέλος κατεστασίασε καὶ μετέστησεν ἐξοστρακισθέντα τὸν Ἀριστείδην

". . . à la fin, triomphant du parti qui lui était opposé, il fit bannir Aristide par ostracisme (Flacelière's Budé translation). "He . . . finally headed a successful faction and got Aristeides removed by ostracism" (Perrin, in the Loeb ed.). Scott-Kilvert has ". . . secured the triumph of the party he

---

[64] *Praec.ger.reip.* 807B; *Vit.pud.* 534E; *Apophth.* 185D.

specifically contrasts the two words: a *diaitetes* is an arbitrator; a *krites* a judge who gives final decisions.

[65] Cf. Synesius, *Ep.* 93 p. 693 Hercher: ἀπηύξατο πᾶσαν ἀρχὴν ἐν ᾗ τῶν ξένων οὐδὲν ἔμελλον πλέον ἕξειν οἱ γνώριμοι. "He [sc. Themistocles] avoided every office in which the *gnorimoi* had no advantage over strangers." Wade-Gery once proposed a historical context for Plutarch's story (*Essays* 176-178), but the absence of any early testimony should make us reject it.

[66] Schol. Pindar, *Ol.* 13.78. Even though the Corinthians were Greeks, the Trojans did not hate them because they fought on both sides in the Trojan War; cf. Plut. *Dion* 1.1; Arist. *Rhet.* I.6, 1363ᵃ15.

[67] Also *IG* i² 927; [Dio Chrys.] 37.18, on which see A. Boegehold, *GRBS* 6 (1965) 179ff.

led" (Penguin ed.). The word καταστασιάζω is normally used by Plutarch to describe the rough and tumble of Roman politics during the late Republic[68] and has no particular reference to partisan politics in Athens. The passage is to be translated simply, "growing powerful and pleasing the many, he finally overthrew Aristeides and caused him to be banished by ostracism" (cf. *Arist.* 25.10; *Arist.Cato comp.* 2.4). Although Plutarch is the earlier writer to say specifically that Themistocles was responsible for the ostracism, it is usually taken for granted. Herodotus said Aristeides was ostracized and that he was Themistocles greatest enemy (8.79), but he did not connect the two data. Neither is a connection made in *AP* 22.7, where it is said that the naval bill and the ostracism took place at about the same time.

In *Arist.* 7.1, Plutarch reports the charge made by Themistocles: that by judging all cases himself Aristeides had destroyed the power of the *dikasteria* and was secretly preparing a monarchy for himself. The story is obviously late and anecdotal because of the anachronistic mention of the *dikasteria*, whose increasing activity still lay in the future. In the 480's, justice in minor cases was undoubtedly still the province of individual aristocrats, as we have seen in the case of Themistocles himself (see above, comment to 5.6-7).

The difficulties of one man getting a specific opponent removed have been pointed out above. In this case we would assume that Aristeides had hopelessly compromised himself by taking the wrong side (pro-Aegina?) in the naval debate; that his momentary weakness with the Demos was exploited; that during the sixth prytany of 483/2 (roughly January 482) an ostracophoria was authorized with Aristeides uppermost in all minds; and that the vote, held in the eighth prytany (roughly, March 482), did in fact go against him. During the two-month interval, we would also assume an organized word-of-mouth campaign against Aristeides,

[68] *Marius* 28.6; *Lys.Sulla comp.* 5.1; *Sert.* 4.5; *Pomp.* 47.2, etc.

concentrating on the charge authorized by the constitution that he was planning a tyranny; but we should not go far wrong in assuming also that his unpopular views on foreign policy would have been given broad currency (if not, in fact, grossly exaggerated).

A counter-campaign by Aristeides and his supporters against Themistocles is probably indicated by the ostraca, especially those of the two men found in conjunction, and it may be to this contest as well that we owe the 190 sherds inscribed in advance with the name of Themistocles.[69]

This is the simplest reconstruction of events. There are two difficulties: (1) no authority actually says that Aristeides opposed Themistocles on the naval bill; (2) there is a chronological problem because of the sequence in *AP* 22.7-8: Νικοδήμου ἄρχοντος (483/2) . . . ὠστρακίσθη ἐν τούτοις τοῖς καιροῖς Ἀριστείδης . . . . τετάρτῳ δ' ἔτει . . . ἄρχοντος Ὑψιχίδου (481/0). The crux can be resolved by emending τετάρτῳ to τρίτῳ[70] or by bracketing ἄρχοντος Ὑψιχίδου. This latter suggestion rests on the assumption that although a decree recalling the exiles was passed in 481/0, they did not actually arrive back in Athens until early the next archon year. *AP* reports their actual date of return; some copyist supplied the archon date of the *decree* rather than the return, and his comment has crept into our text.[71] None of these solutions are totally satisfactory because too many assumptions have to be made. Like so much else in early Athenian history, this episode continues to evade an easy explanation.[72]

---

[69] E.g., *AJA* 37 (1933) 296; cf. Hands, *JHS* 79 (1959) 77.

[70] Wilamowitz, *Aristoteles und Athen* I 25; T. Cadoux, *JHS* 68 (1948) 118.

[71] G. V. Sumner, *CQ* 11 (1961) 33-35. See also Labarbe, *Loi navale* 88ff.; Calabi Limentani *ad Arist.* 8.1; Raubitschek, *Historia* 8 (1959) 127.

[72] See the sensible and conservative conclusions by Podlecki, *Themistocles* 188.

IV

THE INVASION OF XERXES: COMMENTARY TO CHAPTERS 6-11

6.1 Ἤδη δὲ τοῦ Μήδου καταβαίνοντος ἐπὶ τὴν Ἑλλάδα
Both here and in the *Aristeides*, Plutarch skips from the ostracism directly to the invasion. The interval is dated in *Arist.* 8.1: "In the third year, with Xerxes driving toward Attica through Thessaly and Boeotia . . . ." This is not quite accurate, for it is generally assumed that Xerxes did not reach Thessaly and Boeotia until the fourth year had commenced, i.e., July-August 480, which is near the beginning of the archon year of Calliades, 480/79 (Hdt. 8.51). The modern historian will attempt to draw up a rough calendar of Xerxes' march, using the very few indications in Herodotus; this is obviously not true of Plutarch. He is not thinking of the interval between the two events, but simply of the *duration* of Aristeides' ostracism, memorable because it was so short.[1]

τῶν Ἀθηναίων βουλευομένων περὶ στρατηγοῦ
The story of the unworthy Epicydes, bribed to withdraw as a candidate for the strategia, is told only by Plutarch (also in *Nic.Crass.comp.* 3.4; *Apophth.* 185A). Because Plutarch is speaking here of *one* general, and in *Arist.* 8.1

---

[1] For chronological computations, see Hignett, *Xerxes' Invasion* 448-457; A. Dascalakis, *Problèmes historiques autour de la bataille des Thermopyles* (Paris, 1962) 89ff.; Labarbe, *Loi navale* 81ff.; How and Wells ad Hdt. 7.37.

he explicitly called Themistocles *strategos autokrator*, the question has been raised whether the Athenians did appoint a supreme commander for the coming campaign.[2] But it is Plutarch's usual practice to bring his generals to center stage, whether or not the facts warrant it: Themistocles is *the* general at Salamis; Aristeides at Plataea.[3]

The Greeks had been aware of the impending invasion for several years (Hdt. 7.220; Plato, *Laws* 698E) and could have had no doubts once the advance parties began to establish supply depots and to cut the canal through Mt. Athos. Xerxes and the Persian satraps left Susa perhaps in April 481[4] We assume Themistocles was elected general of the Leontis regiment in about June 481, to serve for the following year. Toward the end of summer 481, the Greeks met at the Isthmus to discuss strategy; during these meetings they received the news that Xerxes had arrived at Sardis, had sent out heralds to demand earth and water, and was preparing to go into winter quarters (Hdt. 7.145, 32, 37; Diod. XI 2.3-4).

At the beginning of spring, say, March 480 (Hdt. 7.37), the Persians left Sardis and would have arrived at the Hellespont in April; here they spent about a month. So it would have been at this time that Thessalian envoys appeared before the *probouloi* of the Greeks at the Isthmus and asked for an expeditionary force to stop the Persians at the passes from Macedonia (Hdt. 7.172). The force sent out included Spartans, commanded by Evaenetus (Synetus, in Diod. XI 2.5) and Athenians, led by Themistocles (Hdt. 7.173 and see comment to 7.2). If there was in fact a contest over

[2] This is what Aeschines Socr. seems to be saying, in Aristides II 292; cf. K. J. Dover, "ΔΕΚΑΤΟΣ ΑΥΤΟΣ," *JHS* 80 (1960) 72.

[3] Cf. Fornara, *The Athenian Board of Generals* 13f.

[4] Diod. XI 2.3; the date is possibly that of the eclipse of 18 April 481, if one accepts the suggestion that Herodotus was misinformed about which city Xerxes was leaving when the eclipse occurred, How and Wells ad Hdt. 7.37.

generals in Athens, it would have been over the command of this expedition. According to Plutarch, "they say the others willingly abstained from the strategia, frightened by the risk," and we could well imagine such a situation. But the story of the bribery of Epicydes is an obvious anachronism. It is introduced by the noncommittal "they say"; Epicydes is called a "demagogue skilled at speaking"; the whole mood of corruption and bribery has Theopompan overtones (cf. 19.1, *FGrH* 115 F 85), and if the story is not from Theopompus, it is probably no earlier than his day—the later fourth century. At any rate, Plutarch did not connect the contest for the strategia with the Tempe expedition, for he reserves that for the next chapter.

6.3 ἐπαινεῖται δ' αὐτοῦ καὶ τὸ περὶ τὸν δίγλωσσον ἔργον
Herodotus mentioned four Persian delegations to Greece and/or the Athenians, the elements of which were greatly confused by later writers.

1. In 491, Darius sent heralds to Greece demanding earth and water; in Athens the herald was thrown into the *barathron* (Hdt. 6.48; 7.133). According to Pausanias (III 12. 7), the execution of the herald was moved by Miltiades.

2. In fall 481, while Xerxes was at Sardis preparing to go into winter quarters, he sent heralds on the same task, excluding the cities of Athens and Sparta because of the previous reception (7.32). Diodorus does not note the omission of these two cities (XI 2.3).

3. During the winter of 480/79, Mardonius sent Alexander of Macedon to subvert the Athenians (8.136, 140sq.).

4. In about June 479 (ten months after the first invasion of Attica, Hdt. 9.3), Mardonius returned to sack Athens once more. Hoping to have terrified the Athenians watching from Salamis, he sent a herald to repeat his offer of collaboration. The herald was allowed to depart unharmed but a *bouleutes* named Lycidas counseled medism and was stoned to death (Hdt. 9.4-5). The story was repeated by Demosthenes (18.204), who changed the name to Cyrsilus,

on whose authority we know not. This was the version with greater currency in later times, when Cicero noted it (*De off.* III 11, 48), and the rhetorical handbooks and lexica picked it up (Harpocration, *Suda* s.v. Cyrsilus).

A fifth mission was that of Arthmius of Zelea, discussed below.

Aelius Aristides agreed with Plutarch in saying that Themistocles had an interpreter executed for using his voice in Persian service against the Greeks (*On the Four* II 247; cf. *In Lept.* II 676). But in the *Panathenaicus* (I 198f.), Aristides did not mention Themistocles, and the episode was identified as the mission sent by Darius before Marathon. To this latter passage, the scholiast added some details (III 125): the interpreter was named Mys (or Mysos); he was a Samian who knew Persian and Darius therefore sent him unwilling to Athens with the other heralds. Although the name Mys was probably absorbed from the story about the Carian sent by Mardonius to consult the oracles (Hdt. 8.133sq, How and Wells ad loc.; Paus. IX 23.6), the other details testify to the existence of a variant account of the episode reported by Herodotus as taking place in 491. The original author of the account must remain unknown.

It is obvious the tradition had become hopelessly confounded by Plutarch's day. Elsewhere in his treatment of the Persian Wars he demonstrates that he does not have Herodotus open before him—or even his own essay on Herodotus. Therefore he did not hesitate to insert the "matter of the bilingual man" even though Herodotus had said specifically that heralds were not sent to Athens in 481.

6.4 καὶ τὸ περὶ ῎Αρθμιον τὸν Ζελείτην
There are two problems involving Arthmius of Zelea: what were the true circumstances of his mission to Greece?; how did the tradition develop? It is necessary to investigate this latter question first.

Chronologically, the first "source" for the episode was the bronze stele itself, set up on the Acropolis, bearing a decree worded something like the following:

Κίμων εἶπε· Ἄρθμιον τὸν Πυθώνακτος τὸν Ζελείτην ἄτιμον εἶναι
καὶ πολέμιον τοῦ δήμου τοῦ Ἀθηναίων καὶ τῶν συμμάχων αὐτὸν
καὶ γένος . . . ὅτι τὸν ἐκ Μήδων χρυσὸν ἀπήγαγεν εἰς Πελοπόν-
νησον.[5]

The remaining testimonia may be listed chronologically:

343 B.C.	Demosthenes 19.271sq.
341	Demosthenes 9.41-45.
330	Aeschines, 3.258.
323	Deinarchus, 2.24-25.
c. 300	Craterus, *FGrH* 342 F 14, schol. M Aristides (ad II 287).
2nd century A.D.	Aristides I 310, II 287, 392, 676.
?	scholiast to Aristides III 327 (ad I 310).
6th century A.D.	Nonnus, schol. Greg.Naz. *Adv.Jul.* init.

The orators were fond of reminding their audiences how
an older generation of Athenians had punished bribery:
Arthmius of Zelea (on Propontis) had brought gold from
the Mede to the Greeks (or more specifically, in some
versions, to the Peloponnesus). No indication of date was
given, but Aeschines, adding the information that Arthmius
was an Athenian proxenos and actually living in Athens,
said he was exiled "from everywhere the Athenians rule."
This of course implies a time when Athenian writ ran outside the borders of Attica, i.e., after about 476. That this
implied date was correct was proven by Craterus, who took
the trouble to look at the stele and saw that the decree had
been moved by Cimon (in a scholium to Aristides first
published by Wilamowitz in 1889).

In the centuries between Craterus and Plutarch, the episode found its way into the lexica to the orators and probably the rhetorical handbooks as well. But, first, popular
history had had its way with the story, pulled the context

[5] E.g., a composite from the testimonia; see also Meiggs, *Athenian
Empire* 509.

back to the time of the Persian Wars, and inserted the name of Themistocles. This is the version uppermost in the minds of Plutarch and Aristides; by their day many of the details would have dropped out of the lexica. When the scholiast Nonnus wrote his commentary to Gregory Nazianzenus' Στηλιτευτικὸς λόγος against Julian, he no doubt looked up the word στηλιτευτικός in such a lexicon and copied out what he found there (the bit about Arthmius seems to be Demosth. 9.41-45 with little change).[6] In the *Suda* s.v. στηλιτευτικός one will find Nonnus' first few sentences word for word, proving transmission through the rhetorical lexica, but the story of Arthmius had by that time dropped out.

The true circumstances of Arthmius' journey continue to exercise scholars.[7] The mission has been associated with Pausanias' machinations at Byzantium in the 470's,[8] or with the mission of Megabazus in about 457 when the Athenians were occupied in Egypt.[9]

6.5 μέγιστον δὲ πάντων τὸ καταλῦσαι τοὺς Ἑλληνικοὺς πολέμους Ending wars and discord among Greeks is ascribed here specifically to Themistocles (see also Aristides II 248, 290; Libanius, *Declam.* 10.27), but this is probably only Plutarch's usual device of bringing his subject to center stage. Herodotus (7.145) said only that the Greek *probouloi* decided to end the wars at their first meeting in the fall of 481.

---

[6] Nonnus may be found in Migne, *Patrologia Graeca-Latina* 36, 985; repr. in A. Bauer, *Themistokles*, 2nd ed. by F. J. Frost (Chicago, 1967) 121; see also S. Brock, *The Syriac Version of the Pseudo-Nonnos Mythological Scholia* (Cambridge, 1971) 82.

[7] There is no reason to doubt the authenticity of the episode; I follow the arguments of Meiggs, *Athenian Empire* 510f., opposing C. Habicht, "Falsche Urkunden zur Geschichte Athens im Zeitalter der Perserkriege," *Hermes* 89 (1961) 27.

[8] M. Cary, *CQ* 29 (1935) 177-180.

[9] Thuc. I 109.2. Full discussion by G. Colin, "La déformation d'un document historique dans une argumentation d'orateur," *Rev.Phil.* 7 (1933) 237-260; Meiggs, *Athenian Empire* 508-512; M. B. Wallace, "Early Greek Proxenoi," *Phoenix* 24 (1970) 199-201.

There is a statement in the *Suda*, s.v. ἀνεῖλεν claiming that Themistocles counseled the Athenians to put aside their hatred of the Aeginetans. It must have taken some statesmanship to persuade the Aeginetans to do the same and to accept Athenian leadership. The islanders commanded perhaps the second largest fleet in the Aegean (cf. Diod. VII 11) and they were bitter toward the Athenians even during the war, with good reason (Hdt. 8.92). But their performance in battle was outstanding (Hdt. 7.181; 8.93, 122 pace Isocr. *Paneg.* 72), indicating that perhaps violent anti-Persian sentiment outweighed other considerations.

The last sentence in this chapter is curious: "And they say that in this matter [ending wars among Greeks] Cheileos the Arcadian was especially helpful." It does not seem possible that Plutarch can be referring to the advice of Chileus the Tegean to the Spartans in 479 (Hdt. 9.9, a passage familiar to Plutarch, *De Hdt.mal.* 871EF). The biographer must be citing a tradition with which we are unfamiliar.

Chapter 6 contained an assortment of anecdotes about Themistocles' praiseworthy accomplishments on the eve of the war. Chapters 7-10 commence a more strictly chronological narrative of the opening phases of the war and must be analyzed against the background of the Herodotean chronology of the period summer 481 to summer 480, which Plutarch is consciously following but which he has condensed into a few dramatic moments.

7.1 Παραλαβὼν δὲ τὴν ἀρχήν, εὐθὺς μὲν ἐπεχείρει τοὺς πολίτας ἐμβιβάζειν εἰς τὰς τριήρεις

Plutarch skips quickly by the many months of debate and consultation over the agonizing decisions that had to be made both by Athenians and other Greek states. Curiously enough, he also neglects discussion of the Delphic responses (until 10.3, q.v.), which ought to occur here. For the actual dating of events during the year preceding Salamis, we must rely on Herodotus. According to the historian, when the embassy sent to Delphi (probably in early summer 481) returned to Athens with the "wooden wall" response, Themistocles persuaded the assembly to interpret the wooden wall as meaning the Athenian fleet (7.142-143). Thereupon, the Athenians decided to build more triremes, "to meet the barbarian with their ships, all in unison, placing their trust in the God, together with those Greeks who so wished" (7.144).

In these passages, Herodotus clearly shows that the Athenians had accepted Themistocles' strategy a year before the war. But such an early dating of the Delphic response has bothered scholars, particularly because of the words "O Divine Salamis, you will destroy children of women." I quote Hignett, *Xerxes' Invasion* 442: "If, however, the battle of Salamis really was predicted in B [i.e., the second response], the prediction could only have been made after the Greek fleet had abandoned its advanced position at Artemision, for only then could the decisive battle at sea have been expected to take place so far south as Salamis." And compare Labarbe, *Loi navale* 111: "la Pythie ne peut avoir invoqué Salamine à une époque où l'on ne savait encore absolument rien du developpement des operations militaires." The assumption implicit in these statements is that the priests at Delphi had not the slightest belief in Apollo's power of prophecy, that they ignored the Pythia completely and made up oracles out of whole cloth, based on purely rational political and strategic considerations. I find this cynical notion inconceivable. The account of Herodotus is neither naïve nor chronologically vague. When the Persian threat became real it is only natural to suppose that the Athenians would have consulted Delphi *immediately*—not after Tempe or, even more impossible, after Artemision. I have no idea why the priestess mentioned Salamis—but this is the exact point. If oracular responses could easily be explained, who would go to oracles?

Even so, let us admit, for the sake of argument, that the Delphic priests *were* eminent political and strategic experts.

In that case, they knew two things for certain: the Persian armada was attacking Greece in general and Athens in particular; because of her naval power, Athenian resistance would no doubt take place in Athenian waters. The last attempt to stave off a Persian attack by sea had been during the defense of Miletus in 494. And where had the Ionians centered their naval resistance? On the island of Lade, right off Miletus. Are not the situations very similar? ask our well-informed priests; therefore, let us put in something about the island of Salamis.

There is no reason, therefore, to move the Delphic responses from the time implied by Herodotus. It may also have been during this period that the Athenians began negotiating with Troizen and other states to accept their refugees in case evacuation became necessary. There is no actual testimony for these negotiations but they must be assumed in light of later events (see comment below to 10.5).

7.2 ἐνισταμένων δὲ πολλῶν, ἐξήγαγε πολλὴν στρατιὰν εἰς τὰ Τέμπη A mistaken notion. The Athenian resolution cited above was no doubt primarily responsible for convincing the other Greek states to gather at the Isthmus in late summer 481, just as Xerxes was preparing to go into winter quarters at Sardis (Hdt. 7.37, 145). Plutarch brings all events into one compass; actually, the expedition to Tempe did not take place until April-May 480. Obviously Themistocles did not urge the Athenians to embark on the triremes as early as this.[10]

ἐπεὶ δ' ἀνεχώρησαν ἐκεῖθεν ἄπρακτοι . . . μᾶλλον ἤδη τῷ Θεμιστοκλεῖ προσεῖχον οἱ Ἀθηναῖοι περὶ τῆς θαλάσσης The Athenians had already committed themselves to a general strategy of naval defense; now the time had come to make specific plans for mobilization on one hand and evacuation on the other. The date is probably the latter part of May 480, still during the archon year of Hypsichides.

[10] See How and Wells ad Hdt. 7.172-174; Hignett, *Xerxes' Invasion* 102f.; N. Robertson, "The Thessalian Expedition of 480 B.C.," *JHS* 96 (1976) 100-120.

Tradition held that Themistocles moved and the Athenians passed a decree, or several decrees, incorporating the following provisions:

1. That the city be evacuated and entrusted to the care of Athena.

2. That women, children and possessions be transported to Troizen for safekeeping.

3. That all others of military age were to embark on the triremes and go out to fight on behalf of freedom.

4. That the exiles be recalled to aid the city.

The first three points were quoted most fully by Aristides (*On the Four* II 256), with less detail by Plutarch (below, comment to 10.4). The evacuation was first mentioned (after Herodotus) by Thucydides (I 18.2) and Lysias (2.33). The earliest statement that this was the result of a motion brought by Themistocles is Demosthenes (19.303) in a speech delivered in 343 claiming that Aeschines had had the decree read aloud (cf. 18.204). Point four is alluded to by Andocides (1.107 and cf. 77) and *AP* 22.8, where the return of the exiles is dated to the archonship of Hypsichides.[11]

I join a number of modern scholars in believing that the decree discovered at Troizen in 1959 by Michael Jameson is a mid-third-century B.C. copy, with revisions, of the actual decree moved by Themistocles in the waning months of Hypsichides' archonship. No one doubts there was a fourth-century version of the decree; current debate revolves over whether the text read by Aeschines was a creation of patriotic fourth-century politicians or whether it was a text preserved from the era of the Persian Wars, with only the language modified to conform to later custom. So much has been written on the subject that one hesitates to add to the literature. I doubt that anything I could say would change minds and will limit myself to a few points concerning the spring and summer of 480.[12]

[11] On which, see Stanley Burstein, "The Recall of the Ostracized and the Themistocles Decree," *CSCA* 4 (1971) 93-110.

[12] The inscription was published by Jameson in *Hesperia* 29 (1960)

The middle part of the decree envisions an orderly evacuation and mobilization, ending on lines 40-44 with:

ἐπειδὰν δὲ πεπληρωμέναι ὦσιν αἱ νῆες τα[ἲ]ς μὲν
ἑκατὸν αὐτῶν βοηθεῖν ἐπὶ τὸ Ἀρτεμίσ[ι]ον τὸ Εὐβοϊκὸν ταῖς δὲ
ἑκατὸν αὐτῶν περὶ τὴν Σαλαμῖνα καὶ τὴν ἄλλην Ἀττικὴν ναυλοχεῖν
καὶ φυλάττειν τὴν χώραν.

But Herodotus says that *after* the Athenians returned from Artemision, they made a proclamation for all to preserve their families and possessions as best they could (8.41).

Some critics feel the decree directly contradicts the testimony of Herodotus.[13] This is not necessarily true. When the force returned from Tempe, some sort of arrangement had to be made immediately, an arrangement which the assembly had already agreed to in principle (Hdt. 7.144, cited above). It is entirely in human character that an evacuation be ordered and yet not carried out until the last moment, when the attendant confusion would make observers and participants forget that a plan had been made months before. The decree only states what ought to be done; it is not evidence that its instructions were in fact carried out. Herodotus, on the other hand, was a historian and not concerned with flawed preparations. He simply reported what actually happened.[14]

The decree called for 100 triremes to be sent to Artemision. Herodotus said that 127 were sent, and a second force of 53 arrived later (8.1, 14). Again, there is no real contradiction. All this means is that a change of battle plan took place between the implied date of the decree (May-June) and the actual date of the battles at Artemision in late August. Between the two dates much discussion must have

---

199ff.; rev. ed. *Hesperia* 31 (1962) 311f.; representative bibliography in Meiggs and Lewis, *GHI* no. 23.

[13] W. K. Pritchett, *AJA* 66 (1962) 43-47.

[14] Jameson, *Historia* 12 (1963) 402f.

gone on, not only in Athens but between Athenian and allied commanders over the disposition of fleets and other forces.[15]

The period May-August 480 might be reconstructed as follows:

Themistocles returned from Tempe, followed by reports that all of northern Greece was medizing.

The Troizenians offered to accept Athenian refugees if evacuation became necessary (see comment to 10.5).

In late May or early June the assembly met and passed Themistocles' motion to put into effect his previous interpretation of the Delphic response, i.e., to evacuate the land of Attica and embark upon the fleet with a base at Salamis.

This plan was then taken to the other Greeks meeting at the Isthmus, where it was made part of the general strategy of a land and sea blockade north of Boeotia (Hdt. 7.175). The Athenians were persuaded to adjust their plans in two particulars: they gave the leadership to the Spartans (Hdt. 8.2-3, on which see below, comment to 7.3); they committed 147 of their ships rather than 100, sending an additional 27 in the Athenian contingent and loaning 20 to Chalcis (Hdt. 8.1, 46).

Between this decision and actual embarkation, there was evidently a survey made of possible sites—πάντα σκεψάμενοι, as Herodotus said (7.177)—and a preparation of both land and sea forces, which may have taken up part of June and July.

Finally, at the beginning of August or thereabouts, the Greeks heard that Xerxes had left Therme, whereupon they too moved north to meet him.

Other than these brief remarks on chronology, I can find little to add to the sensible and concise review of the Themistocles Decree controversy by Podlecki.[16]

7.3 τῶν μὲν Ἑλλήνων Εὐρυβιάδην καὶ Λακεδαιμονίους ἡγεῖσθαι κελευόντων

---

[15] Ibid. 399.

[16] *Themistocles* 147-167; Meiggs and Lewis, *GHI* discussion to no. 23 is also valuable.

Themistocles' statesmanlike refusal to press for Athenian leadership on the eve of battle is dramatic but incorrect. Herodotus had shown that the question of command had been settled a year before (8.2-3, and see the statement of the Athenian envoy to Gelon in 7.161: Athens would lead the fleet, but if the Spartans wished this command as well, the Athenians would not oppose them). Plutarch's version, whether based on earlier literature or his own sense of timing, was obviously more memorable: it was repeated more elaborately by Aristides.[17] Diodorus reported that Eurybiades was *nauarchos* but that Themistocles διῴκει δὲ τὰ περὶ τὸν στόλον, which is perhaps intended to mean that Eurybiades was titular commander but that Themistocles was actually running things, an interpretation of Herodotus' narrative with which no one will argue.

7.4 ὡς ἀνδρείᾳ μὲν τῶν πολεμίων, εὐγνωμοσύνῃ δὲ τῶν συμμάχων περιγενομένους

A rhetorical flourish, perhaps suggested by Isocrates, *Paneg.* 71: ἀμφοτέρων κρατήσαντες ὡς ἑκατέρων προσῆκεν, or Lycurgus, *In Leocr.* 70: μόνοι δ' ἀμφοτέρων περιγεγόνασι, καὶ τῶν πολεμίων καὶ τῶν συμμάχων, ὡς ἑκατέρων προσῆκε, κτλ.[18]

7.5 ἐκπλαγεὶς ὁ Εὐρυβιάδης

He was terrified because of the number of Persian ships and the detachment of two hundred sent to encircle Euboea and take the Greeks in the rear. But according to Herodotus (8.4-5), *all* the Greeks were disheartened at first; nor did they find out about the encircling squadron until *after* the bribing episode (8.7). It may be that Plutarch here incorporated all the fears of the Greeks into the person of Eurybiades, in the same way that he made Themistocles the symbol of Athenian *eugnomosyne*.[19] It is also very possible that Plutarch intentionally disturbed the sequence of events: if Eurybiades knew of the encircling squadron, he had a better excuse than pure funk for wanting to withdraw. This same

---

[17] II 252 and cf. I 217, with the note of J. H. Oliver, *The Civilizing Power* (Philadelphia, 1968) 121.

[18] Cf. Aristides I 217; Himerius, *Orat.* 14.29.

[19] Perrin, *Plutarch's Themistocles* 195.

kind of tacit editing of Herodotus can be seen in *Arist.* 5.5 and 17.6, where Plutarch gratuitously corrected what he felt were unkind judgments. In one case, the Alcmeonids had been maligned; in the other, the allies occupying the center of the line of Plataea.[20] On the other hand, there do exist examples of Plutarch reversing sequence simply because of faulty memory (e.g., *Arist.* 12 and 14).

7.6 ὡς Ἡρόδοτος ἱστόρηκε (Hdt. 8.4-5). Plutarch was furious with this story in his essay on the historian (*De Hdt.mal.* 867BC), accusing him of representing the victory as a "work of bribery and fraud." But here in the *Life* he actually added details, like the name of the Euboean emissary Pelagon, not mentioned by Herodotus. The claim that Eurybiades contemplated a withdrawal has frequently been denied for the very reason indicated by Plutarch in *De Hdt.mal.* 867D: "There was no point for them to sit there guarding the sea once the war had got beyond Pylae and Xerxes was master of the passes." In other words, the whole point of the naval expedition had been to guard Leonidas' seaward flank. Although one is usually skeptical of modern armchair strategists' attempts to predicate what ancient strategies must have been,[21] it seems abundantly clear in this instance that Leonidas could not hold Thermopylae if the Persian fleet were to penetrate the straits of northern Euboea—and Eurybiades knew it.[22]

7.6-7 ταῦτα μὲν οὖν Φανίας ὁ Λέσβιος εἴρηκεν Phanias of Eresos *floruit* 336 (*Suda* s.v. Phanias). He was countryman, contemporary, and fellow-peripatetic of Theophrastus (Strabo XIII 2.4). The wide range of his writings may be seen in the fragments collected by Wehrli.[23] Five citations of Phanias in this *Life* have led some to suspect the

[20] His motivation for making the one change is seen in *De Hdt.mal.* 862DE; for the other, *De Hdt.mal.* 872BC.

[21] I am guided by the sensible warnings of N. Whatley, "On the Possibility of Reconstructing Marathon and Other Ancient Battles," *JHS* 84 (1964) 124f.

[22] How and Wells ad 8.4; Hignett, *Xerxes' Invasion* 154f.

[23] *Schule des Aristoteles* 9 (Basel, 1957).

existence of a *Life* of Themistocles by the peripatetic that was heavily exploited by Plutarch.[24] I hope to have demonstrated that this sort of reliance on a single source is contrary to Plutarch's method; the anecdote is likely to have occurred to the biographer first, and then the name of the author.[25]

"Of all the citizens, Architeles opposed him most, a man who was trierarch on the sacred ship." It is usually assumed from this language that Architeles was an Athenian, and the "sacred ship," the *Paralos*. But Gottlieb has noted another anecdote from Phanias about a Corinthian named Architeles who lived at this same time (Athen. 232B, where the story is also attributed to Theopompus, *FGrH* 115 F 193). Moreover, this episode in Plutarch's narrative replaces Herodotus' description of the bribe given to the Corinthian Adeimantus.[26] There is confusion here, but it must be pointed out that it is possibly *our* confusion rather than that of the biographer. Some alternative solutions may be proposed: Plutarch has imperfectly remembered, or combined, one or two anecdotes of Phanias; Phanias did in fact write about two different men named Architeles, one a Corinthian and one an Athenian—and Plutarch is quoting correctly. But our data here permit us to do no more than speculate about Plutarch's citation.

One thing is almost certain: the story, with all its details, is false. The insistence of the crew on being paid, and even the very existence of a "sacred ship" may be anachronistic. We know that in later times, at least, the crew of the *Paralos* was paid four obols a day by the state.[27] It is sometimes claimed that such stories came from the anti-Themis-

[24] L. Bodin, "Histoire et biographie: Phanias d'Erèse," *REG* 28 (1915) 251ff.; R. Laqueur, "Phainias," *RE* 19 (1938) 1567-1586.

[25] Cf. Wehrli, *Schule des Arist.* 9, 34-35.

[26] Gottlieb, *Ausserherodoteische Überlieferung* 105f.

[27] Harpocration s.v. Paralos; cf. Jacoby, *FGrH* IIIb Suppl. ad Philochorus 328 F 47-48. B. Jordan, *The Athenian Navy in the Classical Period* (Berkeley and Los Angeles, 1975) 157ff., discusses the institution but not the founding date of the sacred ships.

toclean tradition current at Athens during Herodotus' day
(How and Wells ad Hdt. 8.4). But some of them may equally well have been put about by Themistocles himself after
the war when he was trying to convince the Athenians that
Sparta was the real enemy. The details about his own en-
richment would have been added later.

8.1 Αἱ δὲ γενόμεναι τότε . . . μάχαι
I believe we can see here an echo of the feeling which
Plutarch expressed so strongly in his essay on Herodotus. I
would translate as follows: "Phanias has in fact told these
stories. Nevertheless [that is to say, despite all these stories
of bribery, deceit, and flagging zeal], the battles that took
place at this time against the barbarian ships in the straits
. . . were of the greatest benefit to the Greeks in the way of
experience." Plutarch must have been torn here. He wanted
to tell the stories as evidence of Themistocles' constancy
and cleverness, and yet he really didn't believe in the
cowardice of the other Greeks—in which he is joined by
most modern scholars, pace Herodotus and Phanias.[28] The
rest of this paragraph is martial music and is no doubt from
Plutarch's own pen.[29]

8.2 ὃ δὴ καὶ Πίνδαρος (fr. 93 Turyn)
Quoted in four other places by the biographer[30] and by
Aristides (II 251). The scholiast to the latter passage (III
600 was reminded of one of Pindar's most famous couplets

ὦ ταὶ λιπαραὶ καὶ ἰοστέφανοι καὶ ἀοίδιμοι
Ἑλλάδος ἔρεισμα, κλειναὶ Ἀθᾶναι, δαιμόνιον πτολίεθρον

and many modern critics believe the four lines belong to the

[28] On Plutarch's faith in panhellenic solidarity, see A. Hauvette,
Hérodote, historien des guerres médiques (Paris, 1894) 101.
[29] Bauer, *Plutarchs Themistokles* ad loc., was reminded of Isocr.
Paneg. 91; Diod. X 34.12; Aesch. *Sept.* 397ff.
[30] *Apophth.Lac.* 232E; *Glor.Ath.* 350A; *Sera num.vind.* 552B; *De
Hdt.mal.* 867C.

same dithyramb.[31] In *De Hdt.mal.* 867C, Plutarch argued that Pindar praised Athens "although he was not from an allied city but from one accused of medism." This is one of his weaker arguments in that essay. Plutarch will have known as well as everyone else the tradition that Pindar was fined by Thebes for praising Athens and that the Athenians paid the fine and otherwise honored the poet.[32]

8.3-4 ἔστι δὲ τῆς Εὐβοίας τὸ Ἀρτεμίσιον . . . . ἔχει δὲ ναὸν Both Plutarch (who knew the area at firsthand) and Herodotus (7.176) called Artemision a beach, with a temple of Artemis nearby. The beach is to be identified with the sandy coastline in the vicinity of the modern resort area of Pevki. Such a strand provided an ideal anchorage for the Greek fleet, even in the face of prevailing north winds. Shallow water extends out to sea for as much as five hundred meters (U.S. Navy Oceanographic Office, chart 54348). Some modern scholars have argued that the Greek fleet was farther west, within the Oreos channel, otherwise the Persian fleet could have outflanked the Greeks to the left and forced an entrance to the channel. This suggestion is adequately blocked by Hignett (*Xerxes' Invasion* 151-154, with references to older literature), who correctly points out that the Persians could not so proceed with the threat of the Greek fleet on their flank. The location had one other advantage: the Greeks, by occupying Pevki Bay, were denying that same anchorage to the Persians, who were forced to cling to the hazardous lee of the cliffs of the Magnesian coast opposite, around τρηχεῖα Ὀλιζών (*Il.* 2.717). The mountains descend steeply into the sea and anchoring is possible only at a number of small coves where the Persian ships must have had to cluster in ranks as Herodotus describes their previous unhappy anchorage off Pelion (Hdt. 7.188). They were no doubt exhausted and half-sick with fear of another storm the whole three days they were

[31] B. Snell's Teubner ed. frs. 76, 77; C. M. Bowra, *Pindar* 142f.
[32] [Aeschines] Ep. 4.3; Eustathius, *Comm.Pind.* p. 93 Westermann, cf. pp. 97, 99 in the other vitae; Isocrates *Antid.* 166.

forced to lie there. Moreover, there is little fresh water along this coast, and thirst must have become a factor during their enforced stay (see below, comment to 9.2).[33]

The site of the temple of Artemis Proseoa was located in 1883 by H. G. Lolling. There is at present a small chapel of Agios Georgios and an even smaller cemetery on a low pine-clad hill just east of Pevki Bay. Just adjacent to the ruins of the shrine, Lolling discovered an inscription dated between 146-75 B.C., honoring a list of donors for gifts toward τὴν ἐπανόρθωσιν τοῦ ἱεροῦ τῆς Ἀρτέμιδος τῆς Προσηῴας.[34] Visiting the chapel and cemetery in the heat and silence of a summer afternoon, I have been struck by a curious feeling that I can only describe as numinous.

8.5 ἐν μιᾷ δὲ τῶν στηλῶν ἐλεγεῖον (also *De Hdt.mal.* 867F) Attributed to Simonides (fr. 109 Diehl) by some editors.[35]

8.6 δείκνυται δὲ τῆς ἀκτῆς τόπος

From the hilltop where the temple stood, Plutarch could see a place on the sandy beach below where, he was told, one could dig up ashes of the Greek wrecks that had been burned on the spot together with the bodies of the dead. We may imagine here a day trip taken from Aedepsus, about twenty miles away, a resort town frequented by Plutarch (*Qc* 4.4, 667Csq). Podlecki has doubts about the location of the shrine, thinking that it lies too far from the water's edge ("perhaps the ancient coastline has receded here . . . .").[36] I cannot share his uncertainty; the present site of chapel and cemetery overlooks the shore from a prominent position and seems perfectly suited to ancient descriptions. The coastline has certainly not receded. In fact,

[33] Fullest discussion in Pritchett, *SAGT* II 13-18, who rightly identified Platania, with its spring, as the most likely headquarters for the Persian fleet. The numbers must have been too large for all to anchor there however.

[34] Now *IG* XII (9) 1189; "Das Artemision auf Nordeuboia," *Ath.Mitt.* 8 (1883) 7-23, map facing p. 12.

[35] Fr. 109 Diehl; cf. Wade-Gery, *JHS* 53 (1933) 73; A. Podlecki, "Simonides: 480," *Historia* 17 (1968) 266.

[36] Podlecki, *Themistocles* 176f.

the sea level has risen about two meters: a small headland about eight kilometers to the southwest, now an island, was indisputably connected to the mainland in antiquity.

9.1 Τῶν μέντοι τὰ περὶ Θερμοπύλας εἰς τὸ Ἀρτεμίσιον ἀπαγγελ-
λόντων

Blass inserted τὰ after Diodorus XI 13.3; neither this nor the variant ἀπαγγελθέντων affect the sense of the phrase. Both Diodorus and Plutarch were probably closer to the true picture than Herodotus (8.18; cf. Plutarch's remarks in De Hdt.mal. 867DE), who once more pictured the Greeks considering retreat *before* they learned the outcome of the stand at Thermopylae. The messenger from the pass was Habronichus, son of Lysicles, who may have been one of those Athenians with a special relationship with Sparta (Thuc. I 91.3).

In their withdrawal, the Corinthians led the van and the Athenians brought up the rear. In *De Hdt.mal.* 868A, Plutarch felt that the historian was thus accusing the Corinthians of cowardice but here in the *Life* he takes a more positive approach: the Athenians were the rearguard because of their valor (cf. Aristides II 255).

9.2 ἐνεχάραττε κατὰ τῶν λίθων ἐπιφανῆ γράμματα

Very nearly the same account as Herodotus (8.22) with the exception that Plutarch had Themistocles place these inscriptions all along the route; the historian said they were situated around the places where drinking water was available at Artemision. When one considers that a hundred thousand or so Persian naval personnel had been cooped up in their ships off the waterless cliffs of Magnesia for three to five days, in the heat of August, it may well be imagined that they flocked to the wells and springs along the strand at Artemision (the area is still well-watered by springs that run all year round).

This was a famous stratagem of Themistocles.[37] It did

---

[37] Justin II 13.3; Polyaenus I 30.7; Aristides I 228, II 255.

not affect the performance of the Ionians (perhaps for the reasons put forward by Xerxes in Hdt. 7.52, written with hindsight by the historian), as we are told by Herodotus (8.85), but some suspicion was generated, at least in the minds of the Phoenicians (8.90).

9.3 Ξέρξου δὲ διὰ τῆς Δωρίδος ἄνωθεν ἐμβαλόντος εἰς τὴν Φωκίδα Herodotus gives the details, including the story of the attack on Delphi (8.31-39). In *De Hdt.mal.* 868B-F, Plutarch was quite aroused by the historian's comment that the Phocians would have done the opposite of the Thessalians in any event (8.30). He would seem to be as much a partisan of Phocis as he was of the other lands watered by the Kephissos.[38] Both Plutarch and Herodotus (8.40) suppose that an infantry stand had been considered by the allies in Boeotia and then abandoned. What actually seems to have happened, as Herodotus himself makes clear (7.203) is that the Locrians and Phocians were decoyed into sending troops to Thermopylae by false reports that the rest of the troops were on the way. This rumor evidently spread to *all* the contingents, and to the surrounding countryside, and halted for the moment the process of Theban medism.

The justification for Theban surrender continued to be discussed throughout antiquity. Herodotus' picture is well known. According to the historian, the Thebans gave earth and water during the winter of 481/0 (7.132), and long before the actual arrival of the Persians they had arranged through the good offices of Alexander of Macedon to have the Boeotian towns protected (8.34). The Thebans under Leontiades at Thermopylae were there under compulsion (7.205-222) and surrendered as soon as they were able (7.233). The Theban nobility fought with distinction at Plataea (9.67) and Timagenidas reminded his fellow citizens that "we all medized together, not just a few of us" (9.87).

But the wrath of the allies was satisfied by the surrender of the chief men of Thebes after Plataea (9.87-88), and after

[38] He had written a life of the Phocian hero Daiphantus, cited in *Mul.virt.* 244B.

the war Thebes was readmitted to the Amphictyony (*Them.* 20.3, q.v. below) probably on the pretext that Thebes had been forced to medize by a "clique of a few powerful men." That this became the official history is confirmed by the Theban spokesman in Thucydides III 62.3-4 (cf. Paus. IX 6.1-2).

By Diodorus we are told that the Thebans at Thermopylae were from the opposite party (XI 4.7). This is accepted by some modern scholars[39] but may be only one of Ephorus' attempts to explain away what he found uncongenial in Herodotus by the exercise of pure reason. Nevertheless, the decision of Thebes to medize because of necessity continued to attract criticism throughout antiquity (Polybius IV 31.5; Favorinus *De exilio* 21.42-47).

Plutarch disregarded the excuse of internal politics and concentrated on the excuse of necessity. Basing his account partly on Aristophanes of Boeotia (*FGrH* 379 FF 5-6) but also, no doubt, on many other accounts (one would assume he commanded all the literature and traditions about his native land) he claimed that the Thebans were as patriotic as any other state at first, sending Mnamias with five hundred troops to Tempe (*De Hdt.mal.* 864E) and fighting bravely at Thermopylae (866F-867A). Only after Xerxes had won at Thermopylae did the Theban leader Attaginus (cf. Hdt. 9.16, 86) arrange with his friend the exiled Spartan Demaratus to medize and thus save Boeotia from destruction (867F).

All this reconstruction of events has to recommend it is patriotic fervor, as it is patently false. We are to believe that with the Persian host storming down the valley of the Kephissos, Attaginus was able to locate Demaratus in the entourage of Xerxes and arrange for a peaceful surrender— all this in one and a half days, as Plutarch himself admits. Then we must believe that Xerxes would accept the sur-

---

[39] L. Pearson's note to *De Hdt.mal.* 865F in his Loeb ed.; Dascalakis, *Problèmes historiques autour de la bataille des Thermopyles* 62, with note.

render of a country that had waited until the last desperate moment before inclining to the victor.

It is difficult to resolve the problem. No doubt the Thebans have been treated unfairly by Herodotus, but they obviously do not deserve Plutarch's spirited defense. There will have been partisan differences among the Thebans but one must not rush to accept the explanation of Diodorus simply because it is reasonable.

9.4-5 ὀργὴ τῆς προδοσίας εἶχε τοὺς ᾿Αθηναίους
Vainly hoping for a unified infantry stand somewhere in central Greece, the Athenians then heard that all allied land forces had withdrawn behind the fortifications being prepared at the Isthmus. But modern critics agree that a stand in Boeotia could never have seriously been considered. If a retreat became necessary in the face of the world's best cavalry it would have turned into a rout and massacre. Once more we are only guessing at ancient strategy, but given the usual Greek dread of being caught in the open by cavalry, the assumption seems logical. Nevertheless, the false promise of infantry support once made to the Locrians and Phocians (Hdt. 7.203, and see comment to 9.3) had done its work too well; the Athenian rank and file had believed it as well and now felt themselves betrayed. That the tradition lingered on is seen first in the language of the Athenian speaker in Thucydides (I 74.2): the Athenians were deserted by the other allies; nevertheless they resolved μὴ ὀργισθῆναι ὅτι ἡμῖν οὐ προυτιμωρήσατε. The spokesman is obviously implying that the Athenians *were* angry but mastered their emotions on behalf of the greater cause.[40]

Herodotus (8.71) described the feverish activity of the myriads who worked night and day piling up the Isthmus wall out of stones, bricks, wood, and "sandbags" (on which see Aeneas Tacticus 32.2). The present remains of fortifications do not meet this description, being well constructed

---

[40] See also Lysias 2.45; Isocr. *Paneg.* 93.

of ashlar masonry, and are from some subsequent attempt to prevent land invasion of the Peloponnesus.[41]

In this passage (and in Chapter 10 as well) Plutarch's sense of timing once more is dramatic rather than historical. We have seen before how he can collapse whole months into a few breathless moments; here he does the reverse. Five days or so after Thermopylae was lost, the van of Xerxes' army was at the borders of Attica, but in Plutarch's account one has the feeling of a far longer period of time. There is time for the Athenians to remonstrate with the allies; the allies pay no attention but begin to withdraw to the Peloponnesos and build the wall (there was confusion in Diodorus XI 15.3, 16.3 over whether the wall had been built yet); then Themistocles has time to persuade the Athenians all over again to evacuate the city and put their trust in the fleet (see below, comment to 10.1).

In the last sentence of this chapter the despair of the Athenians was nicely phrased. The theme that the essence of a city lay not in inanimate possessions but in men who could defend them was at least as old as Alcaeus (in Aristides II 273), but for the moment the Athenians were still preoccupied with shrines and ancestral graves.[42] Later on (11.5) we are to see Themistocles announcing Athenian contempt for such things when freedom is at stake.

10.1 ὥσπερ ἐν τραγῳδίᾳ μηχανὴν ἄρας

Because Plutarch used the same phrase to accuse Phylarchus of theatrics in 32.4, Jacoby suggested that this story too is from a "Themistoclesexkurs" by the Hellenistic historian, who was famous for vivid writing.[43] But Plutarch's criticism

[41] How and Wells ad 8.71; J. G. Frazer, *Pausanias's Description of Greece* III 5-6.

[42] ἠρία Y: ἡρῷα S and most modern editors; the same variants occur in *Cam.* 31.3.

[43] *FGrH* 81 F 76; cf. FF 22, 72, with commentary; so also T. W.

of contrivance in historical or rhetorical writing commonly makes use of this term: τραγικῶς μηχανὴν ἄραντες, ὦ φίλοι, against the use of Peripatetic *topoi* (*Qc* 8.4, 724D); ὥσπερ ἐν τραγῳδίᾳ μηχανὴν αἴρων, against Lysander's use of oracles (*Lys.* 25.1); see also the indictment of Herodotus' use of stage machinery in *De Hdt.mal.* 870C. The use of common Greek phrases to track down sources should be resisted.[44] This whole story is obviously just a reworking of Herodotus 8.41, with Themistocles emphasized. It is difficult to see why the Athenians should need to be tricked into evacuating, with Xerxes only a day or so away. As Herodotus said, the disappearance of the snake was just the last straw to the Athenians.

10.1-2 σημεῖον μὲν λαμβάνων τὸ τοῦ δράκοντος
Some authorities, including Phylarchus (*FGrH* 81 F 72, Phot. *Lex.* s.v. οἴκουρον ὄφιν), said there were two snakes. Plutarch follows Herodotus 8.41, except that he makes Themistocles responsible for the interpretation of the omen. The site was probably the Erechtheion.[45]

10.3 τῷ δὲ χρησμῷ πάλιν ἐδημαγώγει
As noted above (comment to 7.1), this is the first time Plutarch mentioned the famous oracle and Themistocles' interpretation. It was a startling omission from his narrative of war preparations in chapters 6-7. Nor does he mention the argument over the wooden wall in any of his extant works, although it was a quite popular story in antiquity.[46] Perhaps the biographer thought the story had been told well enough and often enough already. This is what he said about the battle of Cunaxa (*Artox.* 8.1); in *De Hdt.mal.*

Africa, *Phylarchus and the Spartan Revolution* (Berkeley and Los Angeles, 1961) 55.

[44] For instance, the cogent criticism of W. R. Connor, *Theopompus and Fifth-Century Athens* 41f.

[45] Thus Phylarchus in a variant of F 72 from Hesychius; Philostratus *Imag.* II 17.6; discussion and other references in Frazer's *Pausanias* II 169.

[46] Nepos, *Them.* 2.7; Polyaenus I 30.1-2; etc.

869C, he said that if there were people living in the an-
tipodes, they had heard of the *bouleuma* of Themistocles.
πάλιν, incidentally, does not mean "he again invoked the
famous oracle" (so Scott-Kilvert, in the Penguin translation); it goes with the verb: "he again tried to win over
the People" (Perrin, Loeb edition).

10.4 ψήφισμα γράφει

For a discussion of the historical circumstances, see above,
comment to 7.2. Plutarch's citation of the decree deserves
some comment.

Plutarch: τὴν μὲν πόλιν παρακαταθέσθαι τῇ Ἀθηνᾷ τῇ Ἀθηναίων
μεδεούσῃ

Decree 4.5: τὴ[μ] μὲν πό[λιν παρ]ακατ[αθέ]σθαι τῆι Ἀθηνᾶι τῆι
Ἀθηνῶμ [μεδεο]ύ[σηι]

Plutarch: τοὺς δ' ἐν ἡλικίᾳ πάντας ἐμβαίνειν εἰς τὰς τριήρεις

Decree 14-15: τοὺς δὲ ἄλλους Ἀθη[ναίους ἅπαντας καὶ τοὺς
ξέ]νους τοὺς ἡβῶντας εἰσβαίνειν ε[ἰς τὰς ἑτοιμασθ]ε[ί]σ[α]ς
διακοσίας ναῦς

Plutarch: παῖδας δὲ καὶ γυναῖκας καὶ ἀνδράποδα σώζειν ἕκαστον ὡς
ἂν δύνηται

Decree 8: [τὰ τέκ]ν[α καὶ τὰς γυναῖκ]ας ε[ἰς] Τροιζῆνα κα-
ταθέσθαι

9-11: τ[οὺς δὲ πρεσβύτας καὶ τὰ] κτήματα εἰς Σαλαμῖνα καταθέ[σ]
θαι

It can be assumed that the decrees read to the Athenians
by Aeschines (Demosth. 19.303) were preserved by literary
transmission as well as by the actual documents. Ulpian's
scholia to Demosthenes (ad loc. p. 155 Dobson) show that
he knew the contents of the decrees mentioned by Aeschines and that either he or his source had looked up some
matters in Philochorus (on Aglauros, *FGrH* 328 F 105-
106). The sections cited by Aristides (II 256, cf. I 226)
repeat the portion of the preamble to the decree cited by
Plutarch, and with greater accuracy. As Jameson has demonstrated (*Hesperia* 29, 201f.), the preamble at least was
well known in antiquity and was frequently alluded to.

It is often claimed that Plutarch is citing this or that de-

cree from Craterus' collection, which he seems to have
known rather well.[47] In this case, however, he is almost
certainly quoting from memory; he has brought in the
phrase σῴζειν ἕκαστον ὡς ἂν δύνηται as if it were part of the decree, whereas it is obviously remembered from Herodotus
and Aristotle (8.41; *AP* 23.1). Naturally, no decree passed
by the people could have contained such a phrase. I have re-
marked elsewhere that no specific source can be identified
for this citation of the decree, and that Plutarch has a dim
recollection of it at best.[48]

   10.5 φιλοτίμως πάνυ τῶν Τροιζηνίων ὑποδεχομένων
Plutarch said the Troizenians voted to support the women
and children at public cost, allow children to pick fruit
anywhere, and pay their teachers. The mover of the decree
was Nicagoras. That he was a citizen of Troizen should
never have been doubted (e.g., by Jacoby, *FGrH* IIIb Suppl.
82), as Hypereides also testified to the circumstances (*In
Athenogenem* 3.32-33): "recalling their kindness in the face
of the Barbarian more than 150 years ago, you thought it
was necessary to protect people who had been helpful to
you in perilous times and who were now out of luck . . .
and to prove that I speak the truth the clerk will read . . .
the decree of the Troizenians which they voted for your
city."

   Good editions of Hypereides in antiquity will have acquired scholia; there was such an MS in the library of
Matthias Corvinus in the late sixteenth century.[49] The
scholia probably included reports of this decree, or even
a "text." Plutarch knew Hypereides well and may have
remembered this information from such an edition.

   So far as I know, modern scholarship has not recognized
the fact that if we did not have Hypereides' and Plutarch's
reference to the decree of the Troizenians, we should have

----

[47] *Arist.* 26; *Cimon* 13.4, and see Jacoby, *Atthis* 209; E. Meinhardt,
Perikles bei Plutarch 70-74.
[48] *Class.et Med.* 22 (1961) 189-192.
[49] Thalheim, "Hypereides," *RE* 9 (1914) 284.

to assume something like it. During the winter of 481/0, the
Athenians must have applied to the Troizenians, with whom
they were related through Theseus' father, Pittheus, asking
for refuge in case an evacuation became necessary. The
psephisma of the Troizenians was the result, although there
is no guarantee for the accuracy of the details reported by
Plutarch. A Hellenistic copy of this decree, or the Troizen-
ian copy of an Athenian decree acknowledging the hos-
pitality of the Troizenians, was discovered in 1847, as reported by K. Pittakes: Τὸ 1847 Ἰουλίου 23, ἐφημίσθη, ὅτι εἰς
Τροιζῆνα ἀνευρέθη ψήφισμα τῶν Τροιζηνίων ὑπὲρ τῶν Ἀθηναίων, ἢ
τῶν Ἀθηναίων ὑπὲρ τῶν Τροιζηνίων, διὰ τὴν ὁποίαν ἔδειξαν πρὸς
αὐτοὺς, κατὰ τὰ Μηδικὰ, φιλοξενίαν (Ἀρχαιολογικὴ Ἐφημερίς 1855:
1273). Unfortunately, despite Pittakes' vigorous efforts to
recover the stone, somebody substituted another inscription
for it (now published as *IG* IV 823a), and the whereabouts
of the original is unknown.[50]

Superficially, it would appear that there is a conflict between the Themistocles Decree and Herodotus: the decree
specifies Troizen as the refuge for all women and children;
Herodotus (8.41) and the rest of our ancient witnesses[51]
give the impression that some families went to Troizen, and
others to Salamis, or Aegina, or wherever they could—
which is probably exactly what happened. But the decree
only specified what was supposed to happen—i.e., what was
official policy, and what had probably been arranged between Athens and the Troizenians in advance. When the
defense of the north failed, Athenians who had not yet
evacuated their families sent them wherever possible at that
late date.

As H. I. Marrou has pointed out, this decree must be
added to the evidence for early public education, which is
usually thought to have begun only much later.[52]

---

[50] I have discussed this episode in "Troizen and the Persian Wars:
Some New Data," *AJA* 82 (1978) 105-107.

[51] Nepos, *Them.* 2.8; Frontinus, *Strat.* I 3.6; *Suda* s.v. ἀνεῖλεν; etc.

[52] *A History of Education in Antiquity* 72; other schools at this

10.6-7 οὐκ ὄντων δὲ δημοσίων χρημάτων τοῖς ᾿Αθηναίοις
A financial crisis which Aristotle said was alleviated by the
Areopagus (*AP* 23.1), Cleidemus, by a stratagem of Themistocles (*FGrH* 323 F 21). The whole passage is fraught
with difficulties. Why did the state require payment for the
sailors during this greatest of all emergencies? Greeks on
duty in the armed forces *normally* brought along their own
food, or bought it on the spot. But certainly no one would
have denied rations to humble rowers in the fleet at this
juncture.[53]

The nature and function of the "public treasury" in early
Athenian history are only dimly perceived. A system of
taxation which contributed to this treasury was described
by Pollux (8.130) and may be Solonian in date, but no one
can be sure. The state had revenue from the Laureion
mines, but this may have all been earmarked for the fleet.
According to *AP* 8.3, the *naukraroi* collected the special
direct tax known as the *eisphora* and supervised expendi-
tures; a five or ten percent tax on land may still have existed
since Peisistratid times (Thuc. VI 54.4; *AP* 16.4). Metics
and artisans were directly taxed until about 477/6, according
to Diodorus (XI 43.3). These are all possible sources of
state revenue.[54] But the only thing we learn from this passage of Plutarch is that there was a financial emergency
of some sort on the eve of Salamis, which Herodotus
thought unnecessary to mention, but which left a trail of
stories to be picked up by Cleidemus and Aristotle's sources.

It is no help that Plutarch has mixed the order of his
authorities, making it appear that Aristotle attributed the
emergency fundraising to the Areopagus, but that Cleidemus replied with the stratagem of Themistocles. The Atthi-

---

approximate date: Hdt. 6.27 (Chios); Paus. VI 9.6 (Astypalaea);
Timaeus *FGrH* 566 F 95 (Acragas).

[53] A. R. Burn, *Persia and the Greeks* 431f., is probably correct in
believing that a part, at least, of the May harvest of grain had been
stockpiled on Salamis.

[54] On the possibility of an *eisphora* during the period of the Persian
Wars, see Rudi Thomsen, *Eisphora* 119ff.

dographer Cleidemus—the first Athenian to write an *Atthis* after the genre had been established by Hellanicus of Lesbos —probably wrote at the end of the fifth century, or very early fourth, as is now well argued by Rudi Thomsen.[55] It is probable that Cleidemus recorded this story simply because it was an interesting incident—not as a reply to an "Areopagus version." At any rate, the tale is absurd for many reasons. For instance, why would everyone's baggage be conveniently all in one place? And what Greek would leave his money in his baggage rather than carrying it on his person? As Labarbe pointed out, the tale is branded as an anachronism by the phrase, "as the Athenians were going down to Piraeus." The only possible site for a *mass* embarkation at this date in Athenian history would have been the usual beach at Phaleron, although people were doubtless boarding vessels of all sorts (as at Dunkirk) from Eleusis to Vouliagmeni. Labarbe also claimed that what Themistocles is supposed to have done amounted to confiscation—"véritable brigandage"—with which we must certainly agree.[56]

Critics in the past have seen the two versions as an illustration of the ingenuity of Themistocles the Democrat, and the oligarchic response, quoted by Aristotle from his usual sources.[57] As I have noted above (Chapter I, F), it is difficult to find political content here.

10.8-9 Ἐκπλεούσης δὲ τῆς πόλεως τοῖς μὲν οἶκτον τὸ θέαμα We should assume that by the time of the final proclamation mentioned by Herodotus (8.41), much of the non-combatant population would already have left for Troizen.[58] The remainder waited till the last moment, buoyed by false

[55] Ibid. 85-89, 115ff.: in F 8 (Photius s.v. *naukraria*), Cleidemus mentioned the hundred symmories of his time—a system that was changed after 378, pace Jacoby, *FGrH* IIIb Suppl. I 58; so also D. Bradeen, *CW* 59 (1966) 245.

[56] *Loi navale* 136f.; Frost, *CSCA* 1 (1968) 108.

[57] Jacoby, *Atthis* 74f.; ad *FGrH* 323 F 21; cf. Hignett, *Athenian Constitution* 147f.

[58] W. den Boer, "Themistocles in Fifth-Century Historiography," *Mnemosyne* 15 (1962) 236.

hopes, or perhaps unable to arrange passage until the fleet returned to Salamis and there were boats available to ferry the refugees across without charge (Hdt. 8.40). In Plutarch's phrase πολλοὶ μὲν οἱ διὰ γῆρας ὑπολειπόμενοι τῶν πολιτῶν ἔλεον εἶχον (the reading of the Seitenstettensis MS), πολλοὶ has been emended by many modern editors to πολύν. Herodotus in fact said that the city was deserted except for the tamiai and a number of other citizens who did not get to Salamis (8.51). But elsewhere (9.99) he noted that Xerxes took five hundred prisoners from Athens. At any rate, Plutarch should not be emended without manuscript authority simply because he disagrees with Herodotus. We must believe that the official position was that published in the Themistocles Decree: elders were to be carried over to Salamis, evidently in order that the rest of the citizens should have the benefit of their wisdom (this clause was quoted from the decree by Aristides II 256). But it is easy to imagine a few pious old men of this generation offering to remain with the priests to help defend the temples on the acropolis to the very end.[59] In my opinion, Plutarch had no intention here either to depart from Herodotus or to revise the tradition; he was simply adding color by writing a stock departure scene. Therefore it was irrelevant for Jacoby to suggest that Plutarch had copied this passage from Cleidemus (*FGrH* IIIb Suppl. I 455).

10.10 ἐν οἷς ἱστορεῖται κύων Ξανθίππου
Another version of this story is found in Aelian, *NA* 12.35, on the authority of Philochorus (*FGrH* 328 F 116) and an unknown work of Aristotle. It differs in two respects— there are several dogs, and they survive the crossing. The actions of animals were often considered significant by experts at divination, as Plutarch once noted rather critically (*De frat.amore* 490D). The precinct of Heracles at Kyn-

---

[59] Nepos, *Them.* 2.8: *arcem sacerdotibus paucisque maioribus natu . . . tradunt*, etc., and see Jameson's remarks on the Themistocles Decree, *Hesp.* 29 (1960) 213f.; G. A. Lehmann, "Bemerkungen zur Themistokles-Inschrift von Troizen," *Historia* 17 (1968) 276-280.

osarges was founded, according to legend, because a dog had carried a sacrifice off to that particular place (*Suda* s.v. Kynosarges). Philochorus was a professional expounder of omens and portents and it is probable that this tale found its way into his *Atthis* because something of the sort actually occurred during the Salamis crossing and its memory was preserved, along with that of other omens, by the expounders of the Persian War generation. Philochorus himself was once called upon to interpret canine behavior (*FGrH* 328 F 67, Dion.Hal. *De Dinarcho* 3). Plutarch's version of the story was probably a popularization of the mantic tradition and the details were added to explain the topographical name of Kynossema, on Salamis. Plutarch repeated this dog story more briefly in *Cato major* 5.4.

NOTE ON THE CHRONOLOGY OF THE SALAMIS CAMPAIGN

There is a substantial literature on the exact date of Salamis, arising from the difficulties in the account of Herodotus. The historian, after having given us a day-to-day chronicle of Xerxes' advance from Therme to the arrival of the fleet at Phaleron (table in How and Wells, II 372f.; cf. Hignett, *Xerxes' Invasion* 379ff.) suddenly becomes vague and implies in his narrative that the battle of Salamis followed closely upon the arrival of the Persian forces in Attica.

There are two meteorological data to aid us. The Olympic Games coincided with the full moon (Pindar, *Ol.* 3.35 with schol.), which in all probability was that of 19 August 480.[60] Herodotus (7.206) said the Spartans sent Leonidas to Thermopylae shortly before the games; the other Peloponnesian contingents heard of the disaster at Thermopylae and marched to defend the Isthmus Ὀλύμπια δὲ καὶ Κάρνεια παροιχώκεε ἤδη (8.72), which would lead us to conclude that the fighting at Thermopylae would have been over about

[60] Busolt, *Griechische Geschichte* I 708 n. 4; Hignett, *Xerxes' Invasion* 452f.

28 August. It took the fleet nine days from that time to arrive at Phaleron (Hdt. 8.23, 25, 66; How and Wells ad 8.66), that is, 6 September.

On 2 October 480, there was a partial solar eclipse which found the Spartans at the Isthmus still celebrating the victory at Salamis (Hdt. 9.10). The date of the eclipse results from astronomical calculation, and the battle of Salamis cannot have taken place much earlier; most commentators follow Busolt in accepting a date somewhere around 27-28 September.[61]

This means an interval of about three weeks during which the Greeks and Persians faced each other across the Salamis narrows, which is very different from the telescoping of events in Herodotus' account. There is nothing inherently improbable in such a delay. On one hand, the Persians would have been unwilling to press on to the Isthmus leaving a hostile fleet intact on their flank.[62] On the other hand, the King and his advisers knew full well that in any concert of Greeks there were those who might eventually seek personal advantage by going over to the Mede, others who would spread defeatism, confusion, and resentment, still others who would decide on their own simply to sail home. There was nothing to be lost therefore by sitting tight for the moment and allowing the inevitable squabbles to break out among the Greeks.

The date of Salamis was also established on the Attic calendar, on the twentieth of Boedromion.[63] This would

[61] *Griech.Gesch.* II 703f., long note 3; a late (19 September) dating of Thermopylae and Artemision is proposed by Kenneth S. Sacks, *CQ* n.s. 26 (1976) 232-248, in order to avoid a long period of waiting in Attica—unnecessarily, I believe.

[62] Hignett, *Xerxes' Invasion* 208f., following R. Custance, *War at Sea: Modern Theory and Ancient Practice* (Edinburgh, 1919) 26f.

[63] Plut. *Cam.* 19.6, quoting from his lost work, *On Days*; his more casual dating of the battle to 16 Mounychion, in *Glor.Ath.* 349F and *Lys.* 15.1—i.e., early spring—is simply wrong. For an explanation, see E. Badian, "The Wrong Salamis?" *RhM* 118 (1975) 233-237,

seem to be confirmed by Herodotus' story about the Iacchus hymn heard from the direction of Eleusis (8.65). The historian specifically dated the incident to some day before that of the battle, but Plutarch said it was the same day (*Phoc.* 28.2; *Cam.* 19.10, where he said that Iacchus was carried to Eleusis on 20 Boedromion). We now know from an inscription of the early third century A.D. that this day of the mysteries fell on 19 Boedromion (*Syll.*³ 885.19f.).

In his description of the Salamis campaign, Plutarch did not mention the capture of the acropolis and the destruction of the temples (Hdt. 8.51-53), but his testimony elsewhere may throw additional light on this episode. In *Frat.amore* 489B (and *Qc* 9.6, 741B), Plutarch said the Athenians τὴν γὰρ δευτέραν ἐξαιροῦσιν ἀεὶ τοῦ Βοηδρομιῶνος ὡς ἐν ἐκείνῃ τῷ Ποσειδῶνι πρὸς τὴν Ἀθηνᾶν γενομένης τῆς διαφορᾶς. The myth is found most fully in Apollodorus III 14.1: Poseidon established a salt pool on the acropolis and Athena, an olive, as tokens of their mastery over the land. The argument was adjudged by the twelve gods and Athena won, but olive and salt pool both remained ever after in the precinct of the archaic Erechtheion.

Two days after the burning of the temples, Xerxes sent the Athenian exiles in his entourage to the acropolis τρόπῳ τῷ σφετέρῳ θῦσαι τὰ ἱρὰ (Hdt. 8.54). I think this occasion may very well have been the anniversary of the contention between Athena and Poseidon (2 Boedromion, or the next day, if the Athenians did in fact skip the second as a *dies ater*), for the exiles went to sacrifice in the Erechtheion and Herodotus specifically mentioned the salt pool and the olive. The exiles reported that the tree had been burnt but had already put out a new shoot (Hdt. 8.55).[64]

The chronology of the Salamis campaign may be tentatively reconstructed as follows:

---

suggesting the battle at Cypriot Salamis associated with Cimon's last campaign.

[64] Cf. A. Mommsen, *Heortologie* (Leipzig, 1864) 208f.

August	19	Full moon, last day of the Olympic Games
	28	Final battle at Thermopylae
September	5	Arrival of Persian forces in Attica
	9	Capture of the acropolis
	11	Athenian exiles sacrifice—3 Boedromion
	27	Iacchus song heard from Eleusis—19 Boedromion
	28	Day of the battle—20 Boedromion
October	2	Partial eclipse of the sun finds the Spartans at the Isthmus still sacrificing for the victory

11.1 Ταῦτά τε δὴ μεγάλα τοῦ Θεμιστοκλέους, καὶ τοὺς πολίτας αἰσθόμενος ποθοῦντας Ἀριστείδην . . . γράφει ψήφισμα
Themistocles wrote the decree recalling the exiles both because the people wanted Aristeides back and because he feared that Aristeides might otherwise take the barbarian side, like the Peisistratids and other Athenian exiles (Hdt. 8.54, 65) in Xerxes' entourage—by no means an idle fear, as is discussed below. Plutarch added a few details in *Arist.* 8.1, where the decree was attributed to the Athenians in general and was extended to *all* exiles, and not just those "exiled for a time."

That such a decree was passed we know from Andocides (*De myst.* 77, 107), although the orator casually muddled the invasions of 490 and 480. The decree was carefully recorded by date in some *Atthis* where it was found by Aristotle (*AP* 22.8), who cited the year—in the archonship of Hypsichides. The legislation is also found as part of the Themistocles Decree, lines 44-49: ὅπως δ' ἂν καὶ ὁμονοοῦντες ἅπαντες Ἀθηναῖοι ἀμύνωνται τὸμ βάρβαρον, τοὺς μὲν μεθεστηκότας τὰ [δέκα] ἔτη ἀπιέναι εἰς Σαλαμῖνα καὶ μένειν αὐτοὺς ἐ[κεῖ ἕως ἄν τι τῶι δήμ]ωι δόξηι περὶ αὐτῶν. τοὺς δὲ [ἀτίμους—That Plutarch thought Themistocles had written two different decrees is probably due to the fact that his knowledge came from a literary source, rather than from a copy of the decree itself.[65] Nepos (*Arist.* 1.5) seems to be saying that there was one decree of recall and another after the battle which restored civil rights: *populiscito in patriam restitutus est. Interfuit autem pugnae navali apud Salamina, quae facta est prius quam poena liberaretur.* All these various testimonia indicate a very confused tradition and what we have is probably only a small part of what was available to Plutarch.[66]

As discussed above (comment to 5.7) it would seem probable that the recall of the exiles was passed near the end of Hypsichides' archon year (481/0) as part of the evacuation decree, after the return of the Tempe expedition (cf. comment to 7.2, above). There may have been exiles living in various areas of northern Greece, and the Athenians preferred them to be home instead of giving Xerxes the benefit of their counsel and rendering the loyalty of their friends and relatives suspect. Often overlooked by those who think in terms of modern war and diplomacy is the question of what would have happened if the Greeks had lost to Xerxes. Contemporary rhetoric no doubt spoke of crushing slavery; modern readers think in terms of enemy occupation, but a Persian victory would have meant no more than it did every generation in the Ionian cities—simple installation of pro-Persian tyrants with subsidies to hire garrisons, and life going on otherwise as it always had. There were undoubtedly important men in all the Greek cities who were wondering if they could successfully betray their city to the Mede and thus become a despot capable of gratifying every whim. By bringing as many exiles as possible home, the Athenians

[65] Frost, *Class.et Med.* 22 (1961) 190-192.

[66] Discussion by Jameson, *Hesp.* 29 (1960) 221f.; A. Raubitschek, "A Note on the Themistocles Decree," *Studi in onore di Luisa Banti* (Rome, 1965) 285-287; Podlecki, *Themistocles* 157; S. Burstein, *CSCA* 4 (1971) 93-110.

no doubt intended to relieve their relatives and other connections of the agony of deciding whether they would be
better off under a Persian-supported tyranny.

11.2 Εὐρυβιάδου δὲ τὴν μὲν ἡγεμονίαν τῶν νεῶν ἔχοντος
Here commences the dramatic story of Themistocles' wise
counsel and its eventual success over the fears of craven
commanders. This particular meeting is the third in Herodotus' scheme. The first was held as soon as the fleets could
collect at Salamis from Artemision, Troizen, and elsewhere
(8.49); it was then resolved to sail to the Isthmus where
their chances of escaping after a defeat were better. A second meeting was held (8.56) in the panic following the
capture of the acropolis and the commanders agreed once
more to sail off to the Isthmus. It was after this meeting
broke up, according to Herodotus, that Themistocles encountered Mnesiphilus, who advised him to go back to
Eurybiades and use any *mechane* to change his mind (8.57).
Plutarch was furious with this account in *De Hdt.mal.* 869C
sq., saying that the historian had brought in Mnesiphilus
merely to diminish the achievement of Themistocles, and
this has been the usual interpretation of Herodotus 8.57
ever since.[67]

The problem is that the entire series of staff meetings as
reported by Herodotus gives a muddled and confused impression. This state of affairs no doubt results from the reports of the historian's informants who, it is often pointed
out, would have been young men at the time of Salamis
and therefore poorly informed about the plans of the high
command (Burn, *Persia and the Greeks* 441). Plutarch here
simply avoids mentioning Mnesiphilus; his purpose was to
highlight without distractions what many thought was Themistocles' greatest achievement.

11.3 ὅτε καὶ τὰ μνημονευόμενα λεχθῆναί φασι
The occasion of two famous apothegms. In *Apophth.Them.*
4, 185B, Plutarch correctly followed Herodotus in attribut-

---

[67] Hignett, *Xerxes' Invasion* 203f.; How and Wells ad Hdt. 8.57;
Gottlieb, *Ausserherodoteische Überlieferung* 98f.

ing the remark about the impatient runners to Adeimantus (8.59); here Eurybiades is made the focus of opposition—a very typical slip for Plutarch.

πάταξον μέν, ἄκουσον δέ

Something of the sort was once said by Diogenes the Cynic to Antisthenes (Diog.Laert. 6.21); Themistocles' retort was reported by no authority earlier than Plutarch.[68] Although probably apocryphal, the remark suited very well Themistocles' characteristic ability to bear fools gladly and to endure humiliation if necessary.

11.5 εἰπόντος δέ τινος ὡς ἀνὴρ ἄπολις

Once again, according to Herodotus, the speaker was Adeimantus (8.61; cf. *Suda* s.v. Adeimantus). Plutarch's reluctance to mention the Corinthian commander is probably based on his recognition of the historian's anti-Corinthian bias (*De Hdt.mal.* 870-871C).

πόλις δ' ἡμῖν ἔστι μεγίστη τῶν Ἑλληνίδων, αἱ διακόσιαι τριήρεις

As in Herodotus 8.61-62, but Plutarch does not mention Themistocles' specific threat to settle at Siris in Italy.[69] The theme that men (and ships) were more important than mere walls and possessions was as old at least as Alcaeus (quoted to that effect to illustrate the situation by Aristides II 273).[70] Plutarch followed Herodotus (8.63) in claiming that the threat of Athenian desertion persuaded Eurybiades to change his mind.

11.6 τοῦ δ' Ἐρετριέως πειρωμένου τι λέγειν πρὸς αὐτὸν

The story is original with Plutarch in extant literature. Perrin (*Plutarch's Themistocles* 203) said aptly that it has been lugged in by the ears. The use of the definite article

---

[68] *Apophth.Them.* 5, 185B; see also Aelian, *VH* 13.40; Aristides II 258, and schol. ad loc.

[69] On Athenian interests in Italy, see How and Wells ad 8.61 (skeptical); Burn, *Persia and the Greeks* 295f., who sees a "training cruise" of the Athenian navy off to the West in 481. How and Wells have the correct approach.

[70] See also Cicero, *Ad Att.* X 8, 4; Favorinus, *De exilio* 10.26-32; Justin II 12.13.

suggests however that the tale was well known by Plutarch's audience.

Ten years earlier a medizing faction had betrayed Eretria to the Persians, who sacked it and carried off the inhabitants into slavery (Hdt. 6.100-101, 119). The survivors contributed seven ships to the Greek fleet (Hdt. 8.1, 46), which shows courage—or at least, a desire for vengeance. By this time, the Eretrians, like the Athenians, were men without a country. We have no way of knowing why this particular Eretrian was supposed to be timid: "like the cuttlefish, you have a sword, but no heart," agreeing with the dubious anatomy of the cuttlefish in Aristotle's *Historia animalium* (4.1, 524^{b}23 sq.). R. Flacelière has ingeniously argued that Themistocles' remark about the *teuthis* referred to the *parasemon* of Eretria, which appears on Eretrian coins before 446 B.C.[71] He claimed that the *teuthis* of the anecdote meant the squid, instead of the cuttlefish, as the squid's "bone" resembles a sword far more satisfactorily than that of the cuttlefish.[72] But Eretrian coins do not depict, as he asserted, a stylized creature which could represent any kind of cephalopod; the coins display an unequivocal octopus. We may attribute the inaccuracy to the unknown raconteur who made the story up.

[71] E.g., C. M. Kraay, *Greek Coins* (New York, 1966) no. 369.

[72] Flacelière, "Thémistocle, les Erétriens et le calmar," *REA* 50 (1948) 211-217.

V

THE BATTLE OF SALAMIS:
COMMENTARY TO CHAPTERS 12-17

12.1 Λέγεται δ' ὑπό τινων τὸν μὲν Θεμιστοκλέα περὶ τούτων ἀπὸ τοῦ καταστρώματος ἄνωθεν τῆς νεὼς διαλέγεσθαι

Cobet deleted ἄνωθεν for no reason that I can see. The picture given by Plutarch is certainly very clear, and this is no doubt the impression he meant to give, whether accurate, grammatical, or not. It is, in fact, not accurate. Herodotus said that Themistocles persuaded Eurybiades to call the generals to their *synhedrion* (8.58), which was certainly not located around the prow of Themistocles' ship. But the discrepancy did not bother Plutarch, who shows minimum concern at the difficulties of fitting anecdotes into the Herodotean framework.

γλαῦκα δ' ὀφθῆναι

If one were trying to catalogue unusual occurrences, a more likely one would be a summer twilight in Greece when *no* owl flew overhead. Greeks were no different from soldiers of all periods of history in looking for portents before battle; to look for an owl flying overhead was a convenient way of reassuring oneself of victory on the eve of battle (especially in the city of Athena). Such omens would naturally be recorded by priests and expounders after the victory (or forgotten after defeat). An owl was also seen before Marathon (Ar. *Wasps* 1085), and owls in general were duly listed in the corpus of proverbs as presaging an Athenian victory.[1]

The fullest notice is found in Ammonius' *Altars and Sacrifices* (*FGrH* 361 F 5), which is repeated in identical form by three late grammarians:[2] οἷον τὰ περὶ τῆς γλαυκὸς ὅτι περὶ τὸν καιρὸν τῆς συμβολῆς ἐφάνη περιπταμένη τὰς ᾿Αττικὰς ναῦς· καὶ τὰ περὶ τῆς περιστερᾶς ὅτι ἐπὶ τῆς Θεμιστοκλέους τριήρους ἐφάνη καθεζομένη, ὅθεν καὶ μετὰ τὴν νίκην ἀπαρχὰς ᾿Αφροδίτης ἱερὸν ἱδρύσατο ἐν Πειραιεῖ, ὡς ᾿Αμμώνιος ὁ λαμπρεὺς[3] ἐν τῷ Περὶ Βωμῶν φησί. Like the owl, the pigeon is an unexceptional visitor. Pigeons are notorious garbage eaters and will follow large and messy congregations of men to the ends of the earth. It is quite possible that the Persians did in fact bring them to Greece for the first time in the wake of their abortive invasion of 492, as we are told by an early informant, Charon of Lampsacus (Athen. 394E; Aelian *VH* 1.15; *FGrH* 362 F 3ab).

It is possible to speak of a body of mantic tradition all through Greek history. We have seen a dog story which was preserved probably because of its significance as an omen (see comment to 10.10, above). These birds need to be given the same respectful attention.

As usual, Plutarch has been selective in his version of the portent. He probably knew Ammonius' work[4] and perhaps another simpler account which described only an owl settling down on the right side of Themistocles' rigging (the source of *Lex.rhet.* 232.30 Bekker). Plutarch will have ignored the pigeon story for one of three reasons: he didn't know it (unlikely); he felt that the pace of his narrative

[1] E.g., Zenobius, 2.89; Diogenianus 3.72 in *Corpus Pareom.Gr.* Cf. Hesychius s.v. γλαῦξ διέπτατο.

[2] Syrianus, *In Hermog.* p. 76.8 Rabe; *Rhet.Gr.* V 533; VI 393 Walz.

[3] λαμπρευς codd: Λαμπτρευς Jacoby et al.

[4] Perrin, *Plutarch's Themistocles* 204, states as a fact that this Ammonius was Plutarch's teacher, but see C. P. Jones, "The Teacher of Plutarch," *HSCP* 71 (1966) 205-215, who shows from *IG* ii² 3558 that Ammonius was from the deme Cholleidae, not Lamptrae (if Lamptreus is in fact the correct reading).

demanded the simplest form of the anecdote; he knew for a fact that Themistocles had never built a shrine to Aphrodite in Piraeus.[5] The latter two explanations are equally probable. A truly absurd story was told by Aelian (*VH* 2.28). Themistocles halted the Athenian forces to watch a cock fight; inspired by their courage the Athenians went out to win. It is a tribute to trivia that this story—least deserving of any sort of credibility—was repeated on the front page of the *Los Angeles Times* (8 February 1971) in a story about cockfighting.

PREFATORY NOTE TO THE SALAMIS CAMPAIGN (12.2-15)

One despairs of adding anything constructive to the enormous literature about the battle of Salamis. Yet anyone who proposes to discuss any of the events of that battle is obliged to take positions, however guarded, on a number of disputed points. For the purposes of this commentary, it is necessary to state in advance my working premises about (1) the sources, (2) the topography of the battle, and (3) the events leading up to the engagement, particularly the Sicinnus incident.

The Sources

Another fifth-century tragedian tells us that Aeschylus fought at Salamis (Ion of Chios, in schol.Aesch. *Pers.* 432, *FGrH* 392 F 7), and there is no reason to doubt this as the poet was still of military age, about forty-five (Marmor Parium A 48). When he presented the *Persae* eight years later, he had not only his own experience to guide him in describing the battle, but also the general consensus of his countrymen about what had happened. While fellow Athe-

---

[5] According to an Augustan inscription, he had built some sort of shrine *before* the battle, *IG* ii² 1035-45:]ακανης δ ἰδρύσατο Θεμιστο-κλῆς πρὸ τῆς περὶ Σαλαμῖνα ναυμαχίας. Davies, *APF* 6669 V suggests that this might have been Themistocles' grave, rather than a shrine, but see the doubts of Podlecki *Themistocles* 178f.

nians would accept a great deal of dramatic license—like
the Strymon freezing in autumn, or Darius presented as an
anti-imperialist, or Xerxes arriving on the scene as if he had
run all the way—it is doubtful they would have appreciated
outright falsification or invention of certain crucial inci-
dents during the battle itself.

I follow Broadhead and Kitto[6] in believing the *Persae* to
be a religious play about hybris and divine punishment
rather than a celebration of victory. An Athenian audience
of Aeschylus' generation would not mind being told that
they were merely the instrument of divine anger; nevertheless, once the drama had reached the question how the
battle started (350), any Athenian audience would have
leaned forward eagerly waiting to hear a familiar tale of
events which had already become the accepted tradition.
This is particularly obvious to one watching a modern production at Epidauros, where it is possible, I believe, to re-
capture some of the anticipation Athenians felt 2,500 years
earlier. For these reasons, I agree with Broadhead (*Persae*
appendix vi 322ff.) that the events described by the Messenger—beginning with the message to Xerxes (353) and
ending with the assault on Psyttaleia (465)—are substantially what all Athenians remembered as having taken place.

Aeschylus was not the only contemporary poet to record
the events of Salamis. Phrynichus' *Phoenissae* had the same
theme (Glaucus, in arg.*Pers.*) and Simonides also wrote
The Sea Battle at Salamis (*Vita Pindari* p. 98 West.; *Suda*
s.v. Simonides), which probably magnified the exploits of
Themistocles.[7] Unfortunately, we know none of the details
and have no way of knowing what, in later accounts, was
derived from Simonides, Phrynichus, and other lesser poets.

Herodotus wrote a good generation later. There were
few aged veterans of Salamis left as informants and much of

[6] H. D. Broadhead, *The Persae of Aeschylus* (Cambridge, 1960)
xv-xxiv; H.D.F. Kitto, *Greek Tragedy* (Garden City, 1954) 38-43.
[7] Podlecki, "Simonides: 480," *Historia* 17 (1968) 266ff.; see below,
comment to 15.5.

what they could add to the solid core of tradition would
have been garrulous exaggeration, on the one hand, and
pure fantasy, on the other. This is a good place to recall
Thucydides' famous *caveat* about battle reporting (VII
44.1) that it is difficult even for the actual participants in a
battle to know what is going on except right in front of
them. Probably Herodotus' most valuable contributions to
the Athenian tradition about Salamis would have been
stories he heard from informants who had fought on the
Persian side. He must have grown up in Halicarnassus hearing about the exploits of Artemisia, for instance, and in his
travels he encountered men like the Samians Theomestor
and Phylacus (or their close acquaintances) who had distinguished themselves at Salamis (8.85).

Nevertheless, Herodotus' account is often bewildering
and seems to betray the historian's own uncertainty about
the course of the battle. Moreover, one must bear in mind
that at the time Herodotus collected his information, neither
Themistocles, nor Spartans, nor Corinthians were any too
popular in Athens among certain groups. This climate, and
his own prejudices, contributed to his uncharitable treatment of the Athenian allies on the one hand, and Themistocles on the other. Every sentence in Herodotus must
therefore be examined on its own merits. If it agrees, more
or less, with the picture given by Aeschylus, and seems
probable of itself, it has been my practice to accept it.

Later writers based their accounts at least in part on
Aeschylus and Herodotus, and so are subject to the same
criticisms. Any details they may supply which are either
original or contradict the testimony of poet and historian
are highly suspect. Ctesias' Cretan archers (*FGrH* 688 F 13
[30] can probably be rejected out of hand, simply because
almost everything else in Ctesias is wrong.[8] When Diodorus
says the Egyptian squadron was sent to close the western
straits, it is easy to claim that Ephorus has supplied this

---

[8] See now the commentary to his contributions by J. M. Bigwood,
"Ctesias as Historian of the Persian Wars," *Phoenix* 32 (1978) 19-34.

detail from an authoritative source; on the other hand, this may merely be an inference to explain the absence of the Egyptians from Herodotus' account of the battle after he had described their distinguished performance at Artemision (8.17).[9] In general, remarks by later writers should be considered useful primarily when they confirm the accounts of Aeschylus and Herodotus.

SALAMIS: THE "STRAITS" AND PSYTTALEIA

All ancient authorities agreed that the battle occurred in waters where the Greeks had the advantage, as their ships were heavier and depended less on maneuver than those of the Phoenicians (*Pers.* 413ff.; Hdt. 8.60; Thuc I 74.1, etc.). And it seems obvious that the action must have taken place somewhere in the long rectangle bounded on the south by the line Cynosura-Lipsokoutali, on the east by Piraeus, on the north by the Attic shore beneath Mt. Aegaleos, and to the west by the indented shoreline of Salamis.

Aeschylus (*Pers.* 447-453) and Herodotus (8.76.2) agreed that Xerxes sent men to Psyttaleia because the little island lay directly in the path of the impending action, and a Persian force (young nobles, according to Aeschylus) could rescue shipwrecked allies and slaughter foes. It would be helpful if there were a small island directly in the center of the rectangle described above. But there is not; therefore

[9] On which see G. Roux, "Quatre récits de la bataille de Salamine," *BCH* 98 (1974) 69f. In this long article (pp. 51-94), Roux has attempted to create a composite picture from the accounts of Aeschylus, Herodotus, Diodorus, and Plutarch. I cannot agree that one can draw eclectically from several accounts as if from some kind of shopping list, taking something that suits the argument from Plutarch, rejecting something from Herodotus, as if all writers were of equal value. By doing this, Roux risks the same mistake others have accused Herodotus of making: "Hérodote aurait recueilli deux récits divergents de la bataille et, incapable de choisir, les aurait mis bout à bout" (58). Nevertheless, his analysis contains some valuable insights, which will be cited where appropriate.

modern discussion has concentrated on two candidates—St. George and Lipsokoutali—one of which would seem to be too far within the straits and the other too far outside. I had once inclined to identify Psyttaleia with St. George, following the arguments of Hammond.[10] Long study of the problem, autopsy, and discussion with other scholars has now convinced me that the island in question must be Lipsokoutali.

Since it was Xerxes who stationed men at night on Psyttaleia, everything depends on what Xerxes thought would happen. It seems to me implicit in the account of Herodotus that Xerxes landed men on Psyttaleia because he was convinced there would be a battle in its vicinity during the hours of darkness and that the battle would result from an attempt by the Greeks to break out of the straits during the night. He stationed his ships "when it was midnight" not necessarily to seal up the straits, but to lie in wait for the Greek fleet trying to escape during the hours of darkness. Herodotus said that these ships were put in place in silence, evidently in order that the Greeks would not realize there was an ambush waiting for them (8.76)—although this contradicts *Persae* 380, τάχις δὲ τάχιν παρεκάλει. This interpretation would seem to call for an island outside the strait, i.e., Lipsokoutali. The second consideration is the description of the topography of the Salamis area by Strabo (IX 1.13-14) which, although confusing at first reading, makes sense if we take into account an approximate two-meter rise in sea level, which has converted at least one ancient peninsula into an island and one island into a semi-submerged reef. St. George and what is now a reef thus become the Pharmakoussae. This is the well-reasoned interpretation of Paul Wallace, with which it is difficult to argue.[11] His

[10] N.G.L. Hammond, "The Battle of Salamis," *JHS* 76 (1956) 33ff.; followed by Broadhead, *Persae* 331ff.

[11] "Psyttaleia and the Trophies of Salamis," *AJA* 73 (1969) 296-303; see also the ingenious interpretation of Alciphron, *Epist.* II 3.11 by E. Bayer, "Psyttaleia," *Historia* 18 (1969) 640.

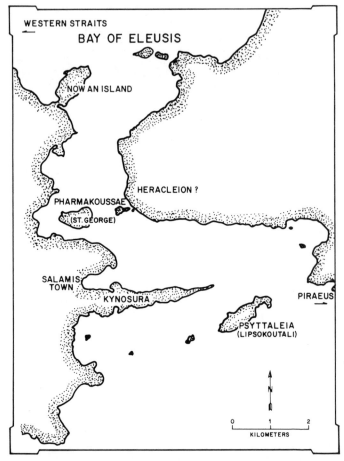

The Straits of Salamis, Indicating Approximate Sea Level in 480 B.C.

Because the sea level has risen about two meters since antiquity, this map was prepared by drawing an outline along the one-fathom-depth contour indicated on USN Oceanographic Chart 54345, *Stenón Salamínos*. What is now a submerged reef thus emerges as a small island—arguably one of the two Pharmakoussae mentioned by Strabo.

Map by Kay Frost

other arguments seem to me decisive: (1) that Lipsokoutali
is an easily explicable corruption, through folk etymology,
of Psyttaleia; (2) that the trophies of the battle, whose remains were seen by early travelers, can be located on Kyno-
sura and Lipsokoutali; and (3) that the testimony of
Michael Akominatos (*Letter* 9 II 13, 14 Lambros) can only
refer to Lipsokoutali.

In any discussion of topography, there is need for cau-
tion. Neither Xerxes, Aeschylus, nor Herodotus had the advantage of our superb topographical maps, naval charts, and
aerial photographs. Moreover, we are so accustomed to
thinking of topography in terms of maps that one looks
down upon from above that it is difficult to understand the
perspective of men who thought in terms of action going
on in front of them, or at least may have found this more
natural than the "bird's-eye" view. I have cruised through
the area under discussion, and studied it from numerous
shore vantage points. Like most seascapes, it offers a decep-
tive idea of distances, particularly relative distances. In the
aftermath of the victory, there must have been many peculiar sketches drawn—in the sand, on chalk boards, on papyrus—as veterans attempted to show what happened and very
naturally adapted the topography to their memory of the
events, rather than vice versa. We must see ancient recon-
structions of the battle of Salamis from this perspective
and entertain the reservation that we may never be able to
relate the action to the topography with any degree of certainty.[12]

MANEUVERS ON THE EVE OF BATTLE

According to Thucydides (I 74.1), Themistocles "was most
responsible for the sea fight ἐν τῷ στενῷ." For this reason, he
added, the Spartans honored him as they had never honored

[12] See recent discussions by W. K. Pritchett, *Studies in Ancient
Greek Topography* I (Berkeley and Los Angeles, 1965) 97ff.; Hignett, *Xerxes' Invasion* 397ff.; Burn, *Persia and the Greeks* 472ff.

a foreigner before. The canonical view (in Athens at least) of the sequence of events during the time Herodotus was writing his history seems to have been as follows: Themistocles kept arguing for a decisive battle where they were, because their ships were best adapted to fighting in a narrow space where their greater size would be an advantage (8.60). When the Persian fleet put out in battle order, however, the size of their fleet once more panicked some Greeks into counseling retreat to the Isthmus (8.70, 74). It was then that Themistocles, by sending Sicinnus, tricked Xerxes into sealing off the straits, thus forcing the Greeks to fight, whether they wished to or not (8.75-76, 83). The historian's exaggeration of Greek panic and cowardice all through the war has been recognized by critics since Plutarch (De Hdt.mal. fin.; cf. How and Wells II 254). But granting that the outline of this story at least must be true—for the Spartans did in fact honor Themistocles for sophia and dexiotes—it is best to review Aeschylus' testimony. What the poet implies, rather than specifically states, is (1) that in terms of sheer numbers, the Persians were bound to win (337-343); (2) it took a trick to tip the scales to the Greeks, a trick described as follows:

355 ἀνὴρ γὰρ Ἕλλην ἐξ Ἀθηναίων στρατοῦ
  ἐλθὼν ἔλεξε παιδὶ σῷ Ξέρξῃ τάδε,
  ὡς εἰ μελαίνης νυκτὸς ἵξεται κνέφας,
  Ἕλληνες οὐ μενοῖεν, ἀλλὰ σέλμασιν
  ναῶν ἐπανθορόντες ἄλλος ἄλλοσε
360 δρασμῷ κρυφαίῳ βίοτον ἐκσωσοίατο.
  ὁ δ' εὐθὺς ὡς ἤκουσεν, οὐ ξυνεὶς δόλον
  Ἕλληνος ἀνδρὸς οὐδὲ τὸν θεῶν φθόνον,
  πᾶσιν προφωνεῖ τόνδε ναυάρχοις λόγον,
  εὖτ' ἂν φλέγων ἀκτῖσιν ἥλιος χθόνα
365 λήξῃ, κνέφας δὲ τέμενος αἰθέρος λάβῃ
  τάξαι νεῶν στῖφος μὲν ἐν στοίχοις τρισὶν
  ἔκπλους φυλάσσειν καὶ πόρους ἁλιρρόθους,
  ἄλλας δὲ κύκλῳ νῆσον Αἴαντος πέριξ·

ὡς εἰ μόρον φευξοίαθ᾽ Ἕλληνες κακόν,
370 ναυσὶν κρυφαίως δρασμὸν εὑρόντες τινά,
πᾶσιν στέρεσθαι κρατὸς ἦν προκείμενον.

(Broadhead's text)

For a Greek man coming from the Athenian force
Said thus to your son Xerxes:
That if the darkness of black night should come
The Greeks would not stay, but leaping
To the benches of their ships, one here,
    another there,
Would save their lives in secret flight.
And the moment he heard this, not understanding
Greek cunning, nor the malice of gods,
To all his admirals he gave this command:
When Helios should cease from warming earth
With rays, and darkness seize the cloister of the sky
Then station a cordon of ships in three ranks
Guarding the exits and the wave lashed channels
And station others round about Ajax's isle.
If the Greeks should elude their evil fate,
Finding some hidden flight with boats,
All would lose their heads, it was decreed.

Lines 366-367 are subject to a number of different interpretations because στοίχοις is such an ambiguous word, but
it may simply refer to the stationing of the main body of
the fleet in the straits. According to the poet, they remained
there all night until they were attacked by the Greeks in
the morning (409), at which time their position was described: ὡς δὲ πλῆθος ἐν στενῷ νεῶν ἤθροιστ᾽ (413f.).
In spite of Hignett's stubborn rejection of the whole
episode, I do not think it is unreasonable to accept at least
the bare bones of this account: that a message was sent dis-
guised as a treasonous communication in order to lure the
Persians into the straits, and that the Persians did in fact

respond in two ways: (1) they sent most of their fleet into the straits during the night; (2) they sent a detachment around to the western strait, where a very few ships could hold the narrow passage against a multitude. This is certainly the meaning of *Pers.* 368. What Aeschylus does not reveal is whether only Themistocles, or all the Athenians, or even all the Greek generals were privy to the trick. The growing horror of the Persians described by the poet as dawn came and they gradually realized that the Greeks were not deserting but coming confidently out to fight (384-405) would seem to imply that the Greeks had never intended flight. This and other details will be discussed more fully in the commentary which follows.

12.2 ἀλλ' ἐπεὶ τῶν πολεμίων ὅ τε στόλος . . . αὐτός τε βασιλεὺς Plutarch's picture is an interpretation of Herodotus 8.69-70.1: Xerxes intended to watch this naval engagement himself; the command was given and the fleet was led out ἐπὶ Σαλαμῖνι. But the hour was late and they put off an attack until the next day.[13]

ἐξερρύησαν οἱ τοῦ Θεμιστοκλέους λόγοι τῶν Ἑλλήνων Following Herodotus 8.70.2: τοὺς δὲ Ἕλληνας εἶχε δέος τε καὶ ἀρρωδίη. Cf. Diod. XI 16.3. This traditional picture must have been highly unpopular among the Peloponnesians in later years; nevertheless, it became an indisputable part of the history of Salamis. The irresolution makes a dramatic contrast with the superb conduct of the Greeks once the battle started, and this may be one of the reasons Plutarch repeated the Herodotean tradition, despite his assertion elsewhere (*De Hdt.mal.* 856BC) that to impugn the motives for fighting is to detract from the glory of the victory. A second reason may be that Themistocles looks so much better if the allies are shown to be on the verge of slinking away.

12.3 ἔνθα δὴ βαρέως φέρων ὁ Θεμιστοκλῆς As in Herodotus 8.75: ἑσσοῦτο τῇ γνώμῃ ὑπὸ τῶν Πελοποννησίων, also Diod. XI 17.1. Aeschylus, in *Persae* 350ff., inferred that

---

[13] On this episode, see Roux, *BCH* 98 (1974) 57-60.

the mission of Sicinnus was from beginning to end a ruse
designed only to get the Persians into the straits. Divisiveness
among the allied Greek commanders he ignored, as was only
natural from his dramatic perspective. But according to
Herodotus, this was also a ruse to keep the Peloponnesians
at Salamis. Whether one believes this ruse was necessary
depends ultimately in the degree of one's faith in Herodotus.
Diodorus' source avoided much of the question by claiming
that the Peloponnesian commanders could no longer control their terror-stricken troops. Unfortunately, no one tells
us when the rest of the allies learned that the closing of the
straits was due to a stratagem of Themistocles; their reac-
tions would have been interesting. According to Herodotus
(8.80), Themistocles told Aristeides that he was responsible for the King's maneuver; did Aristeides inform the other
generals? Or did he and Themistocles wait until after the
ruse had proven successful? As to the allied reaction, the
only clue is that the Spartans later honored Themistocles
for σοφίη and δεξιότης (Hdt. 8.124), and the last word un-
questionably refers to the ruse which forced the Persians
to fight within the straits. If the Spartans so admired the
clever ruse of Themistocles, they were certainly not admitting that they themselves had been tricked by it into remaining at Salamis. In considering this episode, one should bear
in mind that much later, at the time Herodotus was writing
his history, (1) Athenians were quite ready to believe
stories of Peloponnesian cowardice, and (2) in the aftermath of Themistocles' flight to Persia, some people were unkind enough to suggest that Themistocles' private messages
to Xerxes had been equivocal all along.[14]

12.4 ἦν δὲ τῷ μὲν γένει Πέρσης ὁ Σίκιννος αἰχμάλωτος
According to Arrian, the original Sikinnis was a nymph of
Cybele, after whom the Phrygian dance was named.[15]
Others said the originator of the dance was a "barbarian"

[14] Hignett refused to believe the Sicinnus episode, *Xerxes' Invasion*
403-408; cf. Podlecki, *Themistocles* 22f.
[15] Eustathius, schol. *Il.* 16.617, *FGrH* 156 F 106.

named Sicinnus; some said he was Cretan (Athen. 630B). It is possible that Themistocles' servant was a Phrygian and may have known enough Persian to make him the obvious man for the mission. αἰχμάλωτος seems to be original with Plutarch; no other extant source suggests that he was a prisoner. Aeschylus' ἀνὴρ Ἕλλην (355) is of course correct from the perspective of his drama: a Persian messenger would call a Phrygian a Greek.

Herodotus (8.75) said Sicinnus was *paidagogos* to Themistocles' sons (the eclectic Polyaenus specifies τοῖν παίδοιν, I 30.3). If this is true, it implies that Themistocles' sons were in their early teens, and that he married sometime before Marathon. This is worth noting, no matter how tenuous the evidence, for we have so little testimony about the general's early life. Herodotus added that Themistocles had the city of Thespiae make Sicinnus a citizen after the war.[16] This seems to me to reinforce the credibility of the whole episode, as Sicinnus becomes much less anonymous (but note that Plutarch has turned to another source in 16.5).

The story of Sicinnus' mission is remarkable for the fidelity with which it was preserved and passed on by later authors. There were five essential elements in the story: (1) a man came to Xerxes from the Greeks; (2) he was Themistocles' servant, Sicinnus; (3) he said Themistocles was on Xerxes' side; (4) he said the Greeks were going to flee; (5) he urged Xerxes to fight while the Greeks were demoralized. Aeschylus established only points one and four. Herodotus filled in points two, three, and five. These two earliest authorities were followed by almost every later

---

[16] A point overlooked by the author of the *Letters* (4.8, p. 744 Hercher), who has Sicinnus still working for Cleophantus after Themistocles has gone into exile. Podlecki *Themistocles* 22 n. 23, draws our attention to Thespian *proxenoi*, one of them named Athenaeus, in mid-fifth century (*IG* i² 36) and a third-century Thespian named Themistocles (*SEG* 23 no. 271.85).

extant writer.[17] Diodorus (XI 17.1) followed a rather different tradition that said Themistocles persuaded "a certain
man" to desert and to tell Xerxes that the Greeks were
planning to retreat to the Isthmus. This Xerxes believed
"because it was credible" (17.2). In fact the whole narrative of Diodorus is seductively plausible and has therefore
been attributed to Ephorus, who thought that history ought
to make sense and was not above amending his sources to
make it do so.[18]

12.5 ταῦτα δ' ὁ Ξέρξης ὡς ἀπ' εὐνοίας λελεγμένα δεξάμενος (cf.
Arist. 8.2)
This may have been what Xerxes was waiting for—some
indication that there was a party among the Greeks intent on
betrayal. How did Sicinnus deliver the message? And why
was he not held by the Persians to test his good faith? He
certainly cannot have come ashore and delivered the message personally, as many of the later authorities imply, because Xerxes was surrounded by Athenian exiles, who would
have wanted to know exactly who had sent the message and
would probably have suggested that Sicinnus be interrogated
under torture to test his veracity. He probably shouted his
message from a boat and then, as Herodotus said, ἐκποδὼν
ἀπαλλάσετο—a good way of saying that he got away without wasting any time.

   Plutarch did not specify the nationality of the encircling
squadron, but he would seem to be following Diodorus'
source when he gives the number as two hundred.[19] Neither
Aeschylus Pers. 366-368) nor Herodotus (8.76.1) was clear
about the maneuvers ordered by Xerxes, nor it is probable

[17] Nepos, Them. 4.3; Justin II 12.19; Polyaenus I 30.3; Frontinus
II 2.14; Aristodemus 1.1; schol. Aristides III 178, 613.
   [18] J.A.R. Munro, "The Campaign of Xerxes," JHS 22 (1902)
329f., pace Hammond, JHS 76 (1956) 39 n. 26.
   [19] Diod. XI 17.2, described the encircling maneuver by the Egyptians; their numbers were given as two hundred, Diod. XI 3.7; Hdt.
7.89.

that anyone on the Greek side really knew. All movements during the night would have been undetected, except by Aristeides and the Tenian deserter (see below, comment to 12.8), who would have seen only parts of the Persian fleet guarding the straits. Not even Persian prisoners would have been particularly lucid about their own movements, if anyone bothered to question them. It is almost impossible to make out the contours of a surrounding shoreline at night, especially with thousands of small fires winking from both shores and distorting perspective.

12.6 Ἀριστείδης ὁ Λυσιμάχου πρῶτος αἰσθόμενος ἧκεν
As in *Arist.* 8.2. Both accounts followed Herodotus (8.79, 81): Aristeides came sailing through the enemy ships on his way back from Aegina. Although Aristeides was supposed to have spent his exile in Aegina ([Demosth.] 26.6; Aristodemus 1.4), this was not his return, which had been decreed much earlier (see above, comment to 11.1). It has often been suggested that he was returning from a specific mission, the fetching of the Aeacidae.[20] That he was able to penetrate the Persian blockade need not be disbelieved. A single ship would not have the problem facing a large contingent. Or he may simply have landed at one of the small coves on the eastern coast of Salamis and continued overland.[21]

12.6-7 προελθόντι δὲ τῷ Θεμιστοκλεῖ φράζει τὴν κύκλωσιν
The account is a faithful, if abbreviated, rendering of Herodotus 8.79-81 (as is *Arist.* 8.3-5). Hignett's disbelief (*Xerxes' Invasion* 408ff.) was based on a too exact interpretation of the rest of Herodotus' narrative. It is true that the details of what Aristeides and Themistocles said to each other may well have been amplified and improved by He-

[20] J. B. Bury, *CR* 10 (1896) 418; Burn, *Persia and the Greeks* 454; Calabi Limentani, *Vita Arist.* ad 8.2; see the discussion in How and Wells ad 8.79.

[21] In Hdt. 8.81, Aristeides admitted that he was able to sail through unseen only with difficulty. This is another of the stories disbelieved by Hignett, *Xerxes' Invasion* 408-411.

rodotus' day. But it is difficult to see why anyone should
have invented Aristeides' dramatic appearance before the
council of commanders to report that the island was surrounded. His appearance must have been memorable for
exactly the reason Herodotus gives: he was known to be
an enemy of Themistocles and yet he was now telling the
allied command that the strategy urged upon them over
and over by his foe had become inevitable. It is this theme:
deadly enemies laying down their vendetta to face the common peril, that later writers loved to retell.[22]

12.8 Ὁ μὲν οὖν Ἀριστείδης ἐπαινέσας τὸν Θεμιστοκλέα τοὺς
ἄλλους ἐπῄει στρατηγοὺς καὶ τριηράρχους

It was said that the commanders would believe Aristeides
rather than Themistocles (Hdt. 8.80). In *Arist.* 8.6, Plutarch introduces to the debate a certain Corinthian named
Cleocritus, who appears again as a wise statesman in *Arist.*
20.2. This man appears nowhere else in extant Greek literature and is our only evidence that Plutarch was following
sources other than Herodotus here.

ἐφάνη Τενεδία τριήρης αὐτόμολος

Τενεδία is a *lapsus calami* for Τηνία but it is what Plutarch
wrote and therefore should not be emended (as correctly
noted by Flacelière in his Budé edition). That Plutarch
was following Herodotus' story of the Tenian ship is proven
by the fact that he has the captain's name correct (Hdt.
8.82). Once again, Diodorus has followed a conflicting
source. He claimed that the Ionian leaders sent a Samian
deserter swimming to Salamis with information about the
Persian fleet movements and a promise that the Ionians
would change sides during the battle. This may be an attempt of Ephorus to make his fellow Ionians look better, as
Herodotus had specifically reported that the Ionians fought
well for their Persian master (8.85). But if Diodorus was
following Ephorus in this passage (XI 17.3), he ignored

[22] Aristodemus 1.4; Aristides II 258-259; schol. ad loc. III 613f.;
Polyaenus I 31; schol. Lucian, *Calum. non tem.cred.* 27.

his account subsequently, for nowhere in the rest of the description of the battle is anything said about the conduct of the Ionians. That the Tenians fought on the Greek side seems indicated by their appearance (possibly as an afterthought) on the war memorial set up at Delphi.[23]

13.1 Ἅμα δ' ἡμέρα Ξέρξης μὲν ἄνω καθῆστο

We must assume that Xerxes had been waiting all night to be informed that the Greeks were attempting to break out of the straits. Since nothing of the sort happened, he probably concluded that his ambush had been detected and that the Greeks were too craven to test its strength. Believing his enemy demoralized and defeatist, he will then have ordered his fleet into the narrow waters of the strait. Plutarch gives two reports of the site where Xerxes and his entourage gathered. Phanodemus (FGrH 325 F 24) cited the Heracleion, "where the island was separated from Attica by a narrow channel." Neither Aeschylus (Pers. 465-467) nor Herodotus (8.90) mention a specific location (possibly for the reason that Xerxes had not established one in advance, see below). Among extant writers, the first to mention the Heracleion was Ctesias (26) and he certainly meant the southwestern point of this mountainous spur of Attica, although the very fact he said so is enough to cast doubt on it. The same identification was made by Diodorus (XI 18.2) and Aristodemus (1.2) and is usually accepted by modern authors.[24]

Acestodorus, on the other hand, placed Xerxes' seat on one of the Kerata, on the Megarid border. Acestodorus may be identified as a writer of Περὶ πόλεων from Megalopolis.[25]

[23] Paus. V 23.2; Meiggs and Lewis, GHI no. 27.7, with critical note on the late addition of the Tenians.

[24] How and Wells ad 8.90.4; Hammond, JHS 76 (1956) 38; Pritchett, SAGT I 101, are representative.

[25] Steph.Byz. s.v. Megalopolis, cf. s.v. Dodonê in Mueller, FHG II 464. He was cited for the early history of Eleusis by the scholiast to Soph. Oed.Col. 1053 (with Ister, FGrH 334 F 22).

The Kerata are prominent twin peaks, quite obvious to the motorist on the Corinth-Athens highway. It has been suggested that if Xerxes thought the Greeks might flee through the bay of Eleusis, he might have ordered a vantage point set up on the Kerata, where he would have a magnificent view of the entire bay.[26] This explanation makes sense of an otherwise meaningless bit of information, but as in so many cases, this does not make it inevitably the correct explanation (see, for instance, Burn, *Persia and the Greeks* 460 n. 24).

χρυσοῦν δίφρον

It is difficult to find a modern author who does not translate this word as "throne," thus giving a picture of a massive seat of some kind.[27] But if I am not mistaken, the *diphros* was the stool customarily used by Persian monarchs to descend from their chariots, described by Dinon, who knew about such things:[28] "whenever the King gets out of his chariot, he neither jumps down, although it is not far from the ground, nor is he supported by his arms; instead, a golden stool (χρυσοῦς δίφρος) is always placed for him and he gets down by stepping on this.[29]

This makes more sense than a throne (a real *thronos* was mentioned among ancient writers only by Libanius, *Declam.* 9.39 and Tzetzes, *Chil.* I 978). Although confident of victory, Xerxes could not be exactly sure where the most exciting part of the action would take place. He obviously intended to drive in his chariot from one location to another as need be, with his flock of secretaries following to record such events as he should require (Hdt. 8.90.4). For some reason, the stool was left behind and was set up on the

[26] Hammond, *JHS* 76 (1956) 52 n. 83.

[27] Including this author, Bauer-Frost, *Themistocles* 123; most recently, Roux, *BCH* 98 (1974) 85f. Podlecki avoided the mistake in *Aeschylus' Persians* (Englewood Cliffs, 1970) ad v. 466.

[28] In Athen. 514AB, *FGrH* 690 F 26. On Dinon's competence in Persian matters, see Nepos, *Conon* 5.2.

[29] See my remarks in "A Note on Xerxes at Salamis," *Historia* 22 (1973) 118f.

acropolis, whence it was pilfered in the fourth century (Demosth. 24.129). A stool makes more sense in this context as well; one does not idly walk off with a golden throne.

13.2-5 Θεμιστοκλεῖ δὲ παρὰ τὴν ναυαρχίδα τριήρη σφαγιαζομένῳ τρεῖς προσήχθησαν αἰχμάλωτοι

The fact that the attack on Psyttaleia by Aristeides (*Arist.* 9.1-2) with the consequent capture of these prisoners is said by Plutarch to have occurred *before* the battle of Salamis is enough to condemn this story out of hand, as it flatly contradicts the accounts of Aeschylus (*Pers.* 447ff.) and Herodotus (8.95) both in general and in some particulars.[30] Plutarch cites the story from Phanias of Eresos (fr. 25 Wehrli) and repeats it again in a list of human sacrifices (*Pelop.* 21.3). The story probably allowed him to attribute to Themistocles what we assume was his own attitude to such barbaric practices (see *Pelop.* 21.5-6).

Some elements of the story may come from the source of Diodorus XI 57, where it is said that the sister of Xerxes (Mandane, instead of Plutarch's Sandace) begged the King to punish Themistocles as responsible for the death of her sons at Salamis (but there is no inference in Diodorus that their death resulted from anything but the ordinary fighting).[31] The omen of the sneeze may have come down from an expanded version of the mantic tradition (see above, comment to 10.10). Sneezes were significant omens, as had been discovered by Demeter (Philochorus, *FGrH* 328 F 192abc).[32]

[30] Aeschylus and Herodotus both said all the Persians were killed; cf. Paus. I 36.2. According to Hdt. 9.120, Artayctes (who Plutarch said was the prisoners' father) was later crucified by the Athenians at the Hellespont and his son stoned to death before his eyes.

[31] On Plutarch's source, see L. Bodin, "Histoire et biographie: Phanias d'Erèse," *REG* 30 (1917) 118-123.

[32] Perrin, *Plutarch's Themistocles* 210, notes other famous sneezes in *Od.* 17.541 sq. and Xen. *Anab.* III 2.9; cf. Calabi Limentani, *Vita Arist.* ad 9.1-5; Burn, *Persia and the Greeks* 474f.

14.1 Περὶ δὲ τοῦ πλήθους τῶν βαρβαρικῶν νεῶν Αἰσχύλος . . . λέγει ταῦτα

The usually reliable Seitenstettensis MS has the following:

Ξέρξης δὲ, καὶ γὰρ οἶδα, χιλιὰς μὲν νη-
ῶν ἦγε πλῆθος κτλ.

But the lines of Aeschylus which Plutarch purported to cite are:

Ξέρξῃ δὲ, καὶ γὰρ οἶδα, χιλιὰς μὲν ἦν
ὧν ἦγε πλῆθος κτλ.

Modern editors tend to restore the text from Aeschylus, assuming that a copyist has made the mistake. But it is entirely in character for Plutarch to quote the classical authors incorrectly from memory.[33]

Both Aeschylus and Herodotus agreed on the number 1207, which has a nice, exact sound to it. But numbers over a few hundred seem to have been almost meaningless to the Greeks, and it is therefore useless to subject ancient testimony to searching analysis. As How and Wells point out (II p. 365), six hundred seems to be a conventional number for a *normal* Persian naval expedition (Hdt. 4.87, 6.9, 6.95.2, to which I would add Phanodemus, in Plut. *Cimon* 12.6, *FGrH* 325 F 22). Twelve hundred may simply reflect a tendency of even our earliest sources to double the usual number of ships for this extraordinary expedition. On the other hand, prisoners, or Ionian defectors may have reported the number they had been told, soon after the battle. Aeschylus' messenger has been criticized for recording the original number of the ships, as they were enumerated at Doriscus (Hdt. 7.89-95) instead of the number left when they arrived at Phaleron after two storms and heavy action

[33] The reading of the tripartite recension of Plutarch is μὲν ἦν νεῶν τὸ πλῆθος, which should perhaps be preferred.

at Artemision. But I believe the drama allowed Aeschylus to give the largest possible number. After all, the Athenian audience knew what had happened to the Persian fleet on its way south; they also knew that they had been badly outnumbered at Salamis.

Herodotus seems to have accepted Aeschylus' number as the total of the undiminished fleet (7.89, 184), breaking it down into ethnic contingents on the basis of we know not what evidence. After accounting for Persian losses—four hundred in the storm off Sepias (7.190), two hundred on the lee shore of Euboea (8.13), and battle losses at Artemision, which were something greater than thirty (8.11; 8.16)—he said that God intended the Persians to be reduced to near equality with the Greeks (8.13). But on the eve of Salamis, the historian has forgotten God's thoughtfulness, saying that new additions to both fleet and army had brought up the totals to what they had been (8.66). This is patently absurd—the new contingents from medizing states certainly did not contribute anything remotely near six hundred ships.[34]

14.2 τῶν δ' Ἀττικῶν ἑκατὸν ὀγδοήκοντα

Aeschylus said 310 (*Pers.* 339f.) for the whole Greek fleet. Herodotus gave an allied total of 380, of which the Athenians furnished 180 (8.44). Two hundred Attic ships seems to be an unshakable number in Herodotus (or 180, with the Chalcidians manning an additional twenty, 8.1, 46) a number that always remains the same from the time of the Naval Bill (7.144) to Salamis, despite battle losses or new additions (cf. 8.1, 14, 44, 46, 61); this sort of tabulation creates difficulties. Thucydides (I 74.1) said the Athenians furnished

---

[34] See the analysis of How and Wells ad 8.66.2; Roux, *BCH* 98 (1974) 54-57. Most modern critics resort to the *histoire raisonée* approach to Persian numbers: How and Wells, II 364ff.; Hignett, 345, both whittling the Persian fleet down to about six hundred; Hammond, *JHS* 76 (1956) 40f., and Roux, *BCH* 98 (1974) 57, accept Aeschylus' numbers at face value.

two-thirds of a total of about four hundred, a number often emended to three hundred.[35]

There are a number of other difficulties with the Greek tally. For instance, Herodotus gave a complete muster of allied triremes in 8.43-48; he said the total was 378, but when the various items are added up, they come to only 366. It is uncertain if there is some peculiar sort of Herodotean arithmetic involved here (How and Wells, comment to 8.46.1). Even if the number is approximate, it is still far too large to agree with Aeschylus. Roux has proposed that Aeschylus counted only the ships that fought in the straits, thus subtracting the 46 Peloponnesian ships that guarded the bay of Eleusis;[36] I must admit to a certain impatience with attempts to reckon either the Persian or Greek fleets too precisely, as it is obviously an impossible job. Just as one example, nobody ever seems to consider the use of repaired triremes which had been rammed—including triremes captured from the enemy. Timotheus (*Persae* PBerol 9875, line 16) referred to a temporary expedient during battle—πλευρὰς λινοζώστους ὕφαινον—and there must have been a number of ways to patch triremes if they had not been holed too badly.

τοὺς ἀπὸ καταστρώματος μαχομένους

I follow Jameson in believing that the earliest testimony to marines at Salamis is the Themistocles Decree, lines 23-24, 25-26: καταλέξαι δὲ καὶ ἐπιβάτας δέκα [ἐφ' ἑκάστη]ν ναῦν . . . καὶ τοξότας τέτταρας.[37] But one must remember that this plan was published some three months before the battle of Salamis and therefore is not really evidence for what actually happened. Plutarch's figure—fourteen hoplites and four archers—is the only other piece of testimony, and there is no way of telling where he got his information.

[35] Gomme, *HCT* I 234f., with other references.
[36] *BCH* 98 (01974) 54f.; cf. Broadhead ad *Pers.* 339.
[37] M. Jameson, "Provisions for Mobilization in the Decree of Themistokles," *Historia* 12 (1963) 397f.

What we must *not* do is estimate the number of marines
from the numbers given for other battles and then claim
that this was the conventional number. Salamis was an
extraordinary effort and if there was in fact a rulebook, it
was doubtless sacrificed to the course of events. Early
Greek naval warfare seems to have involved large numbers
of marines (Hdt. 6.15), but Thucydides said that Athenian
triremes were not yet decked over at the time of the Persian
Wars (I 14.3) and it might have been difficult to get more
than fourteen non-rowers on board.

14.3 Δοκεῖ δ' οὐχ ἧττον εὖ τὸν καιρὸν ὁ Θεμιστοκλῆς ἢ τὸν τόπ'ον
συνιδὼν καὶ φυλάξας

Plutarch is the earliest authority for this story: Themistocles
chose the exact time at which a sea breeze would begin to
blow and waves would throw the Phoenician ships into confusion. Aelius Aristides and his commentators had also
picked up the tale, and the orator was reminded (II 282)
of Phormion's similar use of the wind off Patras in 429—
the classical instance (Thuc. II 84). But Phormion's stratagem may in fact have been attributed to Themistocles by
later enthusiastic embroiderers of the Themistocles romance.
The scholiast (III 647) was reminded of the myth of Boreas,
who was supposed to aid the Athenians, and he adds, "but
Herodotus does not mention this." Not at Salamis, it is true,
but Herodotus did in fact say that the Athenians invoked
Boreas before the battle of Artemision (7.189). The assistance of the North Wind was probably first commemorated by Simonides in his poem on Artemision[38] and the
poet may have added the detail that the Athenians were
instructed to sacrifice to Boreas by Themistocles.[39]

At any rate, the story is incredible, although Roux seems
to believe it (*BCH* 98, 84). For one thing, it is impossible
to predict weather with any degree of certainty anywhere

[38] Schol. Ap.Rhod. I 211; Podlecki, *Historia* 17 (1968) 262ff.
[39] Aelian, *NA* 7.27; cf. *Anth.Pal.* 9.296 and my comment in "Scyl-
lias: Diving in Antiquity," *Greece and Rome* 15 (1968) 180 n. 4.

in the Aegean, as any yachtsman will attest. For another, Plutarch's conception of wind and wave affecting Persians more than Greeks (and thereby the whole point of the story) is based on a false impression of the difference between these ships: ὅ τὰς μὲν Ἑλληνικὰς οὐκ ἔβλαπτε ναῦς ἁλιτενεῖς οὔσας καὶ ταπεινοτέρας. This directly contradicts Herodotus (8.60), who said the Greeks were heavier and (8.10) that the Persians had ships that handled better (cf. Hignett, *Xerxes' Invasion* 233). It is worth repeating the acute remark of W. W. Tarn about the biographer: that he seems to have believed as a general principle that "the just cause must have the smaller ships."[40] The confusion of the Persian ships is easily explained by excessive numbers in a confined channel (*Pers.* 413ff.; Diod. XI 18.4).

ὁ Ξέρξου ναύαρχος Ἀριαμένης
"A mythical figure conflated from Xerxes' full brother Achaimenes and his half-brother Ariabignes, both of whom were among the four admirals of the fleet at Salamis" (Hignett, *Xerxes' Invasion* 233). According to Herodotus (7.97) there were four admirals (the historian used the term *strategoi*; Aeschylus, *nauarchoi*) who seem to have been equal in rank: Ariabignes was killed in the battle, commanding the Asian Greeks (8.89). But he was not mentioned by Aeschylus and it may be a measure of Greek ignorance about Persian personnel that of all the noble Persians listed in the death roll in *Persae* 303-326, only two are mentioned at all by Herodotus, and it is by no means certain that they are the same people: Arsames (*Pers.* 308; Hdt. 7.69) and Ariomardus (*Pers.* 321; Hdt. 7.67, 78). Syennesis the Cilician was recorded by both (*Pers.* 326; Hdt. 7.98) but *all* Cilician kings were named Syennesis, so there was no way the two writers could come up with different names.

Ariamenes is not a mistake of Plutarch's, as Hignett thought, but the hero of a romance from the noble Persian literature that sprang up in the wake of Xenophon's success

[40] "The Fleet of Xerxes," *JHS* 28 (1908) 208 n. 28.

with the *Cyropaedia*. Plutarch tells the story in more detail in *De frat.amore* 488C-F, leading us to suspect the existence of an even longer version. At Darius' death, Ariamenes was a rival for the throne which Xerxes claimed (see Herodotus' version of the story, 7.2-3, where the rival was named Artobazanes). But when Xerxes was adjudged the rightful ruler, Ariamenes embraced him and personally set him on the throne. Ever after, Ariamenes was Xerxes' most loyal supporter and he died performing great deeds at Salamis. This tale is known only from Plutarch, but Justin also knew the name Ariamenes (spelled Ariaemenes, II 10.2) as a son of Darius.

Unfortunately, both Herodotus' and Plutarch's versions of the tale are pure fantasy. Persian inscriptions show that Xerxes had been officially declared crown prince as early as 498.[41]

14.5 'Αμεινίας ὁ Δεκελεὺς καὶ Σωκλῆς ὁ Πειραιεύς (πειραιεύς Sintenis: πελιεύς, πεδιεύς codd: Παλληνεύς Hdt.)
Herodotus said (8.84, 93) that Ameinias of Pallene was the first to attack and that he was adjudged one of the heroes of Salamis. The historian later recorded Sophanes of Dekelea as the hero of Plataea (9.73). The appearance of these easily confused names and demotics in the early tradition has naturally invited frequent emendation. Kirchner, *PA* 683, thought Plutarch might have been thinking of Sophanes. Flacelière (Budé ed. ad loc.) suggests that Plutarch has transposed the demotics of Ameinias and Socles.

Diodorus (XI 27.2) added the detail that Ameinias was Aeschylus' brother, and he was probably following the same tradition as Plutarch when he claimed that Ameinias killed the Persian admiral. Diodorus is thus the earliest extant writer to identify Aeschylus' brother in this manner, but the tradition was strong by Plutarch's day[42] and we wonder that

---

[41] Cited by A. T. Olmstead, *History of the Persian Empire* (Chicago, 1948; rev. ed. 1959) 215f.

[42] Aelian, *VH* 5.19; *Vita Aesch.* p. 118 Westermann; Aristodemus 1.3; *Them. Letter* 11 p. 751 Hercher.

the biographer did not mention it. But Aeschylus was from the deme Eleusis and his brother would probably not have been old enough at the time of the reforms of Cleisthenes to establish a separate residence in another deme. The problem is most easily resolved by assuming that since the poet's older brother had died at Marathon after distinguishing himself (Hdt. 6.114), the temptation to involve another brother at Salamis was too great to resist. Aelian (*VH* 5.19) even lopped off one of his hands, to match the unfortunate Cynegeirus.

Socles is also mentioned as the first Athenian to ram an enemy ship by the scholiast to Aristides (III 179; Socles BD: Sophilus AC) but this may only mean that the scholiast had read his Plutarch.

καὶ τὸ σῶμα

The end of the Ariamenes romance, called an archetype of brotherly love by Plutarch (*Frat.amore* 489A). But one would think that even the moderate amount of armor worn by Persians would have taken Ariamenes to the bottom like a stone.

15.1-2 Ἐν δὲ τούτῳ τοῦ ἀγῶνος ὄντος φῶς μὲν ἐκλάμψαι μέγα λέγουσιν Ἐλευσινόθεν

This was a famous portent in antiquity and it is curious that Aeschylus, who otherwise emphasized the role of the gods at Salamis (*Pers.* 345-347, 354), did not even hint at the presence of Eleusinian allies. In Herodotus' story (8.65), the portent was seen by two Greek exiles, Dicaeus the Athenian and Demaratus the Spartan, and they concealed its significance from the Persians. It is possible that the story was not yet current at Athens when the *Persae* was produced and that Herodotus heard it much later from informants who had been with the Persian side. Another explanation that must at least be considered is that Aeschylus, although from the deme Eleusis, seems never to have been initiated into the Mysteries. He is supposed to have gotten into trouble by inadvertently revealing a forbidden thing in a drama[43] and perhaps wished to avoid misunderstanding by even hinting at the presence of Iacchus at Salamis.

Whereas Herodotus placed the omen on an unspecified day before the battle, Plutarch said the battle had actually started. Elsewhere (*Phoc.* 28.2; *Cam.* 19.10) he dated the great Iacchus procession to 20 Boedromion, but epigraphical evidence points to the nineteenth.[44] I do not believe the discrepancy between Plutarch's and Herodotus' dating is significant; the most serious disagreement was over the course taken by the cloud. The historian said it was seen and understood only by Dicaeus and Demaratus. But Plutarch said that the cloud came down to the scene of the battle and that in the midst of the cloud were to be seen the shapes of the Aeacidae, who had been invited from Aegina (Hdt. 8.64). Perhaps the proximity of the Aeacidae incident and the cloud incident in the account of Herodotus was responsible for their later combination in the popular tradition. And Plutarch's version is no doubt based on popular tradition, for which no "source" need be sought. This is confirmed by the attribution "they say" and by the host of other authors who had heard some variation of the tale.[45]

At the risk of seeming to offer rational explanations like Ephorus, I might add that the plain around Eleusis, bone-dry at summer's end, is a natural dust bowl because of the

[43] Arist. *Eth.Nic.* III 1.17 and schol. ad loc. quoting Heracleides Pont., *Comm. Arist. Graeca* XX p. 145. Several lost plays are suggested, but the *Oedipus*, which is the only one which can be dated, was produced after the *Persae*, in 468; see arg. Aesch. *Sept.*; schol. Soph. *OT* 733.

[44] *Syll.*[3]885.19 and see the discussion of chronology following comment to 10.10.

[45] Xen. *Symp.* 8.40; Paus. I 36.1 (who added a serpent to the figures in the cloud); Polyaenus III 11.2; Aristodemus 1.8; schol. Ar. *Nub.* 304 (citing Hdt.); Libanius, *Orat.* 30.32; Aristides I 231, schol. ad loc. III 185; II 282, schol. ad loc. III 648. In III 185, the scholiast said that Dicaeus explained the omen to Xerxes, ignoring Herodotus' far more probable and memorable warning (8.65.4-5): "if these words should be carried to the King, he will strike off your head."

effects of the surrounding hills on the winds. It is not unusual today to see whirlwinds whipping the dust hundreds
of feet into the air.

15.3 πρῶτος μὲν οὖν λαμβάνει ναῦν Λυκομήδης
Herodotus (8.11) said that Lycomedes, son of Aeschraeus,
was the first to take a ship—but at Artemision, not Salamis.
The historian said that Ameinias took the first ship in the
latter battle (see above, comment to 14.4). I quote the sensi-
ble judgment of Flacelière (Budé ed. ad loc.): "je crois que
Plutarque avait vu de ses yeux à Phlyées ce sanctuaire et le
Δαφνηφορεῖον (cf. Athenée 10, 24, p. 424F) où se trouvaient
les παράσημα offerts par Lycomédès, sans doute avec une in-
scription où l'on lisait, par exemple: ἀνέθηκεν ἀπὸ Μήδων."
Athenaeus, in the passage cited, quoted from Theophras-
tus *On Drunkeness* concerning the dances at the shrine of
Apollo Daphnephorus. On Plutarch's familiarity with the
Lycomid shrine in Phlya, see comment to 1.4.[46]

15.4 οἱ δ' ἄλλοι τοῖς βαρβάροις ἐξισούμενοι τὸ πλῆθος ἐν στενῷ
One may compare *Pers.* 413f.: ὡς δὲ πλῆθος ἐν στενῷ νεῶν
ἤθροιστ' without concluding that Plutarch consciously copied
the phrase. The confusion of the action is attested by the
shortness of all accounts, Aeschylus being content with sixty
lines; Herodotus with eight short chapters; Plutarch here
with less than an octavo page. No attempts to explain the
course of the fighting can really be satisfactory: e.g., how
did Athenian and Ionian ships, posted on opposite wings
(Hdt. 8.85) eventually come in contact (8.87)? For those
who wish such explanations, I may recommend the account
of Peter Green, *Xerxes at Salamis* 186-196, as the archetype
of enthusiastic, if speculative, battle reporting; second, the
admirable article of N. Whatley, "On the Possibility of
Reconstructing Marathon and Other Ancient Battles," *JHS*
84 (1964) 119-139; and finally, for those with the nerve to
go on, the accounts of Hammond, *JHS* 76 (1956) 45-53,
and Hignett, *Xerxes' Invasion* 230-239 (and the older litera-

---

[46] On his relations with the Lycomids, see W. R. Connor, *Historia*
21 (1972) 569-574.

ture cited therein). On balance, the recent reconstruction by Roux, *BCH* 98 (1974) 70ff. and figure 4, strikes me as most sensible but it is no less speculative; the evidence for a sound reconstruction is simply not there.

ὥσπερ εἴρηκε Σιμωνίδης

Probably in the *Seafight at Salamis*, cited by the Ambrosian *Vita Pindaris* (p. 98.37 Westermann) and ambiguously by the *Suda* s.v. Simonides: γέγραπται αὐτῷ . . . Ξέρξου ναυμαχία καὶ ἡ ἐπ' Ἀρτεμισίῳ ναυμαχία δι' ἐλεγείας, ἡ δ' ἐν Σαλαμῖνι μελικῶς. It is often assumed first, that since surviving fragments of *The Seafight off Artemision* are in fact in lyric verses (Priscian, *De metris Terenti* 2.428, frs 1 and 2, Bergk), the lexicographer has reversed meters and therefore the Salamis poem was actually elegiac; second, that the "Seafight of Xerxes" and that of Salamis are actually the same poem under two different titles.[47]

The difficulty is that nothing that follows Plutarch's attribution to Simonides here is in any kind of meter, lyric or elegiac, except for a few disjointed phrases. This would seem peculiar, considering Plutarch's frequent verbatim citation of Simonides in the *De Herodoti malignitate*.[48]

16.1 Μετὰ δὲ τὴν ναυμαχίαν Ξέρξης μὲν ἔτι θυμομαχῶν
This directly contradicts Herodotus (8.97), who said that Xerxes had already made up his mind to flee and was using the mole as a ruse only to delay pursuit. A third version of the story was offered by Ctesias (26), whom Strabo is probably following (IX 1.13), who said the King had attempted to build a mole *before* the battle. Aristodemus (1.2) also put the attempt before the battle but specified a bridge of boats rather than a mole. The testimony of Herodotus must be preferred here simply on the basis of priority; he would certainly have heard from eyewitnesses the

[47] Podlecki, *Historia* 17 (1968) 266ff.
[48] Five passages in 870E-871A; also 872D, 873B. See Flacelière, Budé ed. ad loc.

description of the mole and the relative date of its construction. As for the mole being only a ruse, however, we should be more cautious and put this in that collection of passages where Herodotus claims to know what went on in the minds of great men.

If for no other reason, Plutarch would have maintained here that Xerxes was still looking for a fight because in his narrative it is Themistocles' subsequent stratagem that dissuaded the King (see comment to 16.2-4).

A hundred years ago, it would have been easy to investigate the existence of a mole—or even the beginnings of one. But at the narrowest point of the Salamis straits, extensive modern construction has effectively eliminated any possible traces.[49]

16.2-4 Θεμιστοκλῆς δ' ἀποπειρώμενος Ἀριστείδου λόγῳ
The same account is seen in *Arist.* 9.5; briefly in *Apophth. Them.* 6, 185B. Curiously, Herodotus was nearly alone in his version of the events both preceding and following the debate over the Hellespont bridges, possibly because of the complexity of the situation, or because later writers could not remember whether Themistocles was pulling off a double-cross or a triple-cross. The historian listed events in the following order:

1. Xerxes, after conferring with Mardonius and Artemisia, had already resolved on withdrawal of most of his forces.

2. The allies pursued the remnants of the Persian fleet as far as Andros.

3. Themistocles, as energetic and imaginative as ever, proposed the destruction of the bridges at Abydos, probably fascinated by the idea of utterly exterminating the barbarian forces.

4. Eurybiades and the Peloponnesian admirals disagreed, offering the "trapped-rat" theory (and possibly thinking of the 250-mile row to the Hellespont with the northern winds of autumn in their faces).

[49] Photos in Pritchett, *SAGT I* plates 90-91.

5. Themistocles then returned to the Athenian contingent, which was still thirsting for vengeance against Xerxes, and used Eurybiades' arguments to dissuade them. His plan, once he saw his original proposal fail, was to turn the situation to his own advantage.

6. This he did by sending Sicinnus and others to Xerxes to say that he had prevented the Greeks from destroying the bridges (Hdt. 8.100-103, 108-110).

This is a complicated series of events; if later writers omitted or reversed any one of the stages, the point was either lost or changed.

The earliest witness to any part of this was Thucydides, quoting Themistocles' letter to Artaxerxes after his flight to Asia, in which the general reminded the King of his good-will in warning the King of (1) the flight of the allies before Salamis, and (2) his prevention of the expedition to destroy the bridges, for which he falsely claimed credit (I 137.4): καὶ μοι εὐεργεσία ὀφείλεται (γράψας τήν τε ἐκ Σαλαμῖνος προάγγελσιν τῆς ἀναχωρήσεως καὶ τὴν τῶν γεφυρῶν, ἣν ψευδῶς προσεποιήσατο, τότε δι' αὐτὸν οὐ διάλυσιν, κτλ).[50] Thucydides also seems to be the source for POxy 1610 fr. 1, 7-12: λέ]γουσι δ' οἱ μὲν ὅ[τι ὑπέ]μνησεν αὐτ[ὸν ὧν] περί τε τῆς ν[αυμα]χίας καὶ τῆς γ[εφύρας προ]ήγγειλε.[51]

Chronologically the next writer to mention the affair, and to begin to confuse it, was Aeschines Socraticus, as quoted by Aristides (II 293). He evidently claimed that it was the Athenians whom Themistocles tried to talk into destroying the bridges. Diodorus came even closer to the story as it was eventually reported by Plutarch: Xerxes was not yet convinced of his defeat, but Themistocles sent him a message to the effect that the allies were going to

[50] This is sometimes translated to mean only the latter message: ". . . the warning to retreat which he had sent from Salamis and of the preservation of the bridges," vel sim., but I agree with Gomme, HCT I ad loc. that both messages were meant.

[51] Modern editors persist in calling this Ephorus, but see T.W. Africa, AJP 88 (1962) 86-89.

destroy the bridges; therefore Xerxes was afraid and evacuated most of his army (XI 19.5-6). This is the general theme of Plutarch's story, but some of the details are different, particularly in the *Aristeides* (9.6) where Themistocles told Xerxes that he had *prevented* the allies from destroying the bridges, but (10.1) Xerxes became frightened and retreated swiftly anyway. The general impression is that Plutarch is not being too careful of the details: what was important to him in the *Aristeides* was to show off that statesman's good advice; in the *Themistocles*, he will show that by following that advice, Themistocles reduced the enormous Persian armament still left in Greece.[52]

16.5 ἔπεμπέ τινα τῶν βασιλικῶν εὐνούχων ἐν τοῖς αἰχμαλώτοις ἀνευρὼν Ἀρνάκην ὄνομα

According to Herodotus (8.110), Themistocles sent from Andros a bunch of hardened adventurers, headed once more by Sicinnus, who is beginning to look like much more than your ordinary *paidagogos*. We find this group later working as Themistocles' secret agents in extorting protection money from the islanders who had medized (8.112). Diodorus seemed to agree on the identity of the agent as Themistocles' *paidagogos* (XI 19.5), as did Justin (II 13.5): *eundem servum ad Xerxem mittit*. Polyaenus specified "another eunuch, Arsaces (I 30.4; the variant spelling is not significant), which would indicate that he is following Plutarch's source. There were many traditions involved here; the one followed by the biographer was implicitly set on Salamis after the battle, rather than on Andros, as Herodotus had said. This should not be surprising when we see later (21.1-2) how badly the biographer has misdated the expedition to Andros.

16.6 καὶ πεῖραν ἡ Θεμοστοκλέους καὶ Ἀριστείδου φρόνησις ἐν Μαρδονίῳ παρέσχεν

The wisdom of Themistocles and Aristeides (in getting

[52] See also Diod. XI 19.5-6; 59.3; Frontinus, *Strat.* II 6.8; Aristodemus 1.7; Nepos, *Them.* 5; Justin II 13.5; Polyaenus I 30, 4; schol. Aristides III 615.

Xerxes out of Greece) was proved by Mardonius, who with such a reduced armament still put the Greeks to the extreme test. This was the logic which evidently led Plutarch to accept this particular variation of the mission to Xerxes. The point is completely different from that made by Herodotus and it would be nice to know when the story was invented. In my opinion, Herodotus' story rings true, as fantastic as it may seem to some scholars. This merits a short discussion.

Many modern writers have seen the story of the second mission of Sicinnus as an attempt to discredit Themistocles, put about by his enemies at Athens and taken at face value by Herodotus (How and Wells ad 8.110; Hignett, *Xerxes' Invasion* 241f.). Various difficulties are proposed: how did Sicinnus, starting from Andros, find Xerxes still in Attica? (Hignett); or, "it is certainly odd that Xerxes should again accept advice from Themistocles when Sicinnus' first message had had such disastrous results" (How and Wells). To the first objection it can be said that the timing is by no means unreasonable. The Greeks could have reached Andros two days after the battle; a fast boat could sail back in something over twelve hours (based on average speeds of modern sailing yachts), and Herodotus said that Xerxes stayed in Attica "a few days" (8.113).

Because of the various deceits intended by Themistocles, we are operating on so many reality levels that it is difficult enough to state the problems, let alone solve them. But Themistocles certainly was the best judge of the circumstances; he would not have sent Sicinnus again to Xerxes unless he thought he still had credibility with the King, and this is not such a hard thing to imagine. For Xerxes did not necessarily know that he had been tricked into entering the straits. The King acted on Sicinnus' first message believing it to be an offer of betrayal by Themistocles and knowing that such treachery was typical of Greeks. But against all expectations the Greeks had fought desperately while Xerxes' own fleet had behaved like women—οἱ μὲν ἄνδρες γεγόνασί μοι γυναῖκες (8.88.3). The King very naturally blamed his own forces for the defeat, which is a human reaction; today in sporting events the losers rarely credit their defeat to the skill of their opponents. The idea that this mission to Xerxes was a discreditable venture of Themistocles and was so played up by his enemies is very nicely countered by Charles Fornara: "What we, in an overprotective way, have taken to be an anecdote derogatory of Themistocles would to his audience have appeared to be the ultimate example of Themistocles' capacity to look after himself."[53] This claim itself may be an over-reaction, but it should warn us to seek a balance: no Greek audience ever saw a thing all in the same way.

17.1 Πόλεων μέν οὖν τὴν Αἰγινητῶν ἀριστεῦσαί φησιν Ἡρόδοτος (8.93)
The historian reported the awards simply and without amplification. He later added the confirming story that Apollo at Delphi asked the Aeginetans to give him the *aristeia* which they had received (8.122). Ephorus is said to have agreed with Herodotus (schol. Pindar *Isth.* 5.63, *FGrH* 70 F 188), but Diodorus, whom most scholars believe to be excerpting Ephorus, described a contest over the *aristeia* between Athens and Aegina (XI 27.2; Strabo VIII 6.16 followed the same tradition): the Spartans, he reported, seeking to weaken the Athenian leadership, influenced the majority of states to vote for Aegina. Among later authors, Aelian (*VH* 12.10) named the Aeginetans as victors; Aristodemus 1.3, 6, and Aristides (I 223) name the Athenians. Plutarch quoted Herodotus here without comment, but in *De Hdt.mal.* 871C, he said that the historian was using Apollo as a device to take the prize from Athens. We must assume that he knew of no such oracular response and

[53] *Herodotus* 72, where *Od.* 13.287-297 is quoted to good effect.

therefore believed Herodotus to be denying the Athenians credit and using the most dishonest means to do so.[54]

No doubt a majority of the Greek states would have been willing to admit that the Athenians had contributed the most to the victory at Salamis. But the *aristeia* was awarded to those who fought most bravely, regardless of numerical contributions. A sense of proportion would lead the electors to award the prize to some city other than the one which had supplied the greatest number of ships. Aegina was no doubt a wise choice: the city had recently been the greatest naval power of the western Aegean,[55] had performed numerous feats of valor at Salamis (Hdt. 8.84, 86, 90, 91, 92) and was, pragmatically, a compromise choice which would hopefully offend neither Athens nor Sparta— as Plataea was later said to be (Plut. *Arist.* 20.1-3).

17.1-2 Θεμιστοκλεῖ δὲ
The story follows the outline of Hdt. 8.123-124.1, with the exception that Plutarch has *every* general voting for Themistocles second—a better story. In *De Hdt.mal.* 871DE, Plutarch said Herodotus should have censured the generals' *philotimia*; here he passes over his previous criticism, as usual. Diodorus surprisingly ignored this story and said the Spartans had the prize awarded to Ameinias (XI 27.2); Aristides and his scholiast have followed Plutarch or his source (II 238, 288; III 574).

17.3 Λακεδαιμόνιοι δ' εἰς τὴν Σπάρτην αὐτὸν καταγαγόντες Εὐρυβιάδῃ μὲν ἀνδρείας, ἐκείνῳ δὲ σοφίας ἀριστεῖον ἔδοσαν θαλλοῦ στέφανον
Herodotus' text (8.124.2) reads ἀριστήια μέν νυν ἔδοσαν Εὐρυβιάδῃ, and Cobet once proposed to read ἀνδρηίης after ἔδοσαν, assuming Plutarch to have seen it in his text of Herodotus. But Plutarch did not usually work from texts, and specifi-

---

[54] Plutarch had a thorough command of the oracular literature, e.g., *De Pyth.orac.* 403EF. If Herodotus was correct in quoting the response, it must have dropped out of the literature, or been excised as spurious by Plutarch's day.

[55] Reflected in the "thalassocracy list" of Diod. VII 11; cf. comment by M. Miller, *The Thalassocracies* (Albany, 1971) 43f.

cally not from a text of Herodotus while writing this life; on the grounds of method alone one must not emend Herodotus from Plutarch.

There is, at any rate, a slight difference in the two accounts: Plutarch said that Themistocles was brought to Sparta by the admiring Spartans; the historian said "he came to Lacedaemon, θέλων τιμηθῆναι," which is not the same thing at all, but is consistent with the general's character as seen elsewhere in Herodotus.

Thucydides let his Athenian spokesman remind the Spartans in 432 of the honors they had paid Themistocles (I 74.1). Diodorus (XI 27.3) agreed on the honors, but said they were given because the Spartans were afraid the Athenians had been offended by losing the *aristeia* to Aegina and therefore wanted to placate Themistocles at least. He also claimed that when the general returned home loaded with honors the Athenians deposed him from the strategia for accepting them. This brings up the question, which many scholars have seen Ephorus trying to answer in this passage of Diodorus: why does Themistocles drop so completely out of Herodotus' history from this point on?[56]

There is an apparently strong circumstantial case to be made for the story of Themistocles' deposition in Diodorus-Ephorus (assuming this *is* Ephorus). First is the silence of Herodotus about any further participation of Themistocles in the war. Second, the spiteful remarks of Timodemus of Aphidnae (Hdt. 8.125) might have been representative of a segment of Athenian popular opinion. Third, Aristeides and Xanthippus were elected to command the land and sea forces during the 479 campaign; it is thought that both were his political enemies. Fourth, an inscription quoted by Plutarch (*Arist.* 10.10) named Cimon, Xanthippus, and Myronides as envoys to Sparta, asking their prompt aid against Mardonius (doubtless the same mission described by Hdt.

[56] How and Wells ad 8.125.1, cf. II 389ff.; Hignett, *Xerxes' Invasion* 275.

9.6-11). It would seem to be a slap in the face to Themistocles to leave him off an embassy to the state where he
had been so signally honored.

On the other hand, the silence of Herodotus is more apparent than real. It is true he never mentioned Themistocles,
but at the same time he mentioned Aristeides—the Athenian
commander in chief at Plataea—only once and that only in
passing (9.28); for the entire campaign of 479, in fact, only
three Athenians were mentioned by name by the historian:
Sophanes of Decelea (9.74), Xanthippus (9.114), and Her-
molycus (9.105). As to Timodemus of Aphidnae, Herodotus specifically stated that he was "enraged by envy,"
which would seem to indicate that his passion was neurotic,
not politically inspired. As to the election of Themistocles'
erstwhile rivals to the generalship and to diplomatic mis-
sions, this must remain one of the puzzles we scarcely have
the right to speculate about, let alone pretend we have
solved. Aristeides and Xanthippus and the others may at one
time or another have been deadly enemies of Themistocles,
but the very next year we find Themistocles cooperating
with Aristeides in deceiving Sparta and otherwise directing
the city's affairs in his usual aggressive manner (Thuc. I
100-103).[57]

17.4 Λέγεται δ' Ὀλυμπίων τῶν ἑξῆς ἀγομένων
Thus Plutarch abruptly ends the Persian Wars in the middle of a chapter—thereby avoiding all problems like the
preceding one. The transition appears smooth at first. The
honors received from Sparta are described, and then we are
told about the aclaim Themistocles received at Olympia.
But then one realizes the Olympian festival of 476 must be
meant, which is a long time after the battle of Salamis. In
fact, the story implies that the games followed fairly soon
after the battle. It is tempting, therefore, to propose the
Isthmian games at which Phylacidas of Aegina won the

[57] How and Wells, II 390; Hignett, *Xerxes' Invasion* 276ff.; Burn,
Persia and the Greeks 491f.

pancration (Pindar, *Isth.* 5), for some editors believe these games to have been held late in 480.[58] But the tradition about Olympia seems too strong to change arbitrarily.[59]

[58] R. Jebb, *Bacchylides* 213 (to *Ode* 12), thought that καὶ νῦν in *Isthm.* 5.60 referred to the recentness of the battle of Salamis; cf. A. Turyn, *Pindari carmina* ad loc.; but my colleague David Young points out that καὶ νῦν means only that Pindar has come to the last item in his catalogue.

[59] Pausanias (VIII 50.3) probably heard his version of the story at Olympia; cf. Aelian, *VH* 13.43; Them. *Letter* 8, p. 748 Hercher.

VI

TRIUMPH AND DECLINE:
COMMENTARY TO CHAPTERS 18-23

18.1 Καὶ γὰρ ἦν τῇ φύσει φιλοτιμότατος, εἰ δεῖ τεκμαίρεσθαι διὰ
τῶν ἀπομνημονευομένων

Perrin has pointed out (*Plutarch's Themistocles* 226) that
this chapter, like the fifth, is a collection of anecdotes designed to illuminate Themistocles' character—as Plutarch
himself summed up in the last sentence of the chapter. As
usual, the biographer was more concerned to collect stories
that were in character than ones that were firmly corrobo-
rated. The first anecdote is an obvious invention. On any
day the fleet was about to leave, its commander would be
busy enough with routine last moment affairs; he certainly
would not have to create an atmosphere of frantic activity
artificially—especially not in the Greek world, where such
an atmosphere accompanies the most routine transaction.

18.2 τῶν δὲ νεκρῶν

Another rather forced story. We may imagine that collection of loot from the Persian casualties was proceeding in a
lively fashion the day after the battle without any need for
encouragement from Themistocles. Nevertheless, the anecdote seemed significant enough to be repeated by Aelian,
VH 13.40, Ammianus Marcellinus, XXX 8.8, and once elsewhere by Plutarch (*Praec.ger.reip.* 808F).

18.3 πρὸς δέ τινα τῶν καλῶν γεγονότων

This is a story we know only from Plutarch (here and in

Apophth.Them. 8, 185C). Antiphates does not appear in our lists of *kalos* names from fine painted pottery.

18.4 Ἔλεγε δὲ τοὺς Ἀθηναίους οὐ τιμᾶν αὐτὸν

It seems to me that the illustration of the plane tree is a botched metaphor in more than one respect. First, the plane tree is far more useful for shade in summer than as a shelter against winter storms.[1] Second, all trees are pruned as they begin to go dormant, *after* the good weather is over for the year. The story is more aptly phrased in *De ipse laud.* 541E, where it is an address to the Athenians.[2]

18.5 Τοῦ δὲ Σεριφίου

Cf. *Apophth.Them.* 7, 185C. Seriphos was legendary for poverty and insignificance during antiquity. The island sent one penteconter to Salamis (Hdt. 8.46, 48) but was nevertheless omitted from the war memorial.[3] This story is obviously another version of the one in Herodotus (8.125) where Themistocles is seen answering the criticism of Timodemus of Aphidnae (a deme in northeast Attica); the story is slightly different:

Herodotus: You would not be honored, *even though you are Athenian.*

Plutarch: You would not be famous *even if you were Athenian.*

The second variation is encountered first in Plato, *Republic* 329E, whence it passed into the tradition (see also Cicero, *De senect.* 3, 8). The story about Themistocles was probably converted to make it more applicable to Cephalus' syllogism about old age in the *Republic*. Plutarch, as always, was more familiar with Plato than with Herodotus and it is no surprise to see him using the philosopher's version of the story (cf. Flacelière, *REA* 50 [1948] 211).

[1] See, for instance, Plato, *Phaedr.* 229a, 230a; Plut. *Cimon* 13.7.
[2] Noted by Perrin, *Plutarch's Themistocles* 227; cf. *Apophth.* 13, 185E; Aelian, *VH* 9.18.
[3] Meiggs and Lewis, *GHI* p. 60; see also Bürchner, *RE* ii 2 (1923) 1730ff.; K. Freeman, *Greek City States* chap. 7.

18.6 Ἑτέρου δὲ τινος τῶν στρατηγῶν

The retort of the Feast Day to the Day After is a trifle. In extant literature, it is found only in Plutarch's works and is no doubt a stock bit of repartee which at some time attracted the name of Themistocles to itself. We find it repeated in *Quaest.Rom.* 270BC, *De fort.Rom.* 320EF, and almost certainly at the beginning of *De glor.Ath.* 345C, where there is a lacuna.[4] These works were all from Plutarch's rhetorical juvenilia and the tale was probably collected from a rhetorician's handbook.

18.7 Τὸν δ' υἱὸν ἐντρυφῶντα τῇ μητρὶ

This story was repeated in *Cato maj.* 8.4-5, where it is said to be translated from the apophthegms of Themistocles. It is also found in *Apophth.Them.* 10, 185D, and in the pseudo-Plutarchean *De lib.educ.* 1C, where the name of the son is given as Diophantus (usually emended to Cleophantus). The story is proven an anachronism by the allusion to the Athenians ruling other Greeks, a concept which would not have occurred to anyone until at least the conquest of Naxos, at which time Themistocles was already in flight.

18.8 Ἴδιος δέ τις ἐν πᾶσι βουλόμενος εἶναι

Tzetzes and a scholion to Hesiod's *Erga* (346: πῆμα κακὸς γείτων, κτλ.) cite this anecdote, probably from Plutarch's commentary to Hesiod (fr. 50 in Sandbach's Loeb edition of the *Moralia*). It is also found in *Apophth.Them.* 12, 185E, and Stobaeus 37.30. This would be a flimsy bit of evidence to prove that land was alienable for fee simple so early in the fifth century.[5]

18.9 Τῶν δὲ μνωμένων αὐτοῦ τὴν θυγατέρα

In Plutarch's version of this story[6] it is Themistocles' daughter. In an earlier tale, found in the fragments of Diodorus

[4] Recognized as long ago as Xylander; cf. Babbitt ad loc. in the Loeb *Moralia*, vol. 4.

[5] But I would not go so far as Hammond, *JHS* 81 (1961) 83-88 in denying that land was inalienable until the late fifth century.

[6] See also *Apophth.* 11, 185E; Cicero *De off.* II 20, 71; Val.Max. 7.2 ext 9; Stobaeus 85.11.

(X 32), an unnamed rich man was looking for a rich son-in-law, but Themistocles advised him to marry his daughter to Cimon, who was still in jail because of Miltiades' fine.

19.1 εὐθὺς ἐπεχείρει τὴν πόλιν ἀνοικοδομεῖν

The fullest and only really reliable account is that of Thucydides (I 89.3-92), which was followed closely and embroidered by Diodorus or his source (XI 39-40). Plutarch began by admitting there was a variant account by Theopompus: Themistocles bribed the ephors not to interfere with the wall building (FGrH 115 F 85). Andocides also said something of the sort in De pace 38: λαθόντες τοὺς Πελοποννησίους τειχισάμενοι τὰ τείχη· πριάμενοι δὲ παρὰ Λακεδαιμονίων μὴ δοῦναι τούτων δίκην. There was obviously an early tradition to this effect.[7]

19.2 ἧκε μὲν γάρ εἰς Σπάρτην ὄνομα πρεσβείας ἐπιγραψάμενος

Thucydides I 90.3, Θεμιστοκλέους γνώμῃ, probably indicates a decree of the people, sending Themistocles and the others as ambassadors, and providing funds. All the clever maneuvering—the delay of the other ambassadors and so on—was doubtless a matter of confidential planning between Themistocles, Aristeides, and the other generals and statesmen. This is probably why the dramatized account in Diodorus emphasized that the advice to the Boule was kept secret (XI 39.5; see Gomme, HCT I 258 ad Thuc. I 90.4).

Thucydides said that he kept putting off discussion of the walls, saying that he had to wait until his fellow ambassadors arrived (I 90.5). These were Aristeides and Habronichus, son of Lysicles (I 91.3), who was perhaps a Spartan proxenus in Athens; he had been with Leonidas at Thermopylae (Hdt. 8.21).[8] The Athenians thus sent at least two ambassadors in whom the Spartans had great confidence. That

[7] Jacoby ad F 85; Connor, Theopompus and Fifth-Century Athens 20f.

[8] We know now that Habronichus was from Lamptrae. More than two dozen ostraca bearing his name have been found in Kerameikos.

they nevertheless fully intended to deceive the Spartans makes two things clear. First, they must have known that they would never again be trusted by Sparta—which became obvious about fifteen years later (Thuc. I 102.2-3). Second, Themistocles and Habronichus were both willing to sacrifice their special status at Sparta—a significant sacrifice, it would seem to us. Domestic political activity at Athens did not exist in a vacuum, and Spartan backing obviously counted for something in the competitive pursuit of honor and esteem that occupied Athenians in public life. It was perhaps at this time that the Spartans began to cultivate Cimon.[9]

Πολυάρχου κατηγοροῦντος ἐπίτηδες ἐξ Αἰγίνης ἀποσταλέντος

Flacelière rightly rejects the proposal of A. Schaefer (*RhMus* 38, 618) to read Polycritus for Polyarchus (cf. Hdt. 8.92). Plutarch's source for this detail must remain unknown.

19.3 γνόντες γὰρ οἱ Λακεδαιμόνιοι τὸ ἀληθὲς

Themistocles' careful planning succeeded in putting Spartan hostages in Athenian hands. The story follows Thucydides I 93-94 exactly. We must wonder if the attitude of distrust was really so great, or if the historian himself was following the tradition of his own day uncritically.

This stratagem took second place only to the ruse at Salamis in the catalogue of Themistocles' memorable deeds. In Bauer's edition of the *Themistocles*, he provided a synoptic collection of testimonia from the following authors: Aristides II 276; Demosth. *Lept.* 20.73; Diod. XI 39-40.4; Nepos, *Them.* 6-7; Justin II 15.1-12; Polyaenus I 30.5; Frontinus I 1.10; Aristodemus 5.1-3; schol. Ar. *Eq.* 814. Such variants as may appear in these accounts are unimportant and are due either to invention or confusion: for instance, Justin and Frontinus said Themistocles put off answering the Spartans, feigning illness; Frontinus, speaking of the walls *quos iussu Lacedaemoniorum deiecerant* is obviously muddling up this and the rebuilding by Conon a century later.

[9] He had been at Sparta on an embassy the year before: inscr. *ap* Plut. *Arist.* 10.10.

ἐκ δὲ τούτου, Πειραιᾶ κατεσκεύαζε

The ancient writers were of course preoccupied with the eventual political and strategic significance of the new harbor district. What is usually ignored is the fact that the Athenians would from now on take care of their ships in an entirely new way. The move from Phaleron is not simply a geographical one; it implies a wholly different method of ship storage. Phaleron was not, in fact, a "harbor"—it was a long beach sheltered from northern gales on which lighter ships could be pulled up. Heavier merchantmen were brought into knee-deep water and loaded or unloaded. This was the usual sort of "harbor" in the Aegean (with a few exceptions like Samos, Hdt. 3.60) until the advent of enclosed ports in the fifth century. But the coves of Piraeus are rocky. The move to Piraeus meant that from now on, ships would be loaded at dockside, and that lighter boats, like triremes, must be stored out of the water in artificial constructions, to keep them from getting waterlogged (on which, see Hdt. 7.59; Thuc. VII 12.3-5).

The remains of the ship sheds at Zea (Pasalimani) are well known. They were first surveyed by Dragatzes and Dörpfeld in the last century (publ. in the *Praktika* for 1885, 63-68) and the plans have been reprinted a number of times. Keel slots were cut in to the bedrock, which was partly graded to accommodate the triremes, partly built up with cut stone. Unfortunately, no one was able to examine the underwater sections, so an unknown part of the slipways has never been studied. The job is now impossible because Pasalimani is little more than a huge open sewer. Up to a meter of vile sludge now covers the underwater portion of the slips, which were once undoubtedly clearly visible. Another consideration: "the possibility of a change in the relative sea level since antiquity has not always been taken into account in discussions of the ship-sheds though if it were established it would affect all the length measurements of the ship-sheds and any conclusions drawn therefrom on the dimensions of the trieres and also the general picture one tries to form of what ancient military harbors looked like."[10]

Thucydides said (I 93-3-4): ἔπεισε δὲ καὶ τοῦ Πειραιῶς τὰ λοιπὰ ὁ Θεμιστοκλῆς οἰκοδομεῖν (ὑπῆρκτο δ' αὐτοῦ πρότερον ἐπὶ τῆς ἐκείνου ἀρχῆς ἧς κατ' ἐνιαυτὸν 'Αθηναίους ἦρξε) . . . καὶ τὴν ἀρχὴν εὐθὺς ξυγκατεσκεύαζε. This is a most difficult sentence, in which the verb ἄρχω and the noun ἀρχή are both used twice, each time with different meanings. Scholars usually agree that this sentence referred to the eponymous archonship (e.g., Gomme, *HCT* I 261-63). Fornara has recently attempted to show that the crucial phrase in the sentence must be translated, "in that magistracy of his which he held yearly," and therefore some other office must be meant.[11] It can be argued that the Greek makes better sense this way (older translations did not). It is true that we know of no other appropriate magistracies that could be held yearly in this period of Athenian history, but we know almost nothing else about pre-Persian War administrative structure either; if Thucydides had said that work went on at Piraeus for several years before the war, Θεμιστοκλέους ἐπιστατοῦντος, no one would have questioned the information for a moment, and this is perhaps what the historian meant. On the other hand, D. M. Lewis and W. W. Dickie, responding to Fornara, have shown by syntactical and epigraphical parallels that the language of Thucydides can mean the eponymous archonship. I am inclined to take the latter view and would add only that I think the most important questions have not been asked and probably cannot be answered until we know more about early Athenian government: were the fortifications begun on the initiative of Themistocles or was

[10] J. Blackman in J. Morrison and R. Williams, *Greek Oared Ships* (Cambridge, 1968) 182 n., and in general, 181-192, pl. 29; cf. K. Lehman-Hartleben, *Die antike Hafenanlagen des Mittelmeeres, Klio Beiheft* 14 (1923) 113ff.; L. Casson, *Ships and Seamanship in the Ancient World* (Princeton, 1971) 363-365, pl. 197.

[11] C. Fornara, "Themistocles' Archonship," *Historia* 20 (1971) 534-540.

he simply in charge as archon? Who paid for the construction? Public works were still in their infancy at Athens and tended to be gifts donated by wealthy men; we know that Themistocles did not control this kind of fortune early in his career. At any rate, it would appear that very little was actually accomplished during 493/2.[12]

19.4 Ἐκεῖνοι μὲν γὰρ ὡς λέγεται πραγματευόμενοι τοὺς πολίτας ἀποσπάσαι τῆς θαλάσσης

We are to believe that the old kings of Athens had tried to keep the Athenians from leading a maritime life by citing the victory of Athena over Poseidon (see above, p. 125). Plutarch was probably quoting interpretations of oligarchic propaganda here, particularly what we can see becoming the hardened party line of the oligarchs at the time of the Thirty (19.6, below): "maritime empire (or rule by sea) is the genesis of democracy." That this interpretation is an absurd anachronism applied to the old kings of Athens is easily demonstrated. As late as the 440's, the maritime imperialists who were running Athens had thought the contest of Athena and Poseidon a fitting theme for the west gable of the Parthenon.[13]

ὥσπερ Ἀριστοφάνης ὁ κωμικός

Eq. 814f: ὃς ἐποίησεν τὴν πόλιν ἡμῶν μεστήν, εὑρὼν ἐπιχειλῆ καὶ πρὸς τούτοις ἀριστώσῃ τὸν Πειραιᾶ προσέμαξεν

Paphlagon had sought to compare himself with Themistocles as a benefactor of the city. Plutarch's point is that of the tail wagging the dog: Piraeus was not stuck to the city; it was the city that was added to Piraeus.

19.5 ὅθεν καὶ τὸν δῆμον ηὔξησε

Once more, a simplistic explanation derived from oligarchic

---

[12] Lewis and Dickie in *Historia* 22 (1973) 757-759. I am not completely convinced by Jacoby that the famous epigram quoted from Philochorus' fifth book by Harpocration refers to the new fortifications by Conon in 395, ad *FGrH* 328 F 40; see Badian, *Antichthon* 5 (1971) 8 n. 20.

[13] Paus. I 24.5; F. Brommer, *Die Skulpturen der Parthenon-Giebel* (Mainz, 1963).

criticism of naval democracy.[14] The creation of a navy requiring as many as 40,000 sailors had revolutionary effects, but they were social and economic; the political effects were symptomatic only.[15] In no case can it be shown that the sailors voted as a bloc (i.e., against rural hoplites). The fleet continued to be commanded by elegant aristocrats like Cimon. Unfortunately we do not even know what percentage of the rowers in any given period were citizens. Many may have been aliens, or even slaves, according to my colleague, Borimir Jordan.[16]

19.6 Διὸ καὶ τὸ βῆμα τὸ ἐν Πνυκὶ

Ziegler and Flacelière emend to πυκνί, but πνυκί may well be Plutarch's own spelling and the spelling of his day, as in Lucian, *Anach.* 17; *Jup.trag.* 11.

K. Kourouniotes and Homer Thompson demonstrated in 1931 that the amphitheatre of the Pnyx had in fact been rebuilt at the end of the fifth century, and that one of the changes was the turning of the entire plan so that the *bema* faced northeast—that is, away from the sea and toward the mesogeion.[17] That this reorientation was meant to be symbolic is, of course, a quaint oral tradition. The strongest impression we get from the rule of the Thirty is that they did not intend to use the Pnyx at all.

20.1 Θεμιστοκλῆς δὲ καὶ μεῖζόν τι περὶ τῆς ναυτικῆς διενοήθη δυνάμεως

The historical expedition into which Plutarch has inserted this anecdote is probably that of Leotychides, sometime dur-

---

[14] As represented in [Xen.] AP 1.2; Plato, *Laws* 707ab; Arist. *Pol.* 1304ª22.

[15] As I have argued in "Tribal Politics in the Civic State," *AJAH* 1 (1976) 70-75.

[16] "The Meaning of the Technical Term Hyperesia," *CSCA* 2 (1968) 183-207. Casson still denies this strenuously. Thuc. I 143.1 shows that a substantial number of rowers were aliens on the eve of the Peloponnesian War.

[17] "The Pnyx in Athens," *Hesperia* 1 (1932) 135f.

ing the years 478-475. Herodotus (6.72) said he could have conquered all of Thessaly but was bought off by a bribe, caught with the money, and exiled from Sparta.[18] In this passage, Plutarch is still in the grip of the late fifth-century oligarchic tradition about naval imperialism and continues with anecdotes that came to mind about Themistocles as the architect of that imperialism. It may be that the story existed in his day in rhetorical handbooks in the form of an *exemplum* contrasting justice and utility.[19]

20.2 τῶν δ' Ἀθηναίων Ἀριστείδῃ φράσαι μόνῳ κελευόντων

Aristeides was the traditional defender of what was δίκαιον as opposed to ὠφέλιμον (Hdt. 8.79). The rhetorical commonplace was pointed out by Perrin (*Plutarch's Themistocles* ad loc.).

20.3 ἐν δὲ τοῖς Ἀμφικτυονικοῖς συνεδρίοις

This story occurs nowhere in extant literature except here and therefore might be peremptorily dismissed as an idle fiction (thus E. Walker, *CAH* V 36). On the other hand, the story fits the historical situation exactly, as Bengtson has pointed out, and reflects the policy of both Sparta and Themistocles.[20]

Herodotus said (7.132) that the Greeks at the Isthmus vowed to fine the states who had given earth and water to Xerxes' heralds and to give the spoils to Apollo at Delphi. There is, however, no hint that this was ever done after the war, although the Amphictyons did take action against Ephialtes of Malis (Hdt. 7.213) and possibly against the

[18] Cf. Plut. *De Hdt.mal.* 859D; Paus. III 7.9-10. On the date, see discussions in How and Wells ad 6.72; Gomme, *HCT* I 365, 406f.

[19] As in Cicero, *De off.* III 11, 49; Val.Max. VI5 ext. 2. The scene is changed in these Latin writers to Gythion (cf. Thuc. I 108.5); it is possible that Plutarch changed this to Pagasae because he knew of the expedition of Leotychides and was already thinking of Spartan punitive activities in northern Greece; see below, 20.3. In *Arist.* 22.2, where Plutarch repeats the story, the location is omitted.

[20] H. Bengtson, "Themistokles und die delphische Amphiktyonie," *Eranos* 49 (1951) 85-92, followed by Flacelière, "Points obscurs de la vie de Thémistocle," *REA* 55 (1953) 19-28.

Dolopes of Skyros (although this is not entirely clear from
Thuc. I 98.2 and Plut. *Cimon* 8.3–4). It is probable that
some kind of reconciliation was arranged between the
medizing states and the Amphictyony. Perhaps even the
Spartans were divided on this question. Plutarch knew a
tradition that claimed a Spartan named Lacrates testified in
favor of medizers (*De Hdt.mal.* 868F).[21]

διδάξας ὡς τριάκοντα καὶ μία μόναι πόλεις

The Serpent Column at Delphi, with its thirty-one inscribed
names, was naturally enough a familiar landmark to Plutarch. As Flacelière points out,[22] nine of the twelve amphictyonic peoples had medized; Athens, Sparta, and Phocis
alone were left, and Phocis had been left off the Serpent
Column, probably because she had made no positive contribution to the war effort. Thus Themistocles' argument
was a strong one.

20.4 διὸ καὶ τὸν Κίμωνα προῆγον ταῖς τιμαῖς

As in the *Cimon* 16.2. See above, comment to 19.2.

21.1 Ἦν δὲ καὶ τοῖς συμμάχοις ἐπαχθής

This is a *locus classicus* of misquotation and in my opinion
a convincing proof that Plutarch often remembered his Herodotus as disconnected anecdotes, and not as a connected
historical narrative. The historian had said (8.111-112) that
after the battle of Salamis, Themistocles had begun to demand money of the islands which had medized. The allies
openly besieged Andros, and Themistocles used this example as a threat to extort money from other cities (Ca-
rystos and Paros, in 8.112). All the islands except the western-
most Cyclades had given earth and water and thus were
fair game for such extortion (Keos, Kythnos, Seriphos,

[21] Plutarch's sources might include the Delphic tradition; Theopompus has also been suggested, Busolt, *Griechische Geschichte* III
i, 30; cf. Bengtson, previous note, 91f.
[22] *REA* 55 (1955) 22.

Siphnos, and Melos fought with the allies; the Naxians gave earth and water but deserted before Salamis, Hdt. 8.46).

But Plutarch dates this episode to a time when the islanders were in fact allies, that it, after 477/6. Themistocles' actions would have been considered piracy. The mistake can be explained. Plutarch, while on the subject of medizing (last chapter) and about to take up the topic of extortion (see below, on Timocreon), happened to remember Herodotus' anecdote about Andros and put it in without checking to see if it really applied. In the *De Herodoti malignitate* (871C), where he was following Herodotus more carefully, he had the episode in the correct chronological sequence.

21.2 Δύο γὰρ ἥκειν ἔφη θεοὺς κομίζων, πειθὼ καὶ βίαν (Hdt. 8.111: Πειθώ τε καὶ 'Αναγκαίην). And the retort; Plut.: εἶναι καὶ παρ' αὐτοῖς θεοὺς μεγάλους δύο, Πενίαν καὶ 'Απορίαν. (Hdt.: πενίην καὶ ἀμηχανίην). The meaning is the same, of course, but Plutarch is obviously quoting from memory (so also Flacelière, in the Budé ed. ad loc.). Andros is today one of the most fertile and prosperous of the Cyclades, producing lemons and silk. But the fertile eastern half seems not to have been exploited in antiquity, probably because it is the weather side and is difficult for shipping.

21.3 Τιμοκρέων δ' ὁ 'Ρόδιος μελοποιὸς
We must regret that we know so little of this memorable poet, glutton, drunkard, and star athlete. He was not a "Rhodian," of course (the polis of Rhodes was to be built long after his lifetime), but a citizen of Ialysos, the second city of the island, and with Lindos, Cameiros, Cnidos, and Cos a member of the Dorian Pentapolis (Hdt. 1.144; schol. Theocr. 17.69). We do not know his dates, but might estimate him to be a younger contemporary of Simonides, with whom he maintained a bitter rivalry (*Suda* s.v. Timocreon; *Anth.Pal.* 13.31). The earliest prose author to mention him, the sophist Thrasymachus of Colophon, said that while once a guest of the Great King (either Xerxes or Darius), he

stuffed himself at table. "When the King asked what he hoped to accomplish, he said that he was going to thrash innumerable Persians. And the next day he defeated many, one by one, and afterward stood throwing punches at the empty air. When queried he explained that he had many such blows left over, if anyone wanted to come forward."[23]

During the Persian Wars, the various Rhodian cities played little part. They are not mentioned at all by Herodotus; only Diodorus mentions forty ships from Rhodes, Cos, and the Dorians of Caria enrolled in Xerxes' fleet (XI 3.8). It is difficult to believe this against the silence of Herodotus, considering his usual care in enumerating the participants of battles. The cities of Rhodes, in fact, may have been able to preserve neutrality during the war, thanks to an agreement reached between Datis and the "god-preserved" Lindians ten years earlier.[24] At any rate, the cities of Rhodes would not have been reckoned medizers by the Greeks, based on the oath taken at the Isthmus in 481 (Hdt. 7.132) because they were in the Persian sphere by compulsion, like the Ionians (Hdt. 9.106). Many personal scores were settled, however, in the period after Mycale, when towns along the Ionian seaboard began to pass legislation against medizing.[25] No doubt Timocreon had been on too good terms with the Persians and the some personal enemy secured his exile on that count.

21.4 'Aλλ' εἰ τύ γα Παυσανίαν

Of all the victors of the war, Timocreon admires Aristeides most—but Themistocles the liar is hated by Leto (the oath-giver, e.g. *Hymn.Hom.* 3.83 sq.; Flacelière, Budé ed. ad loc.). According to Timocreon, Themistocles was his *xenos* but had taken three talents not to restore the poet to

---

[23] In Athen. 415F, Diels-Kranz, *Vorsokr.* II 85 B 4.

[24] For the miraculous preservation of the besieged city by Athena, see the Temple Chronicle of Lindos, *FGrH* 532 F 1D (1).

[25] Teos, *Syll*[3] 37/38 V; Erythrae, *IG* i[2] 10.26; on the situation in general, see J. Wolski, "*Medismos*," *Historia* 22 (1973) 12ff.

his homeland. Returning exiles were always troublesome because they always wanted their lands back and these had usually been confiscated and become the property of someone else. The time of this judgment is unknown, except that it was after the war and after an unspecified Isthmian festival (where the athlete Timocreon may have competed) at which Themistocles evidently provided an unexceptional meal (cold meats).[26]

ἀργυρίοισι κοβαλικοῖσι[27]

Timocreon said that Themistocles had the authority to "restore some unjustly, drive others out and kill some," which hints of a quasi-legal process similar to the "de-nazification" that occurred after the Second World War. The phrase συγκαταψηφισαμένου Θεμιστοκλέους (below, 21.7) sounds like some kind of international tribunal set up to adjudicate cases like Timocreon's. As Plutarch has just been describing a debate before the Amphictyons (20.3), at which penalties for medism were discussed, it is tempting to propose that Plutarch's unknown source also described the episode of Timocreon. In this case, the international authority which made Themistocles competent to hand down such judgments may have been amphictyonic, according to Plutarch's source. But this is only speculative. Meiggs, on the other hand, implies that the only authority Themistocles needed was the presence of the Athenian fleet (*Athenian Empire* 414f.).

21.5-7 μετὰ τὴν φυγὴν αὐτοῦ

After Themistocles was forced into exile, Timocreon gloated over his fate in a poem that found wider currency than the first one quoted by Plutarch: it was cited by an unknown

[26] The editors of *ATL* cautiously suggest that the taking of the bribe, the judgment, and the Isthmian games are all to be dated to 480, on the occasion described by Herodotus (8.123).

[27] κοβαλικοῖσι is read by Flacelière (*Vie de Thém.* ad loc.), following P. Chantraine, *REG* 75 (1962) 389, who compared Ar. *Eq.* 270, ἐκκοβαλικεύεται.

author on proverbs (Page, *PMG* no. 730) and—incorrectly
—by the scholiast to Aristides (III 720).[28]

22.1 Ἤδη δὲ καὶ τῶν πολιτῶν διὰ τὸ φθονεῖν ἡδέως τὰς διαβολὰς
προσιεμένων

This theme has been developed in the last two chapters:
"He became offensive to the Lacedaemonians" (20.4); "he
was also oppressive to the allies" (21.1); and now, "finally,
the citizens, because of envy, eagerly began to believe
criticism of him." Plutarch begins with an anecdote to show
how pompous Themistocles was becoming: "Why [you
lucky people] do you tire of receiving benefits all the time
from me?"[29]

22.2 τὸ τῆς Ἀρτέμιδος ἱερὸν εἰσάμενος

In the summer of 1958, workmen were digging the footings
for what is now number 1, Herakleidai Street, just across
the avenue Apostle Paul, west of the Acropolis and agora.
They came across some ancient blocks which eventually
proved to be one side of what was almost certainly the
shrine of Artemis Aristoboule built by Themistocles.[30] Identification rests on a fourth-century inscription honoring
Neoptolemus of Melite, a well-known figure of the later
fourth century (Davies, *APF* 10652), who was probably
responsible for the shrine's restoration,[31] and on early fifth-
century fragments of votive *krateriskoi* that create a strong

[28] For Timocreon, see testimonia and fragments in J. M. Edmonds,
Lyra Graeca II (Loeb) 418-429; fragments in Page, *PMG* 375-378;
P. Maas, "Timokreon," *RE* ii 6 (1936) 1271-1273; Podlecki, *Themis-
tocles* 51-54.

[29] ὦ μακάριοι was added in the versions of the story told in *De ipse
laud.* 541D; *Praec.ger.reip.* 800B; *Apophth.* 13, 185E. See also Aelian
VH 13.40, who put Themistocles' success and decline in the wrong
order.

[30] Threpsiades and Vanderpool, "Themistokles' Sanctuary of Artemis Aristoboule," *Arch.Delt.* 19 (1964) 26-36.

[31] The decree of the deme of Melite probably honored him for the
restoration, *SEG* 22 (1967) 116.13.

presumption that Artemis was worshipped here in the time of Themistocles (see also *De Hdt.mal.* 869C). Amandry disputed Vanderpool's original assertion that the krateriskoi "prove" the identity of the shrine in Themistocles' day.[32] Perhaps the identity is not proven, but ceramic evidence, inscriptions, Plutarch's eye-witness account, and location in the deme where Themistocles lived combine to make a case only the most fervent skeptics will reject.

22.3 Ἔκειτο δὲ καὶ τοῦ Θεμιστοκλέους εἰκόνιον

In Plutarch's day, there was undoubtedly an "official" portrait bust of the general, like the Roman copy of a Greek original recovered in the Ostia excavations of 1939.[33] Accepting the portrait as genuine has to be a matter of faith; I am inclined to agree with Podlecki that statues were made of Themistocles from life during his later years in Magnesia and that these were the originals for later copies.[34] A statue of Themistocles near the Prytaneion had been reinscribed with the name of a Thracian.[35] There was also a statue in the theatre, flanked by one of Miltiades, although these may have been later additions for the benefit of Roman tourists.[36] So may have been the portrait of Themistocles in the Parthenon reported by Pausanias (I 1.2). There is an excellent discussion of the authenticity of the Ostia herm by Podlecki.[37]

[32] P. Amandry, "Thémistocle à Mélité," *Charisterion eis A. Orlandon* 4 (Athens, 1967/1968) 265-279.

[33] G. Calza, "Il ritratto di Temistocle a Ostia," *Le Arti* 2/3 (1939/1940) 152-161.

[34] See Bauer-Frost, *Themistocles* 135-137; Podlecki, *Themistocles* 145; Gisela Richter, *Portraits of the Greeks* (London, 1965) 97-99.

[35] Paus. I 18.3; and see Cicero, *Ad Att.* VI 1.26 for the custom of reinscription in antiquity.

[36] Schol.Aristides III 535; on these statues, see M. Bieber, *AJA* 58 (1954) 282-284.

[37] *Themistocles* 143-146; also favoring authenticity are M. Cundari, "Un ritratto greco del V secolo a.C., Temistocle," *Studi Classici e Orientali* 19-20 (1970-1971) 400-425; H. Sichtermann, "Der Themistokles von Ostia," *Gymnasium* 71 (1964) 348-381; G. Zinserling, "Themistokles—sein Porträt in Ostia," *Klio* 38 (1960) 87-109 (all the

A NOTE ON THE DOWNFALL OF THEMISTOCLES

Plutarch's explanation of the decline and fall of the general is rather unsatisfying, lacking any analysis of political issues or vendettas pursued among the ruling families of Athens. Many scholars have noted that Themistocles made himself leader and spokesman for an anti-Spartan faction and took no part in the continuing war of Ionian liberation from the Persian yoke. If so, he gambled and lost, for the Spartan threat which had seemed so real at the time of the feverish rebuilding of the walls (Thuc. I 90-92) simply faded away, while the struggle to free the Ionians became not only *the* exciting, popular cause, but an impressive source of wealth for the city as well (Ion of Chios in Plut. *Cimon* 9, *FGrH* 392 F 13).

Did Themistocles simply make a mistake in picking the wrong issue? My feeling is that he had no choice; that sometime during the winter of 480/79, Xanthippus and Aristeides seized the initiative in the Persian conflict by unknown means and that they never relinquished it, except that Xanthippus' place was quickly assumed by the young Cimon. In other words, Themistocles would have loved the chance to lead the crusade against the Mede, but his rival commanders had no intention of allowing him to participate in the glory of these campaigns, forcing him to adopt, by process of elimination, the issue of rivalry with Sparta, which proved ephemeral. Thus, while Aristeides was organizing the Delian League and Cimon was sailing back every fall with tales of new successes and with his ships full of treasure, Themistocles had to make do with bragging about his past exploits at Salamis, which the demos soon tired of hearing, or unsuccessfully attempting to interest

---

above with full bibliography). Representative views opposing an authentic portrait are P. Amandry, "Thémistocle, un décret et un portrait," *Bull.Fac.lett. de Strasbourg* 39 (1961) 413-435; A. Boethius, "The Themistocles Herm from Ostia," *Coll.Ny Carlsberg Glyptothek* III (Copenhagen, 1942) 202ff.

someone in an active anti-Spartan policy. He may even have tried to belittle Aristeides' stewardship of the Delian tribute —at least this is a tradition known by Plutarch (*Arist.* 24.6) —which would have made a bad impression.

Thrown on the defensive. Themistocles may have tried to play down the importance of the campaigns against Persia, claiming that the navy he had created had forever eliminated the Persian threat. But then, several years before the battle of Eurymedon, the rumors began to drift back to Athens of yet another mighty armada being raised by Xerxes to wreak vengeance on the Athenians. It may have been in this atmosphere, when Themistocles' good counsel seemed to have failed him, that the public was roused to bring an ostracophoria against him.[38] Athenians had admired his aggressive style of political behavior and tolerated his lack of balance in other cultural attainments so long as he was successful. He had now made the fatal mistake of pushing what seemed to be the wrong issue at the wrong time. When the previous master of *euboulia* began to offer poor counsel time and again, the Athenians must have considered the whole matter desperately unlucky and could not wait to get him out of the city before the malady proved catching.

22.4 τὸν μὲν οὖν ἐξοστρακισμὸν ἐποιήσαντο

The story of Themistocles' ostracism was reported by many authorities but without most of the details we would consider helpful.[39] It is unfortunate that the new finds of ostraca from Kerameikos are still in the process of cataloguing. They will undoubtedly change a number of preconceptions about Athenian politics and expand our knowledge of political prosopography. Unofficial counts by H. B. Mattingly, Rudi Thomsen, and others, at this date show well over 2,250 ostraca for Themistocles. A very uncertain reconstruction

---

[38] See also G. L. Cawkwell, "The Fall of Themistocles," *Auckland Classical Essays* (1970) 39ff.; Podlecki, *Themistocles* 34-37.

[39] Thuc. I 135.3; Diod. XI 55.1; Plato, *Gorg.*516d; Nepos, *Them.* 8.1-2.

of the candidates for the particular ostracophoria would list the names of the following:

Themistocles.

Cimon, son of Miltiades. Among the hundreds of new ostraca for Cimon, there is one that makes a join with one bearing the name of Themistocles (cf. Plato, *Gorg.* 516d; Plut. *Cimon* 16.2 for the rivalry).

Habronichus Lysicleous Lamptreus (Hdt. 8.21; Thuc. I 91.3; *Letter* 4.743, 10.751 Hercher). Habronichus is said to be a friend of Themistocles in the *Letters.* He was also a candidate for ostracism before 480[40] and was called a medizer on the Kerameikos ostraca.

Leagrus, son of Glaucon of Kerameis. He was a famous *pais kalos* (Beazley, *ARV*² 1591f.), dedicated to the twelve gods (*SEG* 10.319), died at Drabescus as general in 465/4 (Hdt. 9.75; Paus. I 29.5; schol. Aesch. 2.31), and was mentioned as a friend and coeval of Themistocles in the *Letters* (8.747ff. Hercher).

Aristeides, son of Xenophilus, choregus in 477/6 (Simonides, fr. 77 Diehl; Panaetius in Plut. *Arist.* 1.6) probably from Alopeke and a relative of the famous Aristeides (see Davies, *APF* 1695 V).

Other possible candidates represented by extant ostraca are Menon, son of Menecleides of Gargettos, Alcmaeon, son of Aristonymus, and Myronides of Phlya. If all these candidates were in the same ostracophoria, it will be recognized that the mechanics of ostracism were not readily understood by all Athenians. We may imagine that the anti-Themistocleans circulated among the voters reminding them that it was Themistocles they wished to get rid of and to ignore his companions; nevertheless some Athenians still saw ostraca as a sort of curse tablet and to them magic played a higher role in the voting than did mathematics.

For the date of the ostracism, I tend to follow the sensible

[40] A. R. Hands, "Ostraka and the Law of Ostracism," *JHS* 79 (1959) 76-77.

and methodical discussion by R. Lenardon.[41] We know that Themistocles was still in Athens in 477/6 (see comment to 5.5); the next even approximately datable event at which we can place him is the siege of Naxos, in 468 ($\pm$ 1).[42] The conventional way to obtain the date of the siege of Naxos is to work back from the nearest firm date, that of the revolt of Thasos and the expedition to Drabescus in the same year, 465/4.[43] If the Eurymedon campaign (Thuc. I 100.1) occupied the campaigning season of 467 ($\pm$) and the Naxos campaign that of 468 ($\pm$), an approximate interval implied by Thucydides (I 98.4), then we may fit Themistocles' ostracism, his sojourn in Argos, his flight by land and by sea into the period 475-467.

Other indications of chronology begin with Diodorus, under the archon year 471/0 (XI 54.1-3), at which point the writer commences his story of Themistocles' fate. That he goes on and puts the next dozen or so years of Themistocles' life under the same archon year does not totally discredit the date, as Diodorus seems to have worked this way—that is, the very first item mentioned under a year heading may actually belong to that year.[44] The same year

[41] "The Chronology of Themistokles' Ostracism and Exile," *Historia* 8 (1959) 23-48. P. J. Rhodes, "Thucydides on Pausanias and Themistocles," *Historia* 19 (1970) 395-400, argues that none of the ancient evidence traditionally adduced in support of one or another scheme of dating can be used with any confidence, and in effect, throws up his hands at the prospect of dating anything between 478 and 465. It must be admitted that this position is not unreasonable.

[42] Thuc. I 137.2 and my note on this passage, *CR* 12 n.s. (1962) 15-16.

[43] The archon year of Euthymenes, 437/6, when Amphipolis was founded (schol. Aesch. 2.31) was twenty-eight years after the disaster at Drabescus, according to Thuc. IV 102.2-3; cf. Gomme, *HCT* I ad loc., and 390f.

[44] Lenardon, *Hist.* 8 (1959) 24 n. 6 shows that the first item of historical interest in this archon year has to do with Elis, but Diodorus, after reporting Roman consuls and Athenian archons, usually turned to a chronicle of Elis; in Olympiad years this would give the

—471—is cited by Cicero as twenty years after the ex-
pulsion of Coriolanus.[45] The Armenian version of Eusebius,
under Olympiad 77.2 (471/0) gives the information *The-
mestocles in Persas fugit.*

The date 471/0 is obviously traditional for something,
whether Themistocles' ostracism or condemnation. That a
precise date got into the tradition at all would seem to indicate the condemnation rather than the ostracism, for the
actual decree of *eisangelia* was evidently cited by Craterus
in his *Psephismaton Synagoge* (*Lex.Rhet.Cant.* p. 337,
FGrH 342 F 11a), and the decree might have noted the
archon's name. The condemnation rather than the ostracism
seems also to have been uppermost in Diodorus' mind, for he
begins the story of Themistocles' downfall with the Spartan
accusation of collusion with Pausanias (XI 54.2), which occurred *after* the ostracism (Thuc. I 135.2). It must be admitted that Diodorus thought there were *two* such Spartan
embassies, *two* accusations of collusion, and that Themistocles was acquitted of the first. Trying to explain Diodorus
is generally as pointless as it is exasperating; I would suggest only that he is remembering two different accounts of
the same event and interpreting them as two distinct episodes (also the simplest explanation of Cimon's two Cyprus
campaigns in Diodorus, XI 60 sq. and XII 3 sq.). If the
date 471/0 is accepted as the date of condemnation, then
the ostracism will have taken place one or two years previously, if we bear in mind that Themistocles spent some
time in Argos (Thuc. I 135.3) after his exile, and that the
condemnation was a direct result of Pausanias' downfall in
Sparta, which is every bit as difficult to date.

Mary White skillfully argued a late date (470-467) for
Pausanias' death because his son Pleistoanax was still too
young—νέου ὄντος—to command at Tanagra in c. 458/7

---

winner of the *stadion* (e.g. XI 53.1), but from time to time there
were other items as well, in this case, the synoecism of Elis.
   [45] *De amic.* 12.42; cf. Livy II 34.7 sq; Dion.Hal. VII 26.3.

(Thuc. I 107.2) and because Pausanias had time to sire two other sons *after* Pleistoanax (Cleomenes, Thuc. III 26.2; and Aristocles, Thuc. V 16.2).[46] But νέου ὄντος could mean that Pleistoanax was as old as twenty years, which would give him a birth date of 478/8 and plenty of time for Pausanias to sire younger brothers in the next four years. This narrows down Pausanias' death date to the interval from 474/3 to 472/1. I do not believe greater precision is possible. The following table more clearly explains the dates I propose and the reasoning behind them.

477/6	Themistocles produced *Phoenissae* (inscr. *ap. Them.* 5.5: Adeimantus was archon).
476/5	Capture of Eion (schol. Aesch. 2.31).
472 (± 1)	Themistocles ostracized (must precede next event, according to Thuc. I 135.3).
472 (+ 1)	Pausanias condemned and starved to death (between c. 478-472, Pausanias sired three sons).
471 (+ 1)	Themistocles condemned in absentia (must come after previous event; see also Diod. XI 54.1-3; Cicero, *De amic.* 12.42; Euseb.Arm. *Chron.* Ol.77.2).
468 (± 1)	Naxos campaign; flight of Themistocles (based on the order of events in Thuc. I 98.4-100.1).
467 (± 1)	Eurymedon campaign (as above).
465/4	Thasos seceded; disaster at Drabescus (Thuc. IV 102.1-3; schol. Aesch. 2.31).

22.5 κόλασις γὰρ οὐκ ἦν ὁ ἐξοστρακισμός
Plutarch discussed the institution in five other passages.[47] There has been some debate over his sources, Raubitschek making a good case for Theophrastus' Πολιτικὰ πρὸς τοὺς καιρούς, which Plutarch knew well,[48] and Jacoby suggesting

[46] M. White, "Some Agiad Dates," *JHS* 84 (1964) 140ff.
[47] *Arist.* 7; *Nicias* 11; *Alcib.* 13; *Cimon* 17 and *Per.* 10.1; mentioned only in passing in the last two passages.
[48] "Theophrastus on Ostracism," *Class.et Med.* 19 (1958) 73-109.

Ephorus or an *Atthis* (*FGrH* IIIb Suppl. ii n. 12, ad 328 F 30). Ephorus is very likely the source of the description of ostracism in Diodorus (XI 55.2-3), and there was a long discussion in Philochorus' *Atthis* (328 F 30) preserved by three late lexicographers. But there is no need to attribute one single source. Plutarch had read Theophrastus and Ephorus and Philochorus, to say nothing of the *Athenaion Politeia*, and had undoubtedly discussed the practice with other learned men of his day. It is worth noting that he is probably correct in defining six thousand as a quorum, rather than the number a *single* candidate had to receive to make a valid ostracophoria. He also made a typical mistake of memory, discussing ostracism in the *Nicias* (11.8), by calling Hipparchus *Cholargeus* instead of *Kollyteus* (*AP* 22.4).

23.1 Ἐκπεσόντος δὲ τῆς πόλεως αὐτοῦ καὶ διατρίβοντος ἐν Ἄργει, τὰ περὶ Παυσανίαν συμπεσόντα

In a provocative article, W. G. Forrest made a case for the democrat Themistocles being received by the *douloi* of Argos, who had controlled the government since the slaughter of so many aristocrats in the battle of Sepeia (Hdt. 6.77-81, 83; Plut. *Mul.virt.* 245F; Arist. *Pol.* 1303^a6). He felt that Themistocles was then forced to leave Argos when the sons of the aristocrats regained their primacy about 468 (Hdt. 6.83).[49] There is no doubt that the government of Argos changed hands during this period, but I find it difficult to believe in international ideologies in the early fifth century or in solidarity between "democrats" from Athens, Argos, and elsewhere. For one thing, Plutarch differed with Herodotus over the *douloi*, saying that the term referred to newly enfranchised *perioikoi* and not slaves (*Mul.virt.* 245F). For another, men who had been in power in Argos

[49] W. G. Forrest, "Themistokles and Argos," *CQ* 10 (1960) 221-241.

since 494 (the approximate date of Sepeia) would no doubt have become quite aristocratic in life style by the later 470's. The faction that welcomed Themistocles was simply the same one he defended against medism in 479/8 (see comment to 20.3, above).[50]

In the *Letters* (1.741 Hercher) we are told that Themistocles met Nicias, Meleager, and Eucrates, three of his *xenoi* from Argos, on the road and they invited him to Argos, upon hearing of his ostracism, citing his father Neocles' long sojourn in that city (*Letter* 2.741f. goes on to report that he was offered the offices of *strategos* and *epistates*). This fanciful story, whatever its origin, is probably closer to the real situation than Forrest's reconstruction with its ideological assumptions.

According to Thucydides (I 135.2-3), when the Spartans investigated the medism of Pausanias, they found some evidence (see below, comment to 23.4) that supposedly incriminated Themistocles, who had already been ostracised and "was sojourning in Argos, but was also traveling around the rest of the Peloponnesus."

Ὁ δὲ γραψάμενος αὐτὸν προδοσίας Λεωβώτης ἦν ὁ Ἀλκμαίωνος Ἀγραυλῆθεν

Compare Craterus (in *Lex.Rhet.Cant.* p. 337.15, *FGrH* 342 F 11): ἡ κατὰ Θεμιστοκλέους εἰσαγγελία, ἣν εἰσήγγελεν, ὡς Κρατερός, Λεωβώτης Ἀλκμαίωνος Ἀγρυλῆθεν κτλ. Plutarch has also named Leobotes as the accuser in *De exil.* 605E, but without demotic or patronymic. In *Arist.* 25.10 and *Praec. ger.reip.* 805C, however, he gave the name Alcmeon, no doubt by a simple error of memory. There is of course no deme named Agraule, and editors since Cobet have emended to Ἀγρυλῆθεν.[51] But the manuscripts of Plutarch regularly

[50] See the refutation of Forrest by M. Wörrle, *Untersuchungen zur Verfassungsgeschichte von Argos in 5. Jahrhundert vor Christus* (Diss. Erlangen, 1964) 120-123.

[51] There was a precinct of Aglauros, daughter of Kekrops, on the acropolis where the epheboi took their oath, Demosth. 19.303; Plut. *Alcib.* 15.7. But Plutarch would not have confused this with a deme.

have Ἀγραυλῆθεν (cf. *Alcib.* 22.5) so this must be his consistent misspelling of the deme.

P. J. Bicknell makes the point that the name Leobotes is unattested elsewhere in Attica but was the name of an Agid king in Sparta (Hdt. 1.65; 7.204); the family may well have been Spartan proxenoi selected to eliminate Sparta's greatest foe in Athens.[52]

Leobotes Agryleus, Lysander Skambonides, and Pronapes Prasieus were named as accusers by the *Letters* (8.747 Hercher). Pronapes (*PA* 12250) was a famous chariot racer.[53] Lysander is otherwise unknown.

W. Robert Connor has identified three passages from the *Miscellanea* of Theodorus Metochites that name Lycomedes as a demagogue opponent of Themistocles.[54] He draws an intriguing picture of a feud between two branches of the Lycomids, with the part of the clan resident at Phlya attacking Themistocles; perhaps the general's restoration of the family telesterion at Phlya is to be seen as a gambit that did not work.

There is little use speculating on the coalition of families that obtained Themistocles' ostracism and condemnation. He had made enemies to spare, although the tradition shows that some—Aristeides, for instance—were unwilling to add death to exile (*Arist.* 25.10).

23.2-3 Ὁ γὰρ Παυσανίας πράττων ἐκεῖνα

Plutarch's sources were Thucydides (I 128-34) and Ephorus, as becomes clear from *De Hdt.mal.* 855F (*FGrH* 70 F 189). Tracing the story back even further, it would appear that Thucydides reconstructed the story from the "evidence" the Spartans brought to Athens to prove the

[52] "Leobotes Alkmeonos and Alkmeon Aristonymon," *Studies in Athenian Politics and Genealogy*, Historia Einzelschriften 19 (1972) 58.

[53] Raubitschek, *Hesperia* 8 (1939) 158f.

[54] "Lycomedes against Themistocles? A Note on Intragenos Rivalry," *Historia* 21 (1972) 569-574, citing pp. 608, 632, and 802 of the Müller-Kiessling ed. of Leipzig, 1821.

medism of Pausanias and the collusion of Themistocles. As
such "evidence" was routinely obtained (in Athens as in
Sparta) by the torture of household servants, it is plain that
the Spartans could have fabricated any story they wanted—
and probably did. The inconsistencies of Thucydides' narrative have long been recognized and are collected by Mabel
Lang in a provocative analysis.[55] The official story was that
Pausanias, having commenced treasonable correspondence
with Xerxes as long before as 478/7, and having been removed from Byzantium twice, was now at home in Sparta
and had written to Themistocles in Argos, inviting him to
join the conspiracy.[56]

23.4 Οὕτω Παυσανίου θανατωθέντος, ἐπιστολαί τινες εἰς ὑποψίαν
ἐνέβαλον τὸν Θεμιστοκλέα

Considering the care Pausanias had allegedly taken previously to conceal his treason, one must suspect these conveniently located documents. Ephorus, on whatever authority, claimed that Themistocles received Pausanias' invitation,
but refused to have anything to do with it.[57] Mabel Lang
convincingly argues that Pausanias had opened negotiations
with the Persians on Spartan orders. When, for some reason, they decided to dissociate themselves from this policy
the ephors made Pausanias the scapegoat and implicated
Themistocles to settle their old scores against him. This
reconstruction has the advantage of explaining most of the
peculiarities in Thucydides' story, but as Miss Lang admits,
is not on that account necessarily the correct explanation.[58]

[55] M. Lang, "Scapegoat Pausanias," *CJ* 63 (1967) 79ff.
[56] Since Themistocles' response was not preserved, the author of
the *Letters* (2.741, 14.754 Hercher) sought to fill the gap. Unfortunately he was not paying attention to Thucydides' implied chronology and said that Themistocles addressed the letters to Pausanias
at Byzantium, which would have been chronologically impossible.
[57] *FGrH* 70 F 189, *De Hdt.mal.* 855F; this much, at least, Diodorus
has correctly copied in his botched version, XI 54.3-4.
[58] There has been a recent revival of interest in the Pausanias
affair. Podlecki, "Themistocles and Pausanias," *Riv. Fil.* 104 (1976),
reviews recent opinion and suggests parallels in the accounts of the

It is impossible to guess at Plutarch's source for the statement that Themistocles defended himself by letter. This is not one of the *Letters* supplied by the anonymous epistolographer(s), but we can be sure that the rhetorical schools had produced an *Apologia Themistoclis* by Plutarch's day.

23.5 Διαβαλλόμενος γὰρ ὑπὸ τῶν ἐχθρῶν

Themistocles' response sounds like one devised in the sterile atmosphere of the rhetorical schools: how could I, who have always sought to rule and have been unwilling to be ruled, make myself and Hellas subject to barbarians? No contemporary could have invented such a defense. The prosecution would have immediately reminded the court that Hippias and Demaratus were also deposed rulers—but that did not keep them out of Xerxes' entourage.

23.6 Οὐ μὴν ἀλλὰ συμπεισθεὶς

Plutarch believed that the outcome of the trial *in absentia* was an order to arrest Themistocles for judgment "before the Greeks." See also Diodorus (XI 55.4): "before the com-

---

two Persian War heroes (305-307), parallels already proposed as Thucydidean structure by H. Konishi, "Thucydides' Method in the Episodes of Pausanias and Themistocles," *AJP* 91 (1970) 52-69 (which Podlecki seems not to have seen). See also J. F. Lazenby, "Pausanias, son of Kleombrotos," *Hermes* 103 (1975) 235-251; W. G. Forrest, "Pausanias and Themistokles Again," *Lakonikai Spoudai* 2 (Athens, 1975) 115-119, tries to date Pausanias' death as late as 465, but requires the assumption of an ancient editor who revised the text of Thucydides from Ephorus—an unacceptable breach of sound historiography, to say the least. Fr. Cornelius, "Pausanias," *Historia* 22 (1973) 502-504, believes Pausanias and Themistocles were working together for the democratization of Greece, a bizarre notion. A. Blamire, "Pausanias and Persia," *GRBS* 11 (1970) 295-305, comes closest to my own view—that we must take Thucydides at face value for the skeleton of the story he gives us, believing, e.g., that Pausanias was in character vain, arrogant, and ambitious, and that he did in fact open treasonable negotiations with Xerxes; but we can also assume a great deal of double dealing on the part of the ephors, who may have had a hand in the Persian negotiations and who certainly rigged evidence to blacken Pausanias' name (and Themistocles' as well) after his death.

mon *synhedrion* of the Greeks." But according to Thucydides, the Athenians agreed to pursue Themistocles, with nothing said about bringing him before some panhellenic tribunal. The very existence of such a body we know only from the veiled reference in Timocreon's poems (see above, comment to 21.4). In general, the tradition of this whole episode seems to come from the accounts of Thucydides and Ephorus,[59] but by Plutarch's day there had been the inevitable contamination by way of the rhetorical schools (see, for instance, *Rhet. Graec.* II 639, IX 591 Walz).

The legal status of Themistocles in the aftermath of his trial *in absentia* is curiously unclear, as a survey of the available evidence shows. According to Thucydides (I 135.2-3), the Spartans accused Themistocles of complicity in Pausanias' medism and the Athenians agreed to help the Spartans arrest him, the implication being that he was to be arrested so he could stand trial. The historian does not mention a trial *in absentia*.

Craterus, however, had found evidence in the archives at Athens of an *eisangelia* brought against Themistocles by Leobotes (above, 23.1). We are not sure of the jurisdiction of such a case in the 470's. According to Harpocration, an *eisangelia* was tried before Boule and Demos, but before the various restraints imposed upon the Areopagus by Ephialtes[60] the case might still have gone before that body, by solonian law (*AP* 8.4). Harpocration also said that the greatest punishments were provided for those who fled an *eisangelia*. No source specifies a sentence *in absentia*, but Lycurgus (*In Leocr.* 117-118) claimed that in the similar case of Hipparchus, the fugitive was condemned to death *in absentia* by the Demos. Thucydides in a later passage (I 138.6) said that Themistocles was secretly buried in Attica—οὐ γὰρ ἐξῆν

---

[59] Plut. *De cap.ex inim.* 89F; *Praec.ger.reip.* 805C; Nepos, *Them.* 8.2; Aristodemus 6.1; Aristides II 318; schol.Ar.*Eq.* 84.

[60] *AP* 25; but see R. Sealey, "Ephialtes," *CP* 59 (1964) 11ff., warning against assumptions about the powers that were taken from the Areopagus council.

θάπτειν ὡς ἐπὶ προδοσίᾳ φεύγοντος. This still does little to clarify the actual terms of the sentence, or specify what legal body handed the sentence down.

Other testimony in approximate chronological order follows.

Critias, in Aelian *VH* 10.17: his property was confiscated.

Plato, *Gorgias* 516d: he was punished with exile.

Demosth. 23.205: he was driven from the city.

Idomeneus (schol. Ar. *Vesp.* 947, *FGrH* 338 F 1): οἱ μέντοι Ἀθηναῖοι αὐτοῦ καὶ γένους ἀειφυγίαν κατέγνωσαν προδιδόντος τὴν Ἑλλάδα, καὶ αὐτοῦ ἡ οὐσία ἐδημεύθη.

Theophrastus and Theopompus in *Them.* 25.3: his property was confiscated.

Phylarchus in *Suda* s.v. Θεμιστοκλέους παῖδες[61] his descendants were exiled.

Cicero, *Laelius de amic.* 12.42: *in exilium expulsus. Ep.ad Brut.* I 15, 11: the punishment was also applied to his children.

Diod. XI 54-5: reports only his flight. 59.3 (and *POxy* 1610, 3.21): ὑπὸ τῆς πόλεως ἠτιμασμένον.

Schol. Ar. *Eq.* 84: he was exiled.

Idomeneus seems to offer the fullest explanation: the Athenians (which sounds like a decree of the people) sentenced him and his descendants to eternal banishment and confiscated his property. This is the general impression given by the other writers. Note that no source specifically reported a death sentence. Diodorus seems to report a sentence of *atimia*, which was equivalent, but in context he appears to be using the word rhetorically, rather than in a judicial sense.

On the basis of the judgment in 411/0 against Antiphon and Archeptolemus reported in *X orat.vit.* 833E-834, which called for execution, confiscation of all property, demolition of houses, no burial in Attica, and hereditary *atimia*,

<hr/>

[61] For Phylarchus as the source of this excerpt, see Frost, "Phylarchus, fragment 76," *AJP* 83 (1962) 419-422.

M. H. Hansen believes Themistocles was sentenced to death and his descendants to *atimia*.[62] But it is curious that no source said this expressly. The Athenians in control of such matters may in fact have preferred to leave the case in limbo for any number of reasons whose subtlety we can only guess at. We shall see Cleophantus, at least, back in Athens and in control of his property at a later time (Plato, *Meno* 93d, and comment to 32.1, below), which may mean that a relative outside the immediate *genos* was quietly allowed to buy back Themistocles' estate after it had been confiscated by the Demos.

[62] *Eisangelia* (Odense, 1975) 70.

VII

FLIGHT AND EXILE: COMMENTARY TO CHAPTERS 24-32

24.1 Προαισθόμενος δ' ἐκεῖνος εἰς Κέρκυραν διεπέρασεν, οὔσης αὐτῷ πρὸς τὴν πόλιν εὐεργεσίας

With this chapter, the Themistocles romance par excellence begins. The contrast between the reception in Kerkyra and by Admetus in Epirus was told best by Thucydides, who simply noted the facts as he knew them and let his readers draw their own conclusions about the irony of the human condition. But even by Thucydides' day, the legends had begun because of the drama of the contrast: the rich and powerful state of Kerkyra, which had carefully stayed neutral in the Persian Wars, gave in to its erstwhile benefactor's pursuers with indecent haste, while the primitive Admetus, thirsting for revenge, saw his old enemy a helpless suppliant and immediately perceived his obligations under an ancient and honorable code—a code that remained operative even much later, as in Plut. *Pyrrhus* 3.1-3. Only a few miles of water separate Kerkyra from the mainland, but all Greeks knew the true cultural gulf. The northwestern corner of the Greek world was a rugged land where old and rigid tribal codes dictated the proper requital for friend and foe in all situations. Kerkyra was a softer, more civilized place, where expediency could always serve as a higher— and more sensible law.[1]

---

[1] E.g., Hermippus comicus, in Athen. 27F: the Kerkyreans δίχα θυμὸν ἔχουσι.

Thucydides' sources for the tale (I 136-137.1) are difficult to guess, for the story has now become that of a solitary man in flight, and one must speculate how the details of that flight became known. Themistocles himself was the most obvious source, telling the hair-raising stories of his adventures with gusto to his friends and relatives. When his family returned to Athens after mid-century, this version would have become a popular tradition. The pursuers no doubt had their own story to explain their failure. Thucydides may also have heard a Kerkyrean version of the story. We can guess at the vigorous and self-righteous explanation, "after all, what could we have done . . . look, put yourself in our place." A Molossian variation of the tradition may be discounted.

Plutarch explained the *euergesia*: "He was an arbiter when the Kerkyreans and Corinthians had a dispute and he ended the hostility by deciding that the Corinthians should pay a settlement of twenty talents and that both should share Leucas as a colony." The scholiast to Thucydides (I 136.1) also tried to explain. After the war, the allies were about to destroy the Kerkyreans for not having taken part in the war, but Themistocles said that if they destroyed everyone who had not fought, Greece would have been better off with the Persians as victors. This is, of course, a ridiculous theory, as not even the states that actually medized were thus threatened (see above, comment to 20.3-4). As Herodotus explained (7.168), after the war, everyone simply swallowed the Kerkyrean excuse of adverse winds, although he makes it clear that no one believed it.

Plutarch's source is known and was a respectable one: Theophrastus' Πολιτικὰ πρὸς τοὺς καιρούς, on which the biographer had once written an essay (Lamprias catalogue no. 53). The key passage is also quoted for us by a grammarian, in *POxy* vii 1012C, published by Hunt in 1910 (with much assistance from Wilamowitz) from a third-century A.D. papyrus:[2]

---

[2] The text is that of L. Piccirilli, "Temistocle evergetes dei Cor-

Θεόφραστος

[δὲ ἐν τοῖς περ]ὶ καιρῶν φησ[ὶ] δια
[φορὰν ἔχει]ν τοὺς Κερκυραί[ο]υς
[Κορινθίοις] καὶ διαιτητὴν γε
[νόμεν]ον κρεῖναι ἀποδοῦ
ν[αι Κ]ερκυρ[α]ίοις τὸν Κορινθί
ω[ν δῆ]μον εἴκοσι τάλαντα [Λευ]
κ[άδα καὶ κο]ι̣[νῇ νέμειν] ἀ̣[μφοτ]
[ἑρων ἄποικον———]

This information supplements Thucydides nicely, and there is little reason to doubt any part of it except Plutarch's remark (which may be his own interpretation) that the arbitration "ended the hostility." Given the poor condition of relations between the cities, the judgment would seem more likely to perpetuate the feud. It probably found a place in the catalogue of Corinthian grudges against their colony, and while Thucydides did not see fit to mention it (for instance, in I 30.1) the story got into the tradition studied by Theophrastus.

It is difficult for us to see what legal grounds there might have been for dividing Leucas between Corinth and Kerkyra. The sources are unanimous in naming Corinth as the mother city.[3] Some of the colonists may have come from Kerkyrean families at a time when that island was subject to Corinth (Hdt. 3.52) and sending our joint colonies.[4]

---

ciresi," *ASNP* 3 (1973), 317-355, with everything after *talanta* restored *exempli gratia* from Plutarch. Piccirilli has written an exhaustive commentary on this entire episode; cf. his *Arbitrati interstatali greci* (Pisa, 1973) 61-66.

[3] Hdt. 8.45; Thuc. I 30.1; Scylax 34; Strabo X 2.8; in some detail by Nicolaus of Damascus (Const. Porph. *Exc.de insid.* p. 20, 6, *FGrH* 90 F 57): Cypselus sent his illegitimate sons Pylades and Echiades as oecists.

[4] For instance, the colony to Apollonia, Strabo VII 5.8; Ps.Scymnus 439-440 Mue., as suggested by A. J. Graham, *Colony and Mother City* (Manchester, 1964) 129-131.

Plutarch seems to have believed that Leucas was colonized—
perhaps a second time—by Periander (*De sera num.* 552EF)
when he was *de facto* ruler of Kerkyra. Thus the Kerkyreans
in the 480's could have felt that some of their citizens held
legal title to part (or perhaps all) of Leucas. The date of
the arbitration must have been before the Persian Wars.
Corinth would hardly have accepted Themistocles as an
arbiter after his fracas with Adeimantus and the Corinthians
on the eve of Salamis.[5]

Nepos, *Them.* 8.3, and Aristodemus 10.1 also mentioned
Themistocles' visit and rejection by the Kerkyreans. Diodorus (XI 56.1), on the other hand, ignored the sojourn and
had Themistocles skip directly from Argos to Epirus under
the impression that Themistocles and Admetus were old
friends.

24.2-3 Ἐκεῖθεν δ' εἰς Ἤπειρον ἔφυγε
Thucydides has: ἐς τὴν ἤπειρον τὴν καταντικρύ (I 136.1). The
word meaning mainland in general had not yet become the
proper noun for the land of the Molossians by the time of
Thucydides. The historian implied that Themistocles had
been instrumental in persuading the Athenians to turn down
an unspecified request—χρεία τις—of Admetus (I 136.4).
The scholiast adds details: Admetus had once asked the
Athenians for an alliance, which Themistocles had persuaded them to turn down (see also schol. Aristides III
680). Plutarch here simply embroidered Thucydides. The
request of Admetus was not specified, but we are told that
the king went away thirsting for revenge. Like any barbarian warlord, he did not understand considerations of
Machtpolitik but took all differences of opinion personally.

24.4 Ἔχων γὰρ αὐτοῦ τὸν υἱὸν παῖδα πρὸς τὴν ἑστίαν προσέπεσε
This was supposed to be the most powerful form of supplication and impossible to reject (so also Thuc. I 137.1). As
many scholars have noted, Themistocles' supplication re-
calls the story of Telephus, who, wounded by Achilles,

[5] Hdt. 8.59, 61; so also Piccirilli, *ASNP* 3 (1973) 343.

sought out his enemy at the court of Agamemnon as the only man who could cure the festering wound. On the advice of Clytemnestra, he seized the infant Orestes and threatened to kill him unless Achilles healed him (the version of Hyginus, *Fab.* 101). This coincidence has been most thoroughly discussed by Louis Séchan,[6] who believed there were two fifth-century variations of the tale, one by Aeschylus (schol. Ar.*Ach.* 332), in which Telephus held Orestes as a simple act of supplication, that is, *not* threatening to kill him. He believed Aeschylus had written his *Telephus* to commemorate the story of his friend Themistocles, with which everyone was familiar by that time. He suggested this version was illustrated on a pelike from Vulci now in the British Museum. Séchan proposed that a later variation of the *Telephus* by Euripides was more dramatic and portrayed Telephus threatening to kill the infant, as shown on a Cumaean hydria now in the Naples Museum.

This is not an unimportant distinction. A supplicant does not threaten a hostage, nor did Thucydides imply this in any way. The whole point of supplication is complete submission—always a potent form of appeal to the Greeks. Hammond notes the appropriateness of such supplication at the court of a descendant of Neoptolemus, who had killed Priam at the altar and had been slain in return by Apollo.[7] There is a ring of truth to the tale: Admetus the barbarian, simple in his desire for revenge, was just as uncomplicated when faced by his former enemy—now helpless and sitting as a supplicant in time-honored fashion. His obligation was clear and he accepted it. The author of the *Letters* (5.745 Hercher), on the other hand, misses the boat entirely: "Admetus recognized me and well I know he hated me, but he feared for his son and dreaded my knife."[8]

[6] *Etudes sur la tragédie grecque dans ses rapports avec la céramique* (Paris, 1926) 123-127.

[7] Pindar, *Paean* 6.113f.; N.G.L. Hammond, *Epirus* (Oxford, 1967) 492.

[8] C. Méautis, "Thucydide et Thémistocle," *AC* 20 (1951) 297-

24.5 ἔνιοι μὲν
Some said it was Phthia, the wife of Admetus, who suggested the form of supplication to Themistocles (as did
Clytemnestra in the Telephus legend). Plutarch meant
Thucydides here and perhaps the writer consulted by the
scholiast to Aristides (III 680), who followed Thucydides
but improved the simple hearth to the altar of Hestia.

Others said Admetus himself proposed the supplication to
give the persistent pursuers a religious pretext: συντραγῳδῆσαι
τὴν ἱκεσίαν. This was more or less the version of Nepos
(*Them.* 8.4) and Aristodemus 10.2 (Nepos also changed
the child to a daughter and made Admetus and Themistocles old friends; cf. Diod. XI 56.1; Libanius 15.41). The
Letters (5.745 Hercher) made them old enemies and attributed the method of supplication to the queen—named,
in this instance, Cratesipolis.

24.6-7 Ἐκεῖ δ' αὐτῷ τὴν γυναῖκα καὶ τοὺς παῖδας ἐκκλέψας ἐκ τῶν
Ἀθηνῶν Ἐπικράτης ὁ Ἀχαρνεὺς ἀπέστειλεν
This was on the authority of Stesimbrotus (*FGrH* 107
F 3). But Plutarch could show that Stesimbrotus refuted
himself: "he either forgets all this [the presence of Themistocles' wife] or makes Themistocles himself forget it, saying that he sailed to Sicily and asked Hieron the tyrant for
his daughter's hand in marriage, promising to make the
Greeks his subjects." Once more this should remind us what
a peculiar treatise Stesimbrotus must have written. Surprisingly, Epicrates of Acharnae seems to have been a real
person. He has attested descendants much later in the fourth
century: an Epicrates, son of Hippocles of Acharnae (*IG*
ii² 1492B.110-111, 306/5) and a possible nephew of the foregoing: Epicrates, son of Diocles of Acharnae (*IG* ii² 505.5,
302/1).

304, denied any connection with the Telephus legend, proposing
instead that Thucydides accepted the tradition uncritically because
it illustrated Themistocles' adaptability so well; *contra* Wilamowitz,
AA I 150; Beloch, *GG* II.2, 146.

25.1 Ταῦτα δ' οὐκ εἰκός ἐστιν οὕτω γενέσθαι

As Plutarch pointed out, it was not likely that Themistocles would have gone anywhere near Hieron after urging the crowd at Olympia to tear down the tyrant's tent, a story he has from Theophrastus' *On Kingship*. But Theophrastus himself may have his Sicilian tyrants mixed up, as pointed out over a century ago by Arnold Schaeffer: it is hard to see how the crowd could have been sympathetic to an attack on the Sicilian tyrant. Gelon and Hieron had also suffered attack by barbarians and were entitled to as much panhellenic esteem as any of the other allies. Theophrastus must have been thinking of Dionysius, therefore, who was attacked in a speech by Lysias at the 98th Olympiad in 388.[9]

The author of the *Letters* (20.758 Hercher) also knew of Themistocles' intention of asking help from Gelon, "who ruled the Syracusans at that time, had once had substantial connections with me and who would not give in to the Athenians." Just before Themistocles left, however, a messenger arrived to say that Gelon had died and Hieron was on the throne. Besides our usual suspicions of the *Letters*, the chronology brands this story as a fiction, for Gelon died about 478.[10]

25.2 Θουκυδίδης δέ φησι

Plutarch's story is a condensation of Thuc. I 137.2-3, the main elements of which are as follows: Themistocles reached Pydna and took ship on a merchant vessel, unrecognized by anyone on board. A storm came up and drove the ship to the shelter of the island of Naxos, where, as fate would have it, the Athenians were besieging the city. Themistocles, fearing that he would be recognized, revealed himself to the captain and said that if he did not assist him he would tell the Athenians he had been bribed but that if he was saved,

---

[9] Dion.Hal. *De Lysia* 29-30; cf. X *orat.vit* 836D; A. Schaeffer, *Philologus* 18 (1862) 187-190.

[10] Diod. XI 38.7; schol.Pindar, *Pyth.* I inscr.; Eusebius, *Ol* 75.4. Marmor Parium A 53, 55 misdated the accession of both Gelon and Hieron: 478/7 and 472/1.

he would make it worth his while. The captain agreed, let no one off the ship, and after riding out the gale for a day and night sailed off safely to Ephesus. Later on, when Themistocles had received funds from home, he rewarded the captain handsomely. Plutarch follows this scheme except for adding a helmsman and leaving out the later payment to the captain.

Except for Diodorus, who ignored this part of the journey (XI 56.1-4), all other authors who tell the story follow Thucydides closely.[11] There would be no difficulty with this passage except that the normally reliable Seitenstettensis manuscript of Plutarch's *Lives* has θάσον for νάξον. Although the other independent MSS have νάξον, including the older Vaticanus Gr. 138, this variant has been seized upon by those who would like a late dating of Themistocles' flight to make it coincide with the siege of Thasos about 465 (Thuc. I 100.2) rather than with that of Naxos three or four years previously (Thuc. I 98.4, and see comment above to 22.4).[12] As I once pointed out, questions of chronology and paleography must yield to meteorological considerations: it is almost impossible for a ship to be blown at least a hundred nautical miles north of its normal course in the Aegean because the wind simply does not blow in that direction. Even as I write this, in Athens in February, the sirocco has been blowing for a week (including a brief spell at force nine, during which time small craft were not allowed out of port). But the sirocco blows at great force only fitfully, and it weakens the further north one goes in the Aegean. I can still see no reason on the basis of one MS

[11] Nepos, *Them.* 8.5-7, quoting Thuc. in 9.1; Polyaenus I 30.8; Aristodemus 10.3 (where Themistocles threatened to kill the captain instead of implicate him).

[12] Gomme raised the possibility only to reject it, *HCT* I 98f.; the most detailed defense of the Thasos reading is that of Flacelière, *REA* 55 (1953) 5-14; cf. Forrest, *CQ* 10 (1960) 241, and a most forced interpretation in *Lakonikai Spoudai* 2 (1975) 116-119. Mary White, *JHS* 84 (1964) 148 n. 32, proposed Thasos and a northern port of call along the way.

variant to postulate what would be an extraordinary reversal of the normal Aegean weather; the Athenian fleet would have been campaigning only in the summer anyway, and south winds, infrequent in winter, are nonexistent in summer.[13]

Knowledgeable Greek yachtsmen inform me that Naxos does not really make sense either, as there would be far more likely harbors closer to any direct route Themistocles would have taken. And P. J. Rhodes feels the whole story may be a fabrication, or at least embroidery by Themistocles telling his adventures in later years, and that it is not worth the trouble to make any of these problematic data and dates fit together.[14] This is attractive but defeatist. One can still argue that Thucydides had reliable sources and chose not to put in his story any number of details which would have made the episode more believable. I believe we must accept the outline of his account and the chronology it implies: that Themistocles in flight encountered the Athenian fleet besieging Naxos in c. 468, give or take a year.

25.3 Τῶν δὲ χρημάτων

As Thucydides said (I 137.3), the money he had laid up was sent to him in Asia by friends in Athens and Argos (followed by Nepos, *Them.* 8.7, citing Thucydides). For the amount of the estate that had been confiscated, Plutarch cited Theopompus' figure of one hundred talents (*FGrH* 115 F 86) and Theophrastus' figure of eighty talents. Theopompus' source may have been Critias, happily preserved in a citation by Aelian (*VH* 10.17). Plutarch does not cite Theophrastus by title; the work could have been either the *Politica* or *On Monarchy*, both of which were quoted by him in the previous chapter. We also know that Theophrastus believed Themistocles to have been poor as a young man;[15] he may therefore have noted the contrast in the general's fortunes in later life. From Critias as well may come

---

[13] *CR* 12 (1962) 15-16.   [14] *Historia* 19 (1970) 395-400.
[15] *De eligendis magistratibus* I 18-35, ed. by J. J. Keaney, A. Szegedy-Maszak, *TAPA* 106 (1976) 227f.

the claim that Themistocles' fortune before he entered public life was only three talents (three *or* five, in *Cato* and
Arist.comp. 1.4). Actually, three talents was considered a
fair patrimony in the fourth century and would have been
worth more in the fifth.[16] There were many ways for an
Athenian politician to increase his fortune, some of them
even legal.[17] A great increase in the value of land would
not be surprising for the period 500-473. The landed property of Themistocles may have been sold at auction, and
the sale figure was remembered and got into the tradition
about the great man.

CHAPTERS 26-29: INTRODUCTORY REMARKS

These next four chapters should be briefly analyzed as a
unit, for they form the high point of the Themistocles romance: Themistocles at the court of the Great King. Plutarch has changed his style in the telling of this episode. He
has slowed down the action to a sort of *mise en scène* with
dialogue, as if we were watching a drama—probably the
effect he intended. But the drama is interrupted from time
to time by scholarly annotation, as if Plutarch was reminding his audience that he was not simply a storyteller. The
scheme of these four chapters can be analyzed on page 210.

Many years ago, L. Bodin made a good case for the thesis
that all the dramatic action is one unified story and can be
attributed to Phanias.[18] Plutarch cited Phanias for the episode of Artabanus the chiliarch, and Bodin felt sure that
Themistocles' insistence on staying anonymous until he met
the Great King personally was because of the price on his
head; this is to be seen therefore as a reference back to the
previous chapter where the reward was first mentioned. I

[16] Isaeus, 3.18, 3.25; cf. Davies, *APF* xx-xxiv.
[17] The same could be said for Lyndon Johnson, Richard Nixon,
and Gerald Ford.
[18] "Histoire et biographie, Phanias d'Erèse," *REG* 28 (1915) 251-
281; followed by R. Laqueur, "Phainias," *RE* 19 (1938) 1567ff.

(The dramatic narrative is bracketed, the annotations inserted by Plutarch are indented. The arrows indicate which parts of the narrative refer back explicitly to a previous part and therefore identify the story as a unified whole.)

Themistocles landed at Kyme.

The King had set a price of 200T on his head.

He stayed with his friend Nicogenes at Aegae.

Nicogenes' pedagogue uttered prophetic words.

Themistocles had a vision in a dream.

Nicogenes sent him to the King in a closed palanquin.

> Plutarch cited Thucydides and Charon *contra* Ephorus, Dinon, Clitarchus, and Heraclides.

Themistocles and Artabanus discuss *proskynesis*.

He will not reveal his name except to the King.

> Plutarch cited Phanias plus a detail by Eratosthenes.

Themistocles prostrated himself before the King.

He identified himself.

He told about the omens at Nicogenes' house.

The next day he prostrated himself again and was received.

The King said he had earned the 200T reward himself.

Themistocles asked for a year to learn Persian.

> Plutarch concluded the story, added the Demaratus anecdote, cited various writers, Neanthes, Phanias.

would add to this thesis that the emphasis on *proskynesis* is seen repeatedly in these chapters and also seems to demonstrate a unifying theme. There are also two obvious references in the audiences with the King to previous parts of the narrative: the omens at Nicogenes' house and the King's reference to the reward.

This would be a strong argument for the authorship of Phanias except for Plutarch's irrepressible tendency to tell

stories his own way (notice that we have just seen a gratui-
tous *kybernetes* added to Thucydides' account of the merchant ship). Plutarch also tells us that he knows accounts
of this meeting with the King by Charon of Lampsacus,
Ephorus, Dinon, Clitarchus, Heracleides, Eratosthenes,
Neanthes, and possibly Theopompus; it is hard to believe
that he could have preserved a long story by one author
for once in his life without bringing in some details from
others. I do believe that all the bracketed parts of these four
chapters are in fact one unified narrative and that Phanias
had a great deal to do with it. But we cannot exclude the
possibility that some of the details came from some other
author—or perhaps imply an authorless tradition. Details
of this account are treated more fully below.

We still depend on Thucydides for the most likely account of what happened. The historian had the advantage
of knowing a tradition repeated by living relatives of the
great man before the tradition had entirely become a romance. The main problem with Thucydides' version is al-
leged to be the chronology (e.g. Gomme, *HCT* I 397f.). If
Themistocles did sail past Naxos under Athenian siege in,
say 469 or 468, he must then have lingered anonymously at
Ephesus or elsewhere in Asia for at least three or four years,
until Xerxes died and he could write to Artaxerxes. Critics
of this long sojourn in Ionia evidently expect Themistocles
to create a stir wherever he may be (although exactly one
fact is known about his years in Athens between 478 and
about 473—that he produced a play by Phrynichus). We
must simply accept the fact that as he knew in all other
circumstances how to turn matters to his advantage so he
also knew how to live without attracting attention when
his life depended on it.

The rest of the Thucydidean story describes how Themistocles wrote to Artaxerxes. He had doubtless kept himself well informed about the Persian court and had some
idea of his chances of success. We are then told about his
interlude learning Persian and his eventual reception and
exceptional treatment. This is a short, straightforward story

which leaves many questions unanswered. Nevertheless, it
will have to do, for the only alternative is the romance,
with all its obvious fabrications.

26.1 Ἐπεὶ δὲ κατέπλευσεν εἰς Κύμην
This is a sudden switch from the authority of Thucydides,
who had left Themistocles safely at Ephesus. It has been
noted (e.g. by Bodin and Flacelière)[19] that Kyme was the
home of Ephorus and that historian, according to Strabo
(XIII 3.6, *FGrH* 70 F 236) was so eager to bring Kyme into
his account that at one time he added: "at this time, the
Kymaioi were quiet." But Ephorus is only one of many
possible sources (Bodin noted that Phanias, as an Aeolian,
was just as likely to have preferred an Aeolian locale). None
of the other details here—the bounty hunters Ergoteles and
Pythodorus, the bounty itself, Nicogenes the guest friend
of Themistocles from Aegae—appear elsewhere in the extant
testimonia. According to Diodorus (XI 56.4), an extremely
rich man sheltered Themistocles, but his name was Lysi-
theides, who had supposedly entertained Xerxes' whole
army.[20]

26.2-3 μετὰ τὸ δεῖπνον ἐκ θυσίας τινὸς
The pedagogue uttered the prophetic words—*boule* would
come in the night—and the subsequent dream was auspi-
cious: a snake turning into an eagle, which we know was the
emblem of the Persian King (Xen. *Cyr.* VII 1.3; cf. Artemi-
dorus, *Oneir.* II 20).

26.4-6 Πέμπεται δ' οὖν ὑπὸ τοῦ Νικογένους μηχανησαμένου τι
τοιόνδε
Flacelière (Budé ed.) translates οὖν in the sense *quoi qu'il
en soit* = be that as it may. In other words, Plutarch was not
going to make any great claims for the authenticity of the
dream. The exotic palanquin for transporting ladies of the
harem was well known (Xen. *Cyr.* VI 4.11, etc.). In Diodorus (XI 56.7-8) the same means of transport was de-

[19] Bodin, ibid. 262; Flacelière, *REA* 55 (1953) 14.
[20] One is usually reminded at this point of Pythius in Hdt. 7.27.

scribed; this much at least was similar in the accounts of the two writers. The author of the *Letters* (20.760 Hercher), on the other hand, not knowing of the price on Themistocles' head, let him surrender to a Persian satrap named Artabazus, who sent him to Susa on horseback, accompanied by thirteen Persians on camels.

27.1-2 Θουκυδίδης μὲν οὖν καὶ Χάρων ὁ Λαμψακηνὸς (Thuc. I 137.3; Charon, *FGrH* 262 F 11). Of those named, Charon was the earliest source.[21] Interpretation of this passage must begin with a translation: "Thucydides and Charon of Lampsacus in fact record that Xerxes having died, the meeting was between his son and Themistocles; but Ephorus, Dinon, Clitarchus, Heracleides, and many others more say that he came to Xerxes himself. Thucydides seems to correspond best with chronological records (τὰ χρονικά); these, however, are not completely in accord with each other." I read συνταττομένοις here with the UMA group of manuscripts, Gomme (*HCT* I 398 n. 2), Jacoby (*FGrH* 689 F 6, etc.), and *LSJ*⁹ s.v. ἀτρέμα, *contra* συντεταγμένος S: συντεταραγμένοις Cobet, Ziegler (BT, 1957), Flacelière (Budé).[22] The reading of S is ungrammatical, or so it seems to me. συντάττω and συνταράττω are both well attested in Plutarch's vocabulary, but a glance through Wyttenbach's *Lexicon Plutarcheum* will show that the latter verb in Plutarch usually refers to military affairs, that is, physical confusion. συνταττομένοις makes sense as it stands, and a whole group of manuscripts have this reading. For τοῖς δὲ χρονικοῖς, see Plut. *Solon* 27.1: χρονικοῖς τισι λεγομένοις κανόσιν. This was the kind of source Plutarch would have consulted, rather than read and remembered.

[21] See above, chapter I, and n. 25; Podlecki, *Themistocles* 54f.; Jacoby *FGrH* IIIa, ad loc.
[22] συνταττομένοις was also defended by H. Erbse, reviewing Flacelière, in *Gnomon* 34 (1962) 770, and by D. A. Russell, quoted by Forrest, *Lakonikai Spoudai* 2 (1975) 118 n. 2. In his 1960 edition, Ziegler read συντεταγμένοις.

Dinon (*FGrH* 690 F 13) and Heracleides of Kyme (*FGrH* 689 F 6) both lived in the fourth century and wrote *Persika*. Plutarch cited Dinon in eight other places, primarily in the *Artoxerxes*; Heracleides twice—also in the *Artoxerxes*. Clitarchus had a reputation as a colorful writer. He was Dinon's son (Pliny, *NH* 10.136) and seems to have written only one book, his Alexander history.[23] In creating a confrontation between Themistocles and Xerxes, Ephorus and these other writers chose the more dramatic story, but Thucydides was closer to events and Charon came from a city that had been assigned to Themistocles and even continued to honor him and his descendants with an annual festival (see comment to 29.11).

Nepos was also aware of the chronological controversy (*Them.* 9.1): *scio plerosque ita scripsisse, Themistoclen Xerxe regnante in Asiam transisse, sed ego potissimum Thucydidi credo, quod et aetate proximus de iis, qui illorum temporum historiam relinquerunt et eiusdem civitatis fuit.* He went on to quote Thucydides on the letter to Artaxerxes. Other writers following the Artaxerxes tradition were Cicero, *Ad Att.* X 8.7 (citing Thucydides); Aristodemus 10.4; Philostratus, *Imag.* 2.31, *Vit.Apol.* 1.29; Themistius, 15, p. 234; schol. Ar. *Eq.* 84; *Suda* s.v. Themistocles. The author of the *Letters* (20.761 Hercher) did not name Artaxerxes, but quoted him as saying that Themistocles was the reason he and his father did not rule Greece. Diodorus referred to Xerxes throughout, including a citation of "some writers" who said Xerxes planned a new expedition against Greece and wanted Themistocles to lead it (XI 56.5-58.2). Also favoring the Xerxes tradition were Strabo, XIII 1.12; Valerius Maximus, V 3 ext. 3 (although some MSS have Artaxerxes), VIII 7 ext. 15; Libanius, 15.40.

27.2-7 ἐντυγχάνει πρῶτον Ἀρταβάνῳ τῷ χιλιάρχῳ
It is a little disappointing to realize that after the impressive scholarly discussion of the chronological sources and the

[23] T. S. Brown, "Cleitarchus," *AJP* 71 (1950) 134-155; cf. P. Goukowsky, *REA* 71 (1969) 320-337.

recognition that Thucydides' account was more accurate, Plutarch immediately switched to a long account by Phanias, who evidently believed Xerxes was still alive. For the chiliarch Artabanus, plotting to take over the throne, murdered Xerxes and tried to kill Artaxerxes as well, but was slaim in the attempt.[24]

The whole theme of the Artabanus episode was the Persian custom of *proskynesis*—prostration before the King— normally so offensive to the Greeks (e.g., Hdt. 7.136). In later times Conon was unwilling to do obeisance as instructed by the chiliarch Tithraustes and communicated with the King by letter instead (Nepos, *Conon* 3; Justin, VI 2). The same Tithraustes told Ismenias the Theban he would have to prostrate himself; Ismenias got around this by surreptitiously dropping his ring and going to his knees to pick it up (Plut. *Artox.* 22.8 and Aelian, *VH* 1.21, no doubt from the same tradition).

27.8 Οὕτω μὲν ὁ Φανίας φησίν. Ὁ δ᾽ Ἐρατοσθένης ἐν τοῖς Περὶ πλούτου

We see the great polymath here in the unlikely role of adding a trivial detail to a most untrustworthy story. The full title of the work was Περὶ πλούτου καὶ πενίας (*FGrH* 241 F 23, Diog.Laert. 9.66) and seems to have been highly anecdotal. Jacoby (ad F 27) doubted that Eratosthenes misdated Artaxerxes in his better-known chronological work.

28.1 Ἐπειδὴ οὖν εἰσήχθη πρὸς βασιλέα καὶ προσκυνήσας

The emphasis on prostration indicates that this is still part of the same story as the last chapter.

28.2-4 Ἥκω σοι, βασιλεῦ, Θεμιστοκλῆς ὁ Ἀθηναῖος ἐγὼ

Most surviving sources which report the confrontation seem to adopt Thucydides' version of what Themistocles wrote to the King and what was later said during their actual meet-

---

[24] Ctesias 60-61; Diod. XI 69; Arist. *Pol.* 1311b; Justin, III 1. Artabanus ruled seven months, according to the Egyptian king lists in Manetho, *FGrH* 609 F 2-3c, p. 50.

ing although they prefer to eliminate the letter and present Themistocles at court in far more dramatic fashion (Thuc. I 137.4-138.2). There are a few exceptions, and some pure fiction, but there are no traces of an *early* tradition that departs from Thucydides in any significant way (in Diodorus XI 56.8-57.5, the description of an angry Persian mob demanding justice and the appointment of a jury of noble Persians to try Themistocles is sufficient to brand the whole lot as nonsense). It is therefore necessary to discuss Thucydides for a moment, for there are some claims made in the letter to Artaxerxes that that monarch might have found questionable.

It was customary for anyone approaching the King for a favor to claim that they had done the King some benefit in the past (for instance, Pausanias, Thuc. I 128.7). This was Themistocles' claim: γράψας τήν τε ἐκ Σαλαμῖνος προάγγελσιν τῆς ἀναχωρήσεως καὶ τὴν τῶν γεφυρῶν.[25] By mid-century, most Athenians believed that Themistocles' second message was meant to serve more than one purpose, following the same tradition as Herodotus 8.109: Themistocles advised the Athenians not to break the Hellespont bridges "intending to lay up something to his account with the Persian so that he should have a place to turn in case he should suffer something from the Athenians; and indeed it happened." We may assume that Artaxerxes believed the second message to be an authentic warning. But what about the first message, sent by Sicinnus on the eve of Salamis? Could Themistocles actually have thought that Artaxerxes would believe this had been an honest attempt to assist the Persian side? This ruse had been commemorated by Aeschylus in the *Persae* (361-362) in no uncertain terms eight years after the war, and we assume that Themistocles had happily taken credit for it. One did not become Persian King without a certain understanding of human wiles, and Artaxerxes was no exception, although he was young at accession.

---

[25] I agree with Gomme, *HCT* I 441 ad loc., that the two messages, Hdt. 8.75.2 and 8.110.3 are meant.

Moreover, he was surrounded by Greek exiles and flatterers of all kinds who would be bound to resent any newcomer and only too eager to pick holes in his story. Certainly they all knew exactly why Themistocles was famed for his cunning and exactly what verses 361-362 of the *Persae* referred to.

It is difficult to accept Thucydides' reported letter of Themistocles as it stands. On the other hand, there is undoubtedly a great deal that we do not know; Themistocles would never have gone up to Susa on the strength of one exchange of letters. Other arrangements must have been concluded so that he knew exactly what he could expect before he put himself into the King's hands. We might also recognize that Persian Kings took it for granted that top Greek politicians who fell from favor at home would eventually show up at Susa—and that they were all so dishonest in Persian terms that one could only judge them on style rather than promises, explanations, and apologies. Of all the writers who report this meeting, it is surprisingly Libanius, who knew his Thucydides and who had experience of courts something like that of the Persian kings, who interpreted the situation most convincingly: "and [these cities], it seems to me, were the reward for his *megalopsychia*, not for the promises he used to make—to enslave the Greeks to the King." And he added, why would anyone trust a man who had already attempted to betray his own country (15.40)? Antony Raubitschek has also suggested to me the enormous propaganda value the defection of Themistocles represented to Artaxerxes—at a time when Persian prestige was at its lowest.[26]

28.5 τὸ μάντευμα τοῦ Δωδωναίου Διός

Plutarch mentions this as if we should be familiar with it. Evidently a popular tradition which has not survived

[26] See the encounter as reported by schol. Ar. *Eq.* 84; Aristodemus 10.4; *POxy* 1610, fr. 1; *Letters* 20.761 Hercher; and briefly by Themistius, 6 p. 85; once again by Libanius, *Laud.Demosth.* 5.16.

brought Themistocles to Dodona on the way from Admetus' court to Pydna and produced an oracular response
for him there: "proceed to one with the same name as
mine." Both god and King were known as μέγας. Since Plutarch reported this response in the same sentence as the
omens at Nicogenes' house, it would not be surprising if
the detour to Dodona had been part of the Phanias story.
But Plutarch was capable of shifting rapidly from one tradition to another, as we have seen repeatedly, and the tale of
the Dodona response might just as well be one of those
things "that came to mind" (as in Qc 629D).

28.6 Ἀρειμάνιον
Plutarch knew about the dualism inherent in Zoroastrianism:
the struggle of the evil principle (Ahriman) against the
good principle (Ormuzd).[27] He saw Ahriman in the form
of a typical Greek apotropaic deity: one entreats him to
keep on counseling—one's enemies.

29.1-4 is the sequel of the previous chapter. The threatening aspect of the guards and the remark of Rhoxanes the
chiliarch had been added to the tradition somewhere along
the way to heighten suspense. The comparison with the rug
was also noted in *Apophth.Them.* 15, 185E.

29.5-6 ἡσθέντος τοῦ βασιλέως
The King gave Themistocles a year to prepare himself, an
aspect of the tradition that is similar to the year interval reported by Thucydides (I 138.1-2). The phenomenon of a
Greek learning Persian attracted attention from other writers. Thucydides had been realistic: "he learned what he
could" (I 138.1). Nepos was not satisfied; his Themistocles
learned Persian better than the natives (*Them.* 10.1).[28] The
details about his close relationship with the King and his

[27] *De Is.et Osir.* 47, 369F-370C, where Theopompus is cited (*FGrH*
115 F 65).
[28] Cf. schol.Ar. *Eq.* 84; Athen. 535E; Aristodemus 10.4.

mother, and his discussions with the magi are preserved by
Plutarch alone, in extant literature.

29.7 Ἐπεὶ δὲ Δημάρατος ὁ Σπαρτιάτης
This presumptuous request to wear the tiara upright does
not sound like the cautious Demaratus we see in Herodotus
8.65. But it scarcely matters as this story could be told about
any Greek at the Persian court. It was attributed to Phylarchus by various lexicographers.[29] Plutarch may have some
of the additional details from Theophrastus, *On Kingship*,
which he quoted in 25.1; the lexica add the information that
it was Theophrastus in that work who called the tiara a
kitaris, the word used by Plutarch.

29.9 Λέγεται δὲ καὶ τοὺς ὕστερον βασιλεῖς
Themistocles became the honored exile par excellence; later
Kings, trying to recruit Greeks, promised to treat them
even better than Themistocles. Phanias elsewhere gave the
example of Entimus the Cretan (in Athen. 48D-F, fr. 27
Wehrli).

29.10 Ὦ παῖδες, ἀπωλόμεθα ἄν, εἰ μὴ ἀπωλόμεθα
This was frequently cited in ancient literature.[30]

29.11 Πόλεις δ' αὐτῷ τρεῖς μὲν οἱ πλεῖστοι δοθῆναι λέγουσιν
There was a rather standard tradition that Magnesia was
given to Themistocles for his grain, Lampsacus for his wine,
and Myus for his fish.[31] Magnesia was a short way up the
Maeander and was actually on a small tributary of the river.
Myus was close by at the head of what used to be a gulf
guarded by Miletus; even in antiquity this area had begun
to silt up. Lampsacus (modern Turkish Lapseki) is on the
Asian side of the Hellespont. The tradition was reported
first by Thucydides (I 138.5), who also reported the rev-

[29] *FGrH* 81 F 22, *Suda*, Photius, s.v. *tiara*; schol. Ar. *Av.* 487,
where the name Clitarchus has slipped into the MS.

[30] Plut. *De fort.Alex.* 328E; *De exil.* 602A; *Apophth. Them.* 17,
185F; Aristides, I 433; et al.

[31] ὄψον in general means the prepared food that accompanies the
staple bread and wine, e.g., *Od.* 3.480; Plato, *Gorg.* 518C; but here it
must have the other usual meaning of "fish" as in *LSJ*[9] s.v.

enue of fifty talents a year for Magnesia.[32] To this standard list, some authors added Percote and Palaiscepsis, both small cities in Mysia. Plutarch attributed this supplementary information to Phanias (fr. 28 Wehrli) and Neanthes of Cyzicus (*FGrH* 84 F 17ab).

Scholarly controversy has centered about the question how the Persian King could give Themistocles cities which many believe were already in the Delian League? Magnesia was inland and therefore under *de facto* Persian control, but Myus and Lampsacus were on the sea, the first a neighbor of Miletus, which had more reason than most cities to be anti-Persian; the second, right on the Hellespont—an area we usually assume to be well secured by the Athenians, concerned over the safety of their grain supply from the Black Sea. Gomme believed that the King "gave" Myus and Lampsacus to Themistocles without being able to make good on the gift,[33] but Meiggs rightly shows (*Athenian Empire* 53-54) that the relationship of Themistocles to Lampsacus is too well established to be denied, citing a well-known inscription testifying to an annual Themistocles festival at Lampsacus and certain rights enjoyed there by Themistocles' son Cleophantus and his descendants.

As so often, our quandary results from simply not understanding the situation. We are unable to answer satisfactorily two preliminary questions: what was meant by Persian "control" and what were the conditions for membership in the Delian League.

To make the problem more complex, these gifts to Themistocles were not the only examples of cities with divided loyalties. We are told by Xenophon (*Hell.* III 1.6; cf. *Anab.* VII 8.8) that when Thibron was joined by the remnants of the Ten Thousand in the spring of 399, he was able to take

---

[32] The cities were also reported by Nepos, *Them.* 10.3; Diod. XI 57.7; Strabo XIII 1.12, XIV 1.10; Aristodemus 10.6; schol. Ar. *Eq.* 84; Libanius, 15.40. Aesch.Socr. in Aristides, II 292 said only Magnesia; Ammianus XXII 8.4; only Lampsacus.

[33] HCT I 292, followed by the editors of *ATL* III 201, cf. 111f.

the Aeolian cities of Gambreion, Palaigambreion, Myrina, and Gryneion, which were held by the descendants of Gongylus of Eretria, who had been the accomplice of Pausanias in the 470's (Thuc. I 128.6). He also took Pergamon, Teuthrania, and Halisarna, which Xerxes had given to Demaratus of Sparta and which his descendants still held. There is, therefore, a substantial body of evidence testifying to minor but long-lasting dynastic tyrannies, which depended on the loyalty of their rulers to the Great King. But we also have evidence that at least from the date of the first extant tribute list in 454/3 the cities of Lampsacus, Myus, Gryneion, and Myrina paid tribute to the Delian League fairly regularly and are often presumed to have been early members of the League.[34] L. I. Highby[35] argued that because of their Persian connections, the cities of Lampsacus, Myus, Myrina, and Gryneion could not have belonged to the Delian League at the time they were given to Themistocles.[36] But must it be a question of one or the other? I think we share an ancient Athenian prejudice against tyrannies, particularly those supported by Persia, and therefore resist considering the possibility that a Persian-supported dynast could belong to the Delian League. We should remember that small city-states existing precariously in a traditionally contested belt of territory between two major powers would have been less prejudiced against tyranny. In fact, we can readily imagine them actively seeking strong despots with powerful connections. As long as the heirs of Gongylus and Demaratus (and Hippoclus of Lampsacus, see below) could count on Persian arms to ensure the peace and prosperity of their cities, the populace would have had

[34] *ATL* I Register, pp. 216-441, gives attested amounts of tribute as follows: Lampsacus, 12T; Myus, 1½-1T; Myrina, 1T; Gryneion, 1000 dr.

[35] *The Erythrae Decree, Klio Beiheft* 36 (1936) 46-55.

[36] G. Fogazza, "Sui Gongilidi di Eretria," *PP* 27 (1972) 129-130, proposed that the cities defected from the Gongilids from about 452 to the last years of the Peloponnesian War.

no argument with their rule—especially not an ideological argument, which was a luxury they could ill afford.

As to the requirements of League membership, we are on no firmer ground. The testimony for various oaths has been collected by Meiggs (*Athenian Empire* 579); we are informed by *AP* 23.5 that the usual oath applied: to have the same friends and enemies. But in reality, the Athenians may have enforced only two rules: members must remain in the League and they must pay tribute. There is nothing in recorded history against the idea of Persian-supported tyrants at Lampsacus, Myrina, and Gryneion remaining in power but paying tribute to the League as a pragmatic compromise.

There is an additional problem complicating the award of Lampsacus to Themistocles. We have evidence for a dynasty of Persian-supported tyrants already at Lampsacus, and to assign the city to Themistocles we must assume that the line had died out and Artaxerxes needed a new despot to take charge or that he decided to change the ruling family. Under the tyrant Hippoclus, the city had close ties with Darius (Hdt. 4.138). Sometime between 514 and 510, the Peisistratid Hippias married his daughter Archedice to Hippoclus' son Aeantides, who ruled in turn and was eventually succeeded by his own sons.[37] Although the Greeks captured Sestos late in 479 (Hdt. 9.118), we are not informed that they took any action against Lampsacus and from this time forward we know nothing about the city (other than its payments of tribute) until 411, when it was taken rather easily by the Athenians as it was unwalled (Thuc. VIII 62.2). The next year they fortified it as a supply depot (Xen. *Hell.* I 2.15). We have no way of knowing therefore whether Lampsacus was transferred from Hippoclus' descendants to Themistocles, or if he just enjoyed the wine revenues of the city. It has also been proposed that upon Themistocles' death, Cleophantus gave up whatever control

[37] Archedice's epitaph was quoted by Thuc. VI 59.3; Arist. *Rhet.* 1367b attributed it to Simonides (fr. 111 Bergk).

or tribute the city owed him voluntarily and returned to Athens, thus earning the city's gratitude and an eponymous festival every year.[38]

30.1-6 Καταβαίνοντι δ' αὐτῷ πρὸς τὰς Ἑλληνικὰς πράξεις ἐπὶ θάλατταν

There is little to say about this chapter. It is one unified story and is, in fact, almost certainly a foundation-legend that was told to anyone who inquired at the temple of the Dindymian Mother of the Gods (Anatolian Cybele-Cybebe) at Magnesia while it still existed.

The site of Leontokephalon seems well identified as a steep rocky redoubt on the western edge of the Phrygian plateau along the historic route to Sardis.[39] The lion, of course, is symbolic of Anatolian Cybele, with whom the animal is always associated.[40]

In 400 B.C., according to Diodorus (XIV 36.4), the Spartan general Thibron took Magnesia, and thinking the city difficult to defend, moved the whole settlement closer to Mt. Thorax.[41] Strabo also reported that the city was moved and he knew the story of Mnesiptolema being given to the Mother as her priestess, but he was unsure whether she was Themistocles' wife or daughter (XIV 1.40).

Dindymean Cybele and Artemis Leucophryene were both worshipped at Magnesia but they were different deities and should not be confused.[42] The older goddess at Magnesia was Artemis, whose cult came from the nearby shrine of

[38] *ATL* III 113; Davies, *APF* 6669 VI. All these explanations are mere speculation.

[39] Appian, *Mithr.* 19.78; W. R. Ramsay, "Le thema Léontokomeos et le Kaystroupédion," *CRAI* 1935, 127-135.

[40] E. Will, "Aspects du culte et de la légende de la Grande Mère dans le monde grec," *Eléments orientaux dans la religion grecque* (Paris, 1960) 98-102.

[41] J. Kohte, in C. Humann, *Magnesia am Maeander* (Berlin, 1904) 17.

[42] As by Humann, ibid. 1.

Leucophrys, said by Xenophon to be a very holy place (*Hell.* III 2.19). When Themistocles' sons returned to Athens, they dedicated a statue of Artemis Leucophryene on the acropolis (Paus. I 26.4). The cult evidently grew and became the city's most prominent cult after the new location of Magnesia. Toward the end of the third century B.C., the architect Hermogenes built the famous temple, seen by Strabo and described by Vitruvius (III 2.6), whose ruins were excavated by the German Institute in 1891-1893. It attracted courteous attention from as far away as Ithaca (*Syll.*³ 558; cf. a similar Chalcidian decree, ibid. 561). But the *naos* built by Themistocles to Dindymean Cybele represents a wholly different cult and one that was probably eclipsed by Artemis; according to Strabo, it did not survive the relocation of Magnesia to its new site.

31.1 εἶδε καὶ ἐν Μητρὸς ἱερῷ τὴν καλουμένην ὑδροφόρον κόρην χαλκῆν

It was once assumed that the Mother of the Gods/Cybele/ Cybebe (Lydian: KUBABA) was the same as Artemis, and that the impressive temple of Artemis encountered by the excavators of Sardis was the replacement of the temple of Cybebe that had been burned in the Ionian revolt (Hdt. 5.102).[43] But the testimonia to Cybebe began to show up in 1958, pointing to a location of a precinct of the goddess in the vicinity of the synagogue.[44]

τῶν 'Αθήνησιν ὑδάτων ἐπιστάτης

Nothing further is known of this office. Given the eternal

---

[43] G.M.A. Hanfmann, "Lydiaka," *HSCP* 63 (1958) 65 n. 4; cf. G. Radet, "L'Artemision de Sardis," *REA* 6 (1904) 277-289.

[44] *BASOR* 154 (1959) 32 n. 69; *BASOR* 174 (1964) 39-43; cf. L. Robert, *Rev.Phil.* 41 (1967) 34 n. 8. Hanfmann and Waldbaum, "Kybele and Artemis: Two Anatolian Goddesses at Sardis," *Archaeology* 22 (1969) 264-269; M. R. Gusmani, "Der lydische Name der Kybele," *Kadmos* 8 (1969) 158-161; the most recent summary is Albert Henrichs, "Despoina Kybele: ein Beitrag zur religiösen Namenkunde," *HSCP* 80 (1976) 266-276.

problem of water supply in ancient Athens, we should be surprised if there were not some such office. *AP* 43.1 mentions the office of τῶν κρηνῶν ἐπιμελητής as does a fourth-century decree honoring the annual holder of the magistracy (*IG* ii² 338: ἐπὶ τὰς κρήνας).⁴⁵ As a parallel, one might mention the problem of illegal interception of the public water supply at Rome, extensively described by Frontinus (*De aquis* II 75-76; 112-115). The hydrophorus type in sculpture is well known.⁴⁶

According to Plutarch, "either because he was deeply touched by the capture of his dedication, or because he wanted to show the Athenians what honor and power he enjoyed in barbarian affairs, he submitted a request to the Lydian satrap asking to send the *kore* to Athens." This anecdote is inconsistent with the last chapter. Themistocles had just come through a narrow escape for which he owed his life to the warning he received from the Mother of the Gods. One would think that he would have visited the temple of the Mother in Sardis the moment he arrived, not because he had spare time on his hands (we can see Plutarch the perpetually fascinated tourist here), but because this was the first chance he had to pay his respects. We should expect at least this much piety from a man who had just promised his daughter to the service of the Mother. Can we imagine that he would ask the release of this dedication for a prideful and wholly secular purpose? I do not believe so. If there is any truth in the story at all, it must be that Themistocles asked that the *kore* in the Metroon be released in order that she might be dedicated to the Mother in the temple he was going to build at Magnesia.

31.2 Χαλεπαίνοντος δὲ τοῦ βαρβάρου

It was perhaps the jealous satrap who said he would write

⁴⁵ See the excellent treatment of Athenian public water supply by Mabel Lang, *Waterworks in the Athenian Agora* (Princeton, 1968), in the Agora excavations picture-book series.

⁴⁶ E.g., *Hesperia* 22 (1953) pl. 19; T. Wiegand, *Milet* I, v (Berlin and Leipzig, 1919) 60.

to the King reporting that Themistocles wanted to send the *kore* back to Athens. But this is just speculation and there is no need to go any further trying to straighten out this anecdote. The detail about dispensing bribes in the harem to influence the satrap sounds suspiciously like the fragment of Eratosthenes (*On Wealth*) cited above, 27.8.

31.3 Οὐ γὰρ πλανώμενος περὶ τὴν ᾿Ασίαν ὥς φησι Θεόπομπος

Connor notes that Theopompus in this passage seems as usual to have something different to say from the rest of the tradition, but there is no use trying to guess what.[47]

περὶ τὰς ἄνω πράξεις

Artaxerxes was the youngest son of Xerxes. An older brother named Hystaspes was satrap of Bactria (Diod. XI 69.2) and would have been in line. Ctesias (62) tells us that Bactria rose against Artaxerxes, although he says another Artabanus was the satrap. These sources are unreliable, but we may accept the general picture on the basis of probability; most Persian kings had to face minor revolts upon accession.

31.4 ῾Ως δ᾿ Αἴγυπτός τ᾿ ἀφισταμένη

Plutarch erroneously combined the beginning of the Egyptian revolt in 460/59 with the period "when Cimon ruled the seas," which can be before—e.g., 469-466, or later, around 451/0, but not at this time because Cimon had been ostracized and was living in exile (*Cimon* 17.3). Plutarch may have wanted to draw a picture of a sudden crisis for Persia in the Mediterranean to contrast with the former period noted in the previous paragraph. On the other hand, Plutarch may just be mistaken about the sequence of events and the relative chronology in this period of history.[48] Thucydides described the situation we believe Plutarch had in mind: Egypt revolted under Inaros and an Athenian fleet of two hundred ships campaigning in Cyprus was diverted to assist the rebels (I 104).

[47] W. R. Connor, *Theopompus and Fifth-Century Athens* 22.
[48] As seems obvious in *Cimon* 13; cf. *Class.et Med.* 22 (1961) 192-194.

31.5 ἄριστα βουλευσάμενος ἐπιθεῖναι τῷ βίῳ τὴν τελευτὴν πρέπουσαν

By Thucydides' day, the tradition had already reported that Themistocles was bidden to take charge of the Hellenic war for the King, but despaired of success. The historian said unequivocally, "becoming ill, he died" (I 138.4). He did admit there was another tradition, with the attribution, "some say."

31.6 ὡς μὲν ὁ πολὺς λόγος αἷμα ταύρειον πίων

Unlike so many other anecdotes, it is possible to trace the evolution of this tradition rather accurately. The first literary allusion we know is Aristophanes' *Equites* 83:

> βέλτιστον ἡμῖν αἷμα ταύρειον πιεῖν
> ὁ Θεμιστοκλέους γὰρ θάνατος αἱρετώτερος

The scholiast informs us, on the authority of the second century A.D. commentator Symmachus, that this allusion was thought to be derived from Sophocles' lost play Ἑλένης ἀπαίτησις (fr. 178 Jebb):

> ἐμοὶ δὲ λῶστον αἷμα ταύρειον πιεῖν
> καὶ μή γε πλείους τῶνδ' ἔχειν δυσφημίας

We would assume, then, that the average Athenian, by the last quarter of the fifth century, had heard that Themistocles committed suicide by drinking bull's blood.

Gardner long ago proposed an ingenious theory that the story of Themistocles' suicide was deduced by ignorant people from a monument in Magnesia. This monument, as reconstructed from an Antonine coin depicting it,[49] showed Themistocles with a newly sacrificed bull at his feet and a vessel in his hand. The uninformed, reasoned Gardner, might have assumed this statue to have depicted the suicide

---

[49] A. Rhousopoulos, *Ath.Mitt.* 21 (1896) 22.

of Themistocles.⁵⁰ Bull's blood, although totally harmless and in fact a diet staple in parts of East Africa, was supposed to be poisonous because it congealed so rapidly.⁵¹

In Cicero's *Brutus* (11.42-43), we see Atticus recommending historical criticism of rhetorical exaggeration: Clitarchus and Stratocles had supposedly made up the popular version of Themistocles' death, but Thucydides should be followed because he was nearly contemporary. I can add little to this judgment. The citation of Clitarchus may have come from the same work noted by Plutarch (above, comment to 27.1).⁵² Regardless how the story got started, it was nevertheless extremely popular in antiquity.⁵³

πέντε πρὸς τοῖς ἑξήκοντα βεβιωκὼς ἔτη

The lifespan was approximately 525-460. See the discussion of dates following comment to 2.8 (cf. Davies, *APF* 6669 III).

31.7 Τὴν δ' αἰτίαν τοῦ θανάτου

Plutarch conceded that this was the popular story, but he seems to have approved of it nonetheless. If the story did evolve in the fifth century, the family of Themistocles may have encouraged it. Claiming that the general had committed suicide rather than take up arms against his own people would have hastened the rehabilitation of Themistocles' memory among the Athenians. As the author of the *Letters* (20.762 Hercher) put it, alluding to the King's proposed campaign against the Greeks, headed by Themistocles: "Many things may be, but this never."

---

⁵⁰ "A Themistoclean Myth," *CR* 12 (1898) 21-23.

⁵¹ Pliny, *NH* XI 222; cf. Arist. *HA* 3, 520b; references were collected by W. Roscher, "Die Vergiftung mit Stierblut," *Neue Jahrbücher* 29 (1883) 158-162; see the comments of Frazer, *Pausanias* IV 175.

⁵² *FGrH* 137 F 34. Jacoby ad loc. believed it to be the source of Diodorus XI 58.1.

⁵³ Val.Max. V 6 ext. 3; Aristodemus 10.5; Euseb. *Chron.* Ol. 78.3; *Suda* s.v. νῶιν ἡμῖν; cf. Nepos, *Them.* 10.4, who knew the story but once more preferred the authority of Thucydides, as befitted an admirer of Atticus.

Actually, it is difficult to see how Artaxerxes could have used Themistocles, an elderly man with his best days behind him, who had not commanded men in battle for almost twenty years. We know Artaxerxes' first reaction to the Athenian adventure in Egypt: he sent money to Sparta hoping to persuade the Spartans to invade Attica (Thuc. I 109.1-3).

32.1 Ἀπέλιπε δὲ Θεμιστοκλῆς παῖδας
This raises a preliminary question of when Themistocles' family was allowed to return to Athens? One assumes that some members never had to leave—Diocles, for instance, who had been adopted into the family of his maternal grandfather, and the family of Themistocles' brother (see below). As for Themistocles' immediate descendants, Davies (*APF* 6669 VI) suggests any time after 459 in what he calls "the changed political climate of the Ephialtic revolution." I am not as sure as Davies what this climate was, but there were, in fact, two events that affected the future of the family of Themistocles. First was the diplomatic reversal of 462 when the offended Athenians broke off relations with the Spartans and allied themselves with Argos instead (Thuc. I 102.4). Second was the ostracism of Cimon and thereby the elimination from the city of the most powerful pro-Spartan leader. The time was ripe for friends of Themistocles to start the delicate negotiations required to safeguard the return of the family. Davies does not think the original condemnation would have required a formal decree of rehabilitation. This may be so, but Athenians often did not know what the law actually was until someone brought litigation and left it up to a jury to decide. The family may have wanted to avoid this but we do not know what legal steps might have been necessary. One assumes an act of the deme Phrearrhioi restoring descendants' names to the roll of citizens and some action by the proper phratry of the Lycomids restoring tribal rights.

I am pleased to see that Davies, in preparing his Themistoclean genealogy (*APF* 6669), while not having available
the stemma I prepared in Bauer-Frost, 132-134 (published
in 1969), independently produced an almost identical family tree. I simply reproduce here a slightly revised stemma
from Bauer-Frost, with revisions reflecting the work of
Davies.

1. Neocles Phrearrhios. See comment to 1.1: "his father
was Neocles, not one of those prominent in Athens."

2. Lysander Alopekethen. Father of Themistocles' first
wife Archippe and adoptive father of Themistocles' son
Diocles. The most probable reason for such an adoption was
that Lysander had no male heirs (Flacelière, *Vie de Them.*
ad loc.).

3. An uncle of Themistocles, very dubious in *Letters*
(8.749 Hercher).

4. Archippe, daughter of Lysander Alopekethen, probably the mother of Themistocles' five sons. She could have
married Themistocles almost any time between about 505-
490.

6. Another wife, mother of Mnesiptolema (q.v.) and
other daughters. There is a possibility of a third wife, but
this is only speculative. The women in Themistocles' life
stayed very much in the background.

7. Agesilaus, the brother of Themistocles according to
Agatharchides of Samos (in [Plut.] *Parall.min.* 305D; Stobaeus, III 764, *FGrH* 284 F 1). Undoubtedly a pure fiction.

8. A brother of Themistocles. See Phrasicles, below.

9. Neocles died a child. One may safely ignore, as Plutarch does, the story of Neocles and Demopolis (Phylarchus,
FGrH 81 F 76 = *Suda* s.v. Θεμιστοκλέους παῖδες).

10. Diocles, adopted by his grandfather Lysander. He
and his descendants will therefore have been enrolled in
his grandfather's deme, Alopeke. See 20, below.

11. Polyeuctus. Only a name to us. Some of these sons
were old enough in 480 to require a *paidagogos* (Hdt.

THE FAMILY OF THEMISTOCLES

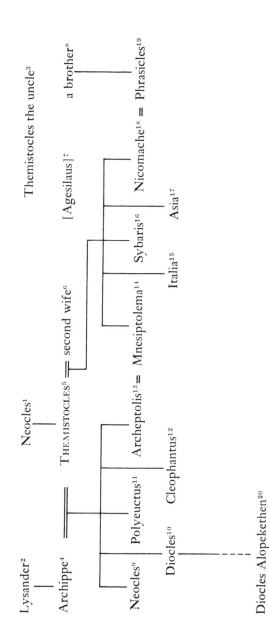

The Genealogy of Themistocles

8.75), therefore I assume Themistocles married and had sons before about 490.

12. Cleophantus. Plato said he was a good horseman. (*Meno* 93d). This implies that he was living in Athens in the later fifth century and that he had the kind of wealth required for *hippotrophia* (Davies, *APF* p. 218).

13. Archeptolis married his half-sister Mnesiptolema. ὁμοπάτριοι marriages were allowed, but not ὁμομήτριοι.

14. Mnesiptolema was priestess of Dindymean Cybele at Magnesia. There is no use speculating why she married her half-brother. Such marriages were usually to preserve within the family the property that went with a widow or spinster.

15. Italia. Married Panthoides of Chios (see a possible reference in Ion of Chios, *FGrH* 392 F 11).

16. Sybaris. These two girls are often proposed as evidence for Themistocles' connections in Italy.[54] Sybaris eventually married an Athenian named Nicodemus (thus the reading of S; another group of MSS has Nicomedes. This is the same crux as *AP* 22.7).

17. Asia was the youngest and was adopted by her uncle, Phrasicles.

18. Nicomache. See the next entry.

19. Phrasicles was Themistocles' ἀδελφιδοῦς, often meaning "brother's son" (*LSJ*[9] s.v.). There is nothing to contradict this assumption and it has been accepted by Davies, *APF* p. 214. Phrasicles was a member of the family who had not been exiled, for he sailed to Magnesia upon the death of Themistocles and married Nicomache, probably for the same reason Archeptolis married Mnesiptolema—to keep the estate in the family.

20. Diocles Alopekethen, *IG* ii[2] 124.23 (357/6); Demosth. 21.174. Possibly a descendant of Themistocles' son (10, above). Davies (*APF* 6669 VII) is hesitant, feeling the name may be a coincidence.

[54] Hdt. 8.62; Piccirilli, *ASNP* 3 (1973) 339.

There are a number of men named Themistocles in later
Attic prosopography who may be descendants. Pausanias'
mention of a Θεμιστοκλῆς Πολιάρχου, τρίτος ἀπόγονος Θεμιστοκλέους (I 37.1) led Boeckh to conjecture that Poliarchos
was a slip for Archeptolis (13, above) and that Pausanias
was counting generations inclusively (quoted and accepted
by Kirchner, *PA* 2383). See doubts about this and other
proposals by Davies, *APF* 6669 VI.

Inscriptions testify to other possible candidates. Rau-
bitschek, *Hesperia* 12 (1943) 37-48, no. 8, fr. L, line 42:
Θ[ε]μισ[τ]ο[κ]λ[ές], restored from Wheler's transcription
ΟΜΙΟΣ Λ of a lost casualty list.

IG ii² 1742.53: a catalogue of *prytaneis* from the tribe
Leontis. See Davies, *APF* p. 219.

A. Skias, *Arch.Eph.* 1896, p. 51, no. 49: φρεαρριο[I]
ΝΘΕΜΙΣ[τοκλ-, said to be II B.C.

Margaret Thompson, *The New Style Silver Coinage of
Athens* (New York, 1961) 221ff.; 568f., 604. A second-
century mint magistrate named Themistocles. See Davies,
APF, p. 219.

Finally, and most important for Plutarch's knowledge of
the family, Themistocles of Athens, Plutarch's contemporary. See below, comment to 32.6.

32.4 καὶ τάφον μὲν αὐτοῦ λαμπρὸν ἐν τῇ ἀγορᾷ Μάγνητες ἔχουσι
Thucydides (I 138.5) mentioned a *mnemeion*; Nepos
(*Them.* 10.3) both a sepulchre near the town and *statua
in foro*. Diodorus (XI 53.2) referred to both a grave and a
mnemeion "remaining to this day," which must mean they
were moved to the new location of Magnesia. This would
seem to be supported by the evidence of the Antonine coin
depicting the monument.[55] Andocides' story of Athenians
despoiling the grave at some unspecified time was rejected
by Plutarch. Nothing else is known of this episode unless a
notice in the scholion to Aristophanes' *Eq.* 34 preserved a
memory of an older tradition which Andocides misrepre-

[55] See above, comment to 31.6 nn. 49, 50.

sented: "when the Athenians were suffering from a plague, the God told them to bring home the bones of Themistocles. When the Magnesians did not agree, the Athenians asked to honor the grave for thirty days. And putting tents around the place, they secretly dug up and transported the bones away."[56] A number of epigrams on the subject of Themistocles' tomb at Magnesia are preserved in the Anthology.[57] They are fatuous exercises in mock bereavement.

ἅ τε Φύλαρχος (*FGrH* 81 F 76)

Phylarchus had told some theatrical tale about Neocles and an otherwise unknown son named Demopolis seeking to arouse *agon* and *pathos*. Plutarch did not tell the story, but I feel sure it is the same as that related by the *Suda* s.v. Θεμιστοκλέους παῖδες: "Neocles and Demopolis competed in the *epitaphios* games at Athens and having won, were crowned, not being recognized. Neocles won the long race, Demopolis the stadion. But being recognized after the contest, they were in danger of being stoned by Themistocles' enemies, who reminded the Athenians about the laws regarding fugitives." I have set out my arguments for attributing this to Phylarchus elsewhere.[58]

32.5-6 Διόδωρος δ' ὁ περιηγητὴς ἐν τοῖς Περὶ μνημάτων (*FGrH* 372 F 35)

Thucydides reported the family tradition that Themistocles himself had asked his relatives to bring home his bones to Attica for burial (I 138.6). The historian did not know the location, possibly, as Davies and others have suggested, because it was not recognized and improved until the rebuilding of the walls by Conon in 395 (Davies, *APF* 6669 V). The site of the tomb, which Diodorus the Periegete thought Platon the comic poet referred to, has been described with full discussion by Paul Wallace.[59] Wallace pointed out that

---

[56] See Podlecki, *Themistocles* 177f.

[57] *Anth.Pal.* 7.73, 74, 235, 236, 237. [58] *AJP* 83 (1962) 419-422.

[59] "The Tomb of Themistokles in the Peiraieus," *Hesperia* 41 (1972) 451-462.

only three ancient authors mentioned the site, Aristotle,
HA 6, 569B, Pausanias I 1.2, and Plutarch (who was actually
quoting Diodorus, who in turn was citing Platon). I agree
with Wallace that the identification of a Themistocleion by
Aristotle must be mistaken, for he is speaking of places
which are shady and marshy, and the site on the southern
promontory of Piraeus is neither. Platon was therefore the
earliest writer to allude to the tomb and Diodorus the earliest to discuss it specifically. Pausanias was more certain
than Diodorus that there was a grave of Themistocles "by
the biggest harbor," which is only natural. Diodorus was in
Athens during a troubled period; Pausanias, during an era
of peace and prosperity when there was a tendency for
cities to label and otherwise promote their antiquities. The
Greek government has recently done some cosmetic reconstruction, although no one seems to be sure when.
There is now an inscription: ΘΕΜΙΣΤΟΚΛΕΣ ΝΙΚΟΚΛΕΟΣ
ΦΡΕΑΡΡΙΟΣ [*sic*].[60] As with decree, bust, and shrine of
Artemis Aristoboule, belief in the tomb in Piraeus must re-
main a matter of faith.

Τοῖς δ' ἀπὸ γένους τοῦ Θεμιστοκλέους
Hereditary honors were still enjoyed by Themistocles of
Athens, a stoic philosopher (*Qc* I 626F), friend, and former
schoolmate of Plutarch. Possis of Magnesia (in Athen.
533DE, *FGrH* 480 F 1) described some of the Athenian
festivals imported to Magnesia and reported that the great
man had held the office of *stephanephorus*, no doubt considered quite an honor by Magnesians, but an ironic role
for the victor of Salamis. I am reminded of the last lines of
Cavafy's *Satrapeia*:

Ἀλλὰ ζητεῖ ἡ ψυχή σου, γι' ἄλλα κλαίει·
τὸν ἔπαινο τοῦ δήμου καὶ τῶν Σοφιστῶν,

[60] There is a curious tendency to get Themistocles' father wrong.
Kahrstedt, "Themistokles," *RE* ii 5 (1934) 1686, reported the name
as Neanthes!

τὰ δύσκολα καὶ τ᾽ ἀνεκτίμητα Εὖγε·
τὴν Ἀγορά, τὸ Θέατρο, καὶ τοὺς Στεφάνους.
Αὐτὰ ποῦ θὰ στὰ δώσει ὁ Ἀρταξέξης,
αὐτὰ ποῦ θὰ τὰ βρεῖς στὴ σατραπεία·
καὶ τί ζωὴ χωρὶς αὐτὰ θὰ κάμεις.

FREQUENTLY CITED EDITIONS OF PLUTARCH'S *LIVES*

Adolf Bauer, *Plutarchs Themistokles für quellenkritische Übungen* (Leipzig: Teubner, 1884); 2nd ed. with additional material by F. J. Frost (Chicago: Argonaut, 1967)

R. Flacelière, ed., *Plutarque: Vie de Thémistocle* (Paris: Presses Universitaires de France, 1972)

R. Flacelière et al., eds., *Plutarque: Vies* II (Paris: Les belles lettres, 1961) The "Budé" edition

B. Perrin, *Plutarch's Themistocles and Aristides* (New York: Scribners, 1901)

K. Ziegler, *Plutarchus: Vitae parallelae* I.1 (Leipzig: Teubner, 1957, 1960)

ABBREVIATIONS OF FREQUENTLY CITED WORKS

AC	*L'Antiquité Classique*
AJA	*American Journal of Archaeology*
AJAH	*American Journal of Ancient History*
AJP	*American Journal of Philology*
APF	J. K. Davies, *Athenian Propertied Families* (Oxford, 1971)
Arch. Delt.	*Archaiologikon Deltion*
Arch. Eph.	*Archaiologike Ephemeris*
Aristides	W. Dindorf's 1829 Leipzig edition
ARV²	J. Beazley, *Attic Red-figure Vase-Painters* (Oxford, 1963)
ASNP	*Annali della Scuola Normale Superiore di Pisa*

ATL	B. Meritt, H. T. Wade-Gery, M. McGregor, *The Athenian Tribute Lists* (Harvard, Princeton, 1939-53)
BASOR	*Bulletin of the American Schools of Oriental Research*
BCH	*Bulletin de Correspondance Hellénique*
BSA	*Annual of the British School at Athens*
CAH	*The Cambridge Ancient History*
CJ	*Classical Journal*
Class.et Med.	*Classica et Mediaevalia*
CQ	*Classical Quarterly*
CR	*Classical Review*
CRAI	*Comptes rendus de l'Académie des Inscriptions et Belles-Lettres*
CSCA	*California Studies in Classical Antiquity*
CW	*Classical World*
FGrH	F. Jacoby, *Fragmente der griechischen Historiker* (Berlin, Leiden, 1926-58)
FHG	C. and T. Mueller, eds., *Fragmenta Historicorum Graecorum* (Paris, 1848-73)
GRBS	*Greek, Roman and Byzantine Studies*
Hesp.	*Hesperia*
HSCP	*Harvard Studies in Classical Philology*
IG	*Inscriptiones Graecae*, various editions (Berlin, 1913-40)
JHS	*Journal of Hellenic Studies*
JRS	*Journal of Roman Studies*
LCL	Loeb Classical Library
*LSJ*⁹	H. G. Liddell, R. Scott, H. S. Jones, *Greek-English Lexicon* (Oxford, 1940)
PA	J. E. Kirchner, *Prosopographia Attica*² (Berlin, 1901)
POxy	B. Grenfell, A. Hunt. eds., *The Oxyrhynchus Papyri*
PP	*Parola del Passato*
RE	A. Pauly, G. Wissowa, W. Kroll, *Real-Encyclopädie der klassischen Altertumswissenschaft* (1893—)
REA	*Revue des Etudes Anciennes*
REG	*Revue des Etudes Grecques*

RhM	*Rheinisches Museum*
Riv.Fil.	*Rivista di Filologia e di Istruzione Classica*
SEG	*Supplementum Epigraphicum Graecum*
Syll.[3]	*Sylloge Inscriptionum Graecarum*, 3rd ed. by H. Dittenberger (Leipzig, 1915-24)
TAPA	*Transactions of the American Philological Association*
WS	*Wiener Studien*

SELECTED BIBLIOGRAPHY

Titles are limited to those cited more than once in the notes.

T. W. Africa, "Ephorus and Oxyrhynchus Papyrus 1610," *AJP* 83 (1962) 86-89.

E. Badian, "Archons and *Strategoi*," *Antichthon* 5 (1971) 1-34.

R. H. Barrow, *Plutarch and His Times* (London, 1967).

H. Barth, "Das Verhalten des Themistokles gegenüber den Gelde," *Klio* 43-45 (1965) 30-37.

A. Bauer, *Themistokles* (Merseburg, 1881).

K. J. Beloch, *Griechische Geschichte* (Strassburg, 1893-1904).

H. Bengtson, "Themistokles und die delphische Amphiktyonie," *Eranos* 49 (1951) 85-92.

E. G. Barry, "The Oxyrhynchus Fragments of Aeschines," *TAPA* 81 (1951) 1-8.

M. Bieber, "The Statues of Miltiades and Themistokles in the Theater at Athens," *AJA* 58 (1954) 282-284.

L. Bodin, "Histoire et biographie: Phanias d'Erèse," *REG* 28 (1915) 251-281; *REG* 30 (1917) 117-157.

D. Bradeen, "The Fifth Century Archon List," *Hesperia* 32 (1963) 187-208.

H. D. Broadhead, *The Persae of Aeschylus* (Cambridge, 1960).

A. R. Burn, *Persia and the Greeks* (New York, 1962).

S. Burstein, "The Recall of the Ostracized and the Themistocles Decree," *CSCA* 4 (1971).

J. B. Bury, "Aristeides at Salamis," *CR* 10 (1896) 414-418.

G. Busolt, *Griechische Geschichte*² (Gotha, 1895-1897).

T. Cadoux, "The Athenian Archons from Kreon to Hypsichides," *JHS* 68 (1948) 70-123.

I. Calabi Limentani, *Plutarchi vita Aristidis* (Florence, 1964).

J. Carrière, "Communicazione sulla tragedia antica greca," *Dioniso* 43 (1969) 169-174.

M. Casevitz, *Diodore de Sicile: Bibliothèque historique*, livre XII (Paris, 1972).

G. L. Cawkwell, "The Fall of Themistokles," *Auckland Classical Essays Presented to E. M. Blaiklock* (London, 1970) 39-58.

W. R. Connor, "Lycomedes against Themistocles?" *Historia* 21 (1972) 569-574.

———, *Theopompus and Fifth-Century Athens* (Washington, 1968).

———, "Theopompus' Treatment of Cimon," *GRBS* 4 (1963) 107-114.

A. Dascalakis, *Problèmes historiques autour de la bataille des Thermopyles* (Paris, 1962).

J. K. Davies, *Athenian Propertied Families* (Oxford, 1971)

J. Day and M. Chambers, *Aristotle's History of Athenian Democracy* (Berkeley and Los Angeles, 1962).

W. den Boer, "Themistocles in Fifth Century Historiography," *Mnemosyne* 15 (1962) 225-237.

H. Diels and W. Kranz, *Die Fragmente der Vorsokratiker*[6] (Berlin, 1951).

——— and W. Schubart, *Didymos Kommentar zu Demosthenes* (Berlin, 1904).

H. Dittmar, *Aischines von Sphettos* (Berlin, 1912).

N. A. Doenges, *The Letters of Themistocles* (Diss. Princeton, 1953).

K. J. Dover, "ΔΕΚΑΤΟΣ ΑΥΤΟΣ" *JHS* 80 (1960) 61-77.

R. Drews, "Diodorus and His Sources," *AJP* 83 (1962) 383-392.

G. Ferrara, "Temistocle e Solone," *Maia* 16 (1964) 55-70.

R. Flacelière, "Sur quelques points obscurs dans la vie de Thémistocle," *REA* 55 (1953) 5-28.

C. Fornara, *The Athenian Board of Generals*. Historia Einzelschriften 16 (1971).

———, *Herodotus* (Oxford, 1971).

———, "Themistocles' Archonship," *Historia* 20 (1971) 534-540.

W. G. Forrest, "Pausanias and Themistokles Again," *Lakonikai Spoudai* 2 (Athens, 1975) 115-119.

———, "Themistokles and Argos," *CQ* n.s. 10 (1960) 221-241.

J. G. Frazer, *Pausanias's Description of Greece* (London, 1913).

F. J. Frost, "Pericles, Thucydides, Son of Melesias and Athenian Politics before the War," *Historia* 13 (1964) 385-399.

——, "Phylarchus, fragment 76," *AJP* 83 (1962) 419-422.

——, "Some Documents in Plutarch's Lives," *Class.et Med.* 22 (1961) 182-194.

——, "Themistocles and Mnesiphilus," *Historia* 20 (1971) 20-25.

——, "Themistocles' Place in Athenian Politics," *CSCA* 1 (1968) 105-124.

——, "Tribal Politics and the Civic State," *AJAH* 1 (1976) 70-75.

A. W. Gomme, *A Historical Commentary to Thucydides* I (Oxford, 1945).

G. Gottlieb, *Das Verhältnis der ausserherodoteischen Überlieferung zu Herodot* (Frankfurt, 1963).

P. Green, *The Year of Salamis* (London, 1970).

C. Habicht, "Falsche Urkunden zur Geschichte Athens im Zeitalter der Perserkriege," *Hermes* 89 (1961) 1-35.

N.G.L. Hammond, "The Battle of Salamis," *JHS* 76 (1956) 32-54.

——, "The Two Battles of Chaeronea," *Klio* 31 (1938) 186-211.

A. R. Hands, "Ostraka and the Law of Ostracism," *JHS* 79 (1959) 69-79.

M. H. Hansen, *Eisangelia* (Odense, 1975).

A. Hauvette, *Hérodote, historien des guerres médiques* (Paris, 1894).

K. Herbert, *Ephorus in Plutarch's Lives* (Diss. Harvard, 1954).

C. Hignett, *A History of the Athenian Constitution* (Oxford, 1952).

——, *Xerxes' Invasion of Greece* (Oxford, 1963).

G. Hill, R. Meiggs, and A. Andrewes, *Sources for Greek History 478-431 B.C.*[2] (Oxford, 1951).

W. How and J. Wells, *A Commentary on Herodotus* (Oxford, 1928).

F. Jacoby, *Atthis* (Oxford, 1949).

——, "Herodotos," *RE* Supplb. II (1913) 205-520.

——, "Some Remarks on Ion of Chios," *CQ* 41 (1947) 1-17.

M. Jameson, "A Decree of Themistokles from Troizen," *Hesperia* 29 (1960) 198-223.

————, "Provisions for Mobilization in the Decree of Themistokles," *Historia* 12 (1963) 385-404.

C. P. Jones, *Plutarch and Rome* (Oxford, 1971).

————, "The Teacher of Plutarch," *HSCP* 71 (1966) 205-215.

B. Jordan, *The Athenian Navy in the Classical Period* (Berkeley and Los Angeles, 1975).

————, "The Meaning of the Technical Term *Hyperesia*," *CSCA* 2 (1968) 183-207.

W. Judeich, *Topographie von Athen*² (Munich, 1931).

J. Labarbe, *La loi navale de Thémistocle* (Paris, 1957).

M. Lang, "Scapegoat Pausanias," *CJ* 63 (1967) 79-85.

G. Lehmann, "Bemerkungen zur Themistokles-Inschrift von Troizen," *Historia* 17 (1968) 276-288.

R. Lenardon, "The Archonship of Themistokles," *Historia* 5 (1956) 401-419.

————, "Charon, Thucydides and Themistokles," *Phoenix* 15 (1961) 28-40.

————, "The Chronology of Themistokles' Ostracism and Exile," *Historia* 8 (1959) 23-48.

F. Leo, *Die griechisch-römische Biographie* (Leipzig, 1901).

M. A. Levi, *Plutarco e il V secolo* (Milan, 1955).

D. Lewis, "Themistocles' Archonship," *Historia* 22 (1973) 757-758.

H. I. Marrou, *History of Education in Antiquity* (English trans., New York, 1956).

R. Meiggs, *The Athenian Empire* (Oxford, 1972).

———— and D. Lewis, *Greek Historical Inscriptions* (Oxford, 1969).

E. Meinhardt, *Perikles bei Plutarch* (Frankfurt, 1957).

B. Meritt, H. T. Wade-Gery, and M. McGregor, *The Athenian Tribute Lists* (Cambridge, Mass. and Princeton, 1939-1953).

E. Meyer, "Die Biographie Kimons," *Forschungen zur alten Geschichte* II (Halle, 1899) 1-87.

A. Mosshammer, "Themistocles' Archonship in the Chronographic Tradition," *Hermes* 103 (1975) 222-234.

J.A.R. Munro, "The Chronology of Themistocles' Career," *CR* 6 (1892) 333-334.

A. T. Olmstead, *History of the Persian Empire* (Chicago, 1948).

D. Page, *Poetae Melici Graeci* (Oxford, 1962).

M. Pavan, *La grecità politica* (Rome, 1958).

B. Perrin, *Plutarch's Themistocles and Aristides* (New York, 1901).

L. Piccirilli, "Temistocle evergetes dei Corciresi," *ASNP* 3 (1973) 317-355.

A. Podlecki, "Simonides: 480," *Historia* 17 (1968) 262-274.

———, *The Life of Themistocles* (Montreal and London, 1975).

W. K. Pritchett, *Studies in Ancient Greek Topography* I, II (Berkeley and Los Angeles, 1965, 1969).

A. Raubitschek, *Dedications from the Athenian Akropolis* (Cambridge, Mass., 1949).

———, "Meeresnähe und Volksherrschaft," *WS* 71 (1958) 112-115.

———, "Theophrastus on Ostracism," *Class.et Med.* 19 (1958) 73-109.

P. J. Rhodes, "Thucydides on Pausanias and Themistocles," *Historia* 19 (1970) 395-400.

N. Robertson, "The Thessalian Expedition of 480 B.C.," *JHS* 96 (1976) 100-120.

G. Roux, "Quatre récits de la bataille de Salamine," *BCH* 98 (1974) 51-94.

D. Russell, *Plutarch* (London, 1975).

F. Sartori, *Le eterie nella vita politica ateniese del vi e v secolo A.C.* (Rome, 1957).

F. Schachermeyr, "Das Bild des Themistokles in der antiken Geschichtsschreibung," *XIIe Congrès international des sciences historiques, Vienna. Rapports* IV (1965) 81-91.

R. Schmitt, "Die achaemenidische Satrapie TAYAIY DRAYAHYA," *Historia* 21 (1972) 522-527.

E. Schuetrumpf, "Die Folgen der Atimie für die athenische Demokratie," *Philologus* 117 (1973) 152-168.

R. Sealey, "The Origins of *Demokratia*," *CSCA* 6 (1973) 253-263.

C. Theander, *Plutarch und die Geschichte, Bulletin de la Société Royale des Lettres de Lund*, 1950-51, I.

R. Thomsen, *Eisphora* (Copenhagen, 1964).

J. Threpsiades, E. Vanderpool, "Themistokles' Sanctuary of Artemis Aristoboule," *Arch.Delt.* 19 (1964) 26-36.

J. Travlos, *Pictorial Dictionary of Athens* (London, 1971).

E. Vanderpool, "A Lex sacra of the Attic Deme Phrearrhioi," *Hesperia* 39 (1970) 47-53.

——, "Ostracism at Athens," *Louise Taft Semple Lectures* II (Cincinnati, 1970).

H. T. Wade-Gery, *Essays in Greek History* (Oxford, 1958).

M. White, "Some Agiad Dates: Pausanias and His Sons," *JHS* 84 (1964) 140-152.

U. von Wilamowitz-Moellendorf, *Aristoteles und Athen* (Berlin, 1893).

J. Wolski, *"Medismos,"* *Historia* 22 (1973) 3-15.

K. Ziegler, *Plutarchos von Chaironeia* (Stuttgart, 1949).

INDEX

Acestodorus, 148
Adeimantus, 6, 7, 129
Admetus, King, 12, 200, 203-205
Aeacidae, 146, 158
Aeantis tribe, 52
Aedepsus, 110
Aegina, 99, 165-66; war with
  Athens, 82-84
Aelian, *Varia Historia*, 37
Aelius Aristides, 96, 102, 105,
  117, 154
Aemilius Paulus, 51-52
Aeschines rhetor, 97, 102, 117
Aeschines Socraticus, 20, 69,
  162-63
Aeschylus, 4, 49, 156-58; *Persae*,
  133-34, 136, 139-45, 148, 151-
  53, 155, 159, 216; at Salamis,
  133
Agesilaus, brother of Themisto-
  cles, 230
Ahriman, 218
Alcibiades, 10, 20-21
Alcmaeon, 188
Alcmeonids, 9, 29
Alexander I of Macedon, 5, 95,
  112
Alexander III of Macedon, 52
Ameinias of Pallene, 156, 159
Ammianus Marcellinus, 76
Ammonius, 47, 49; *On Altars
  and Sacrifices*, 132

Amphictyons, 179-80
Anaxagoras, 16, 19, 20, 67
Andocides, 126, 173, 233; herm
  of, 50
Andros, 7, 8, 163, 180-81
Androtion, 26
Antiphates *kalos*, 171
Aphrodite, in Piraeus, 132
Archeptolis, son of Themisto-
  cles, 232
Archippe, wife of Themistocles,
  230
Architeles, 107
archon list, Athenian, 4
archonship, 74-75
Areopagus, 23, 24, 28, 120-21
Argos, 192
Ariamenes, 155-56
aristeia, 8, 165-67
Aristeides, 7, 27-28, 72-73, 78,
  167-68, 173, 179, 182, 186-87,
  194; and Aegina, 84; and
  Hellespont bridges, 161, 163-
  64; ostracized, 90-92; and
  Psyttaleia, 150; at Salamis,
  126-27, 146-47
Aristeides, son of Xenophilus,
  188
Aristophanes, 18, 177, 227
Aristophanes of Boeotia, 113
Aristotle, 65, 80-82, 120; decree
  recalling exiles, 126-27; school

Library of Congress Cataloging in Publication Data

Frost, Frank J   1929-
  Plutarch's Themistocles.

  Bibliography: p.
  Includes index.
  1. Themistocles, ca. 524-ca. 459 B.C.   2. Plutarchus
Vitae parallelae. Themistocles.   3. Greece—History—
Persian Wars, 500-449 B.C.   4. Greece—History—
Athenian supremacy, 479-431 B.C.   I. Plutarchus. Vitae
parallelae. Themistocles.   II. Title.
DF226.T45F76   938'.03   79-3208
ISBN 0-691-05300-6